HISTORY OF
THE HIGH CONSTABLES
OF EDINBURGH
1920-2008

W. R. Ferguson
Past Moderator

Published by the Society of High Constables of Edinburgh July 2008

ISBN 978-0-9558703-0-9

Cover and book design by the City of Edinburgh Council,
Typeset and printed by the City of Edinburgh Council, Print Services
Bookbinding by Hunter & Foulis

CONTENTS AND INDEX

INTRODUCTION

This book is intended to complement and extend the information contained in the two excellent volumes previously written about the history of the Society of High Constables of Edinburgh. The first, written by James Marwick, City Clerk of Edinburgh, covered the period from 1611 to 1865 and was printed for private circulation in 1865. The second, written by David Robertson, Depute Town Clerk, covered the period from 1865 to 1924, was printed for private circulation in 1924 and sold to members at 15/- per copy. This latter book also includes extensive information on the early watching, cleaning and policing of the city.

Minutes of society meetings since 1755 are still held by the City Archivist, but these records are somewhat incomplete and accordingly the historic value of the two aforementioned histories cannot be underestimated. Copies can still be found occasionally in antiquarian book shops, and a society copy of each of the two books is passed on to successive moderators.

The information set out in the succeeding chapters summarises the evolution of the society over the last 80 years. As a member for some 38 years and as a Past-Moderator, I hope I may be excused for highlighting some details of the internal administration of the society. This has been done with a view to informing discussion about the society's future development as we approach our 400th anniversary.

In order to give an indication of the role played by the constables in earlier years, a short resumé of the complete history of the High Constables of Edinburgh is included as appendix 1.

Virtually all material has been sourced from earlier histories of the society and from official minutes of committee and general meetings. In the latter sections of the book I have supplemented the text from my own recollections.

It is regrettable that no minutes of society meetings are available for the period 1923 to 1932. Several individual wards have fortunately shown great prudence by retaining old minutes of their meetings and these indicate that no major changes took place at that time.

At the conclusion of his history David Robertson commented that "The society may with confidence look forward to the future and may hope to discover new methods of practising the ideal it has held and cherished throughout the centuries of its existence, namely, service to the City of Edinburgh".

85 years later the society is still dedicated to serving the City of Edinburgh, and the type of service given and the practices adopted do not yet vary greatly from those in vogue at the end of the First World War. Indeed it is this constancy which gives strength and appeal to this ancient society and it is noticeable from perusal of the minutes that change has been very gradual and that it has often been difficult to introduce new ideas – "status quo" being the initial preferred option by many of the members.

Although the 85 years have seen unimaginable change and progress in lifestyle and new technology, it is comforting to know that in this age of instant world-wide communication and readily available travel round the globe the High Constables of Edinburgh still follow the straightforward pattern and values set out by our forebears so long ago. It is to be hoped that these values will sustain members for many years to come, and that this unique and ancient society will continue to evolve and to play its part in the civic and social life of Edinburgh.

W R Ferguson
July 2008

ACKNOWLEDGEMENTS

The story of constables in Edinburgh has been ongoing for some 400 years and is not likely to stop in the near future. Compilation and publication of this book has spread out over a number of years and it has been difficult to decide on the optimum time for publication. Accordingly my thanks are due to Moderator Robert Forman for his initiative in encouraging the society to proceed with publication at this time and for expediting the printing process.

Thanks are also due to Past-Captain Hamish Coghill, Ward XVIII for editing the final text and to Past-Custodier Colin Cargill, Ward XI for carrying out the detailed inventory of equipment.

The enthusiasm of Chief Executive Tom Aitchison in its production and his authorization of a substantial financial contribution by the City of Edinburgh Council is greatly appreciated by the society. This contribution has been given in recognition of the special role played by the High Constables in the life of the city. My thanks are also due to his colleagues Jim Inch and Isabell Reid who ensured that all necessary arrangements for publication were in place.

I am indebted to several other staff at the city council who have been very supportive. City Archivist Richard Hunter has taken great care of society records, retrieved them as necessary and given sound advice throughout. Ian Farmer and Simon Goundry gave the artistic input necessary for design graphics and layout of the book and its cover. Details of the printing and production process were carefully thought through and organized by Jacqui Liddle and the laborious task of typesetting and photographic layout was graciously undertaken by Ian Van Der Velde.

Successive city officers have been unfailingly helpful in allowing me access to the City Chambers and society equipment.

Several records and photographs retained in the minute books are in the form of newspaper cuttings from local newspapers and warm thanks are due to Kerry Black of "Scotsman Publications Ltd" for her patient and courteous help in researching their archive. Acknowledgements for all images displayed are given alongside the associated captions.

W R Ferguson
July 2008

CHAPTER 1

THE YEARS FOLLOWING THE FIRST WORLD WAR

This chapter incorporates the latter part of David Robertson's history and gives an introduction to the changing role of the High Constables and to their relationship with Edinburgh Town Council.

The constables' year had been substantially the same since 1866 and comprised three drills in June followed by an inspection, and three drills and an inspection in November. Committee meetings were held regularly throughout the year and a nomination meeting was held in March followed by a general meeting for election of office-bearers on the first Monday in April.

Constitution

In 1924 the strength of the society had been increased from 192 to 276 members as a result of implementation of the Extension Act of 1920. This extended the city to include the Burgh of Leith and other suburban districts. A total of 7 new wards were created, namely:

No XVII	South Leith
No XVIII	North Leith
No XIX	West Leith
No XX	Central Leith
No XXI	Liberton
No XXII	Colinton
No XXIII	Corstorphine /Cramond.

It was anticipated that the membership of Leith High Constables would be incorporated into the new wards of the Edinburgh society following the precedent of earlier extensions to the city boundaries, and accordingly negotiations were held with office-bearers of Edinburgh High Constables. In November 1920 the secretary of Edinburgh High Constables gave a short report to committee of the meeting that the moderator, vice-moderator, treasurer and he had had with representatives from the society of Leith High Constables, and the committee meeting agreed "to leave further negotiations in the hands of the executive."

The intention to incorporate the constables of Leith into the Edinburgh society did not come to fruition, and accordingly the town council authorised the appointment of twelve new constables for each of the four new Leith wards. The society of the High Constables of the Port of Leith therefore continued as a separate society within the bounds of the City of Edinburgh. This society established a role for itself within Leith, and although independent of links with any local authority it still flourishes and retains a very friendly relationship with the Society of Edinburgh High Constables.

Members of the new wards created within the Society of Edinburgh High Constables were elected in November 1921 and all the nominations at that time were proposed by the recently elected councillors in accordance with the terms of the society constitution. For many years previously, the council had been content to allow the society to nominate new members but it is interesting that the councillors wished to exercise their rights on this occasion when new areas were being incorporated. The right to nominate citizens to become members of the High Constables of Edinburgh had been a source of conflict between the city and the society for many years and had caused a major rift in 1857 when the council dismissed all the constables and re-elected a new complement.

In the 1920s, constables elected to the society were still limited to a three-year term of service but were eligible for election immediately thereafter. Accordingly, one third of the constables for each ward, the four at the top of the list, demitted office annually but could rejoin immediately if they so wished. This practice continued until 1975 when the constitution was amended.

Drills
Drills and inspections were held at various venues such as the old Corn Exchange, George Watson's playground at Lauriston, George Heriot's School, Waverley Market and Portobello. Dress for these occasions for office-bearers and captains was black tie, tied sailor knot, and a frock or morning coat, and it was recommended that members should wear black felt bowler hats if possible.

Charity
Reference is made by David Robertson to the large sums of money raised by the society in the years of the Great War, to the practical assistance given at the Grassmarket Mission and to the help given at dinners arranged by the Courant Fund for thousands of poor children. In addition the High Constables were of great assistance at outings for disabled children. These outings were suspended during the war years but reinstated in 1920 when 450 children were entertained. At this type of event members' lady friends were made most welcome in view of their knowledgeable and helpful support when dealing with the children, and it was noted in 1924 that this was the first time that there had been no accidents, the see-saws having been dismantled.

Dinner
The custom of holding an annual dinner to entertain the lord provost, magistrates and other gentlemen of the city was first recorded on 12 May 1796 and during the first quarter of the 19th century it is noted by James Marwick in his history that the legendary Neil Gow and his band frequently provided musical entertainment.

David Robertson indicates that in 1870 it was agreed that the annual dinner be held in the month of October, but it then became the custom to hold the dinner on the first Thursday in December depending on the availability of the lord provost. He also recorded that "the dinners were graced by the presence of many distinguished guests and were productive of much eloquence and enjoyment. As many as fifteen or sixteen toasts appear on the old dinner programmes, but the modern fashion is towards shorter programmes and less formal speeches".

Because of the Great War, the annual dinner was stopped in 1914 and restarted in 1919. The venue was the Freemasons' Hall, but in response to a request from Lord Provost Sir Thomas Hutchison it was dropped again for a year in 1921 "in view of the seriousness of the times."

Social
The first full society excursion had taken place to Melrose in 1849 and excursions continued annually apart from the war years 1914-1919. They restarted in 1920 when an outing to Callander and the Trossachs Hotel was enjoyed. Proposals to include lady friends in such events were made at various times from 1899 onwards, but until 1928 all such proposals were steadfastly rejected in order to ensure that the outing continued to remain an all male event.

This restriction did not apply to individual ward outings, as evidenced by the photograph at the end of this chapter.

Ceremonial
In continuation of a long-standing custom, office-bearers and captains continued to celebrate the King's Birthday at the invitation of the lord provost. The society attended the lord provost and council to many commemorative and other services at St Giles Cathedral and they assisted at ceremonies to confer the Freedom of the City in 1918 and 1923. In 1922, the office-bearers attended Lord Provost Sir Thomas Hutchison in welcoming their Majesties King George V and Queen Mary on their arrival at the Caledonian Station, and captains acted as stewards at Holyrood Palace at the unveiling of the memorial to the late King Edward VII .

Equipment
The equipment held in trust by each individual High Constable was the same as it is today – namely a large decorated wooden baton, a small ebony baton with silver end pieces, a badge and a whistle, whistles having been introduced by an Act of Council in 1909. Each item was marked with a ward number and a membership number, and when a member died or resigned from the society, these items were returned to the custodier who reissued them to the new member elected to fill the vacancy in that particular ward.

With respect to other equipment in the possession of the society, a detailed inventory of the situation in 1924 is given in appendix 3 of David Robertson's history. Much of the equipment recorded in 1924 is still intact and many of the ceremonial silver batons on this list are still used today by office-bearers on parade. A complete list of society equipment in 2002 is included as appendix 2 and appendix 3.

Sport
Regarding recreational activities, the society had run an active golf club since 1895 and in the early years this was very popular with membership being in excess of 100. Over the years many trophies were presented for competition both among the members and against other golf clubs.

A bowling club had been formed prior to 1907, and in 1914, at the start of the Great War, it was agreed to form a rifle club and to run it on somewhat the same lines as the golf and bowling clubs. Moderator Thomas Ferguson presented a shield for annual competition and although the rifle club no longer exists, this trophy and several others are still held in the City Chambers.

Ward XX, Central Leith – Picnic to Aberfoyle, 14 June 1922
(Courtesy of Ainslie J. W. Nairn whose grandfather, William Brown Nairn is sitting with elbow
leaning on charabanc)

CHAPTER 2

THE YEARS LEADING UP TO
THE SECOND WORLD WAR
1924 – 1939

Following the addition of 7 new wards in 1924 the activities of the High Constables settled into their routine pattern and the new wards very quickly took a full part in the life of the society.

Constitution
The formal society year consisted of the following 10 events requiring the attendance of members:-

The annual meeting for nomination of office-bearers and captains of wards,

The annual meeting for the election of office-bearers and captains of wards,

Three summer drills and one summer inspection and

Three winter drills and one winter inspection.

The lord provost was generally present at the annual election meeting and the two inspections, the turn-out of members being generally in the order of 200 at nomination meetings and 220 at election meetings

The procedure adopted for installation of office-bearers at the annual election meetings also remained unchanged for many years and took the following form :-

The lord provost installed the new moderator,

The moderator installed the vice-moderator,

The vice-moderator installed the treasurer,

The treasurer installed the secretary,

The retiring surgeon installed the new surgeon,

The new secretary installed the custodier.

It was also customary for the retiring moderator to be presented with a token of esteem from the members of the society when demitting office.

In February 1912 the Dunbar Trophy had been presented to the society by ex-captain Thomas Dunbar in honour of his father William T Dunbar who had been the first captain of Ward XIII Dalry. The trophy was to be awarded annually to the ward with the greatest number of attendances at society meetings and drills, and this award has been made annually since its inception. The terms of the gift were such that any ward winning the trophy twice in succession would be ineligible to hold it for a third year, though making the largest number of appearances. This rule was brought into effect in 1932 when Ward XXIII Corstorphine / Cramond won for the third year running with 114 out of a maximum of 120 attendances, and again in 1937 when Ward XIX, West Leith under Captain Murdoch McDonald won for the third year with 115 attendances. A list indicating the winners of this competition is shown as appendix 7.

Control of the affairs of the society was regulated by the bye-laws of 1922 which are included as appendix 4. They were amended as follows in respect of entry requirements and included the requirement to have a member suitably qualified as an accountant to be appointed as auditor.

Bye-law 15 required that prospective members should be householders, or "be in business on their own account" within the ward which they wished to join. This requirement was relaxed in 1932 to consider applicants who were "in business within the said ward", thus extending eligibility to gentlemen employed within the ward boundary but not necessarily running their own business.

Prior to March 1937, bye-law 11 required accounts to be audited by 3 members of the committee specifically appointed to do so, but at the annual general meeting that year it was felt that this arrangement was inadequate. This was partly because no auditor could be appointed other than a committee member, and partly because there was a strong feeling that the work should be carried out by a qualified accountant, several of whom were members and would be willing to do this work on a voluntary basis. Accordingly, it was unanimously agreed to amend this bye-law and to replace the specified three members of committee with "an auditor of the accounts of the society to be appointed at the annual election meeting in each year ". This motion was put forward by Hunter Smart, C.A., Ward X, St Stephen's, and he was subsequently appointed as the first auditor of accounts of the society.

Long-service awards were not given in 1932 but reference was made at that time to 8 members who had joined before 1900, the longest serving being James Russell, a confectioner, who had been a member of Ward I, Calton for 43 years. The practice of presenting long-service medals did not start until 1959.

In March of each year the committee was required to make nominations for office-bearers for the following year, and at this stage all existing office-bearers left the room until the captains of the wards had agreed on the nominations to go forward to the next general meeting of the society.

The other regular practice was to authorise the custodier to carry out the "ringing of batons". This was always done at the first committee meeting of the year in April and was necessary to keep the silver ceremonial batons up to date with the names and dates of office-bearers.

There must also have been a proposal that the High Constables should act in co-operation with the Special Constables in the early 1930s because Moderator John Davidson had discussed this with Chief Constable Roderick Ross. However, no action was taken on this proposal and there are no recorded reasons why the society did not wish to participate.

Within the room in the City Chambers where the committee of captains held all their meetings two wooden panels listing the names of all moderators since 1707 were erected. These panels were installed in 1931 with assistance from Lord Provost Sir Thomas B Whitson, and a ceremony to unveil the panels was carried out by Lady

Whitson in October 1931. This was a very cheerful and happy event to which the magistrates and councillors were also invited. These panels were continually updated, with the names of outgoing moderators being added in gold leaf. Society members were given an opportunity to inspect the new panels at the nomination meeting in March 1932, and a copy of the billet calling the meeting is shown at the end of this chapter. The form of this billet differs little from that in use today.

Following the last drill of the year it was customary for the roll to be purged, and the circumstances of members with excessive absence from meetings and drills was discussed in committee. In cases where some leniency could be exercised the matter was referred back to captains for resolution at ward level, but in certain cases the committee agreed to strike the name of the offending member from the roll of membership and to instruct him to return his equipment to the custodier. Failure to attend strictly in accordance with the requirements of the constitution was regarded as a serious matter, and in December 1931 captain George Bee was asked to bring to the next meeting a more satisfactory reply from a delinquent in Ward XV St. Leonard's. Strict rules were also applied to members wishing to rejoin the society at the termination of their three years in office, and in November 1933 a member of Ward IX Broughton was called upon to hand over his baton and badge because he had failed to attend in April of that year to be sworn in, and therefore was no longer a member of the society in view of his breach of bye- law 28.

In April 1938 there was a significant change to the method of recording society events. Prior to this time all minutes had been carefully recorded in handwriting, each secretary having his own individual style. There is no formal comment in the minutes regarding the change in 1938 to typed minutes, and the new secretary David H M Jack presumably introduced the change on his own initiative. There is a certain loss of individuality occasioned by the use of typed minutes, but there is no doubt that research into the society history has been made easier by this change.

In addition to the formal relationship between the society and members of the town council at general meetings and inspections, there were also smaller gatherings where this relationship was strengthened. Meetings in the City Chambers were always held between office-bearers and the lord provost following any change of office, and every year the moderator and office-bearers would visit the City Chambers to join the lord provost in drinking the King's health on his birthday prior to sending him a telegram. The last telegram to King George IV before his death was sent on 3 June 1935 in the following terms: "According to ancient custom the High Constables of Edinburgh toast your Majesty's health and respectfully tender cordial congratulations on the happy occasion of your birthday and beg to renew their expression of loyalty and devotion - Thomas Menzies, Moderator." All aspects of this visit to Lord Provost Sir William J Thomson were fully reported in the "Evening News" including the office and names of all the High Constables who attended.

Another convivial custom enjoyed over the years was the informal gathering of all members following the annual election meeting when light refreshments were provided by the moderator and vice-moderator. The form of refreshment in the 1930s is not recorded.

Leadership of the society went through a difficult phase in the early 1930s. Moderator Andrew Reid was elected in April 1932 but died in November of that year. Ex-Moderator John Davidson acted as interim moderator until the following elections in April 1933, but during this period Vice-Moderator Alexander Fulton also died. James Jackson was elected moderator in April 1933 having previously held the office of treasurer, secretary and custodier but he died in March 1934.

This appears to be one of the few breaks in the practice of progressive office-bearing which started at the time of the First World War.

In spite of these sad losses, the numerical strength of the society remained high, it being recorded in March 1933 that there was only one vacancy.

Apart from the entrance money paid by members there were no funds to defray ongoing expenses, and the payment for each society activity was collected from the wards as and when it was required. A proposal was made in September 1934 that a subscription of 5/- per annum should be levied and although it was agreed that this should be put to a general meeting no further action seems to have been taken at this time.

In 1936 when alterations were to be carried out to the City Chambers, Lord Provost Louis S Gumley tactfully suggested that the High Constables might wish to consider providing a stained glass window. The suggestion was readily taken up and in March 1938 two windows were unveiled on the main staircase. One was unveiled by Lady Gumley, and the other by the moderator's wife, Mrs George W Adams. This ceremony was attended by many bailies, councillors and High Constables, and the windows depicted designs by Miss Margaret Chilton which represented Queen Margaret and Malcolm Canmore. The coat of arms of the High Constables was incorporated in a separate smaller window and later in the year a small brass plaque was added. The total cost was about £190 and was entirely funded by the members of the society. The windows are still intact and greatly enhance that section of staircase.

By 1932 there was only a handful of copies of David Robertson's history remaining, and it was agreed on Moderator Andrew Reid's suggestion that one should be included as part of the equipment of each office-bearer in order that they should not be lost but be retained in perpetuity. At the present time only one remains as society property and that is held by successive moderators.

At various times during the period leading up to the Second World War official studio photographs of the office-bearers, the society committee and of individual wards were taken, but sadly very few of these remain. Throughout this period, the society continued the custom of contributing annually towards the cost of the lord provost's portrait.

Drills
At each of the three drills preceding each inspection, committee meetings were held, and excuses for absence at the drills were all scrutinised by the moderator to ascertain whether fines should be paid or not.

Inspections were generally carried out by the lord provost, but in his absence this duty was undertaken by a bailie. For instance in the summer of 1935 the inspecting officer was the senior magistrate, Bailie Lawrence Raithby who was formerly a High Constable. He complimented Moderator Thomas Menzies on the support of office-bearers and 10 past-moderators, and guests included other councillors, Chief Constable Ross, Lord Dean of Guild Wilson and the lord provost's secretary. Hospitality was provided by the moderator and office-bearers and the occasion was fully reported in the press as were many other activities of the High Constables at that time. Reports of inspections invariably commented on the appreciation of the council for the good works carried out by the constables, especially in relation to their assistance with poor and disabled children.

In November 1922 Lord Provost Thomas Hutchison requested a surprise parade to be held. Ward captains were to be contacted and instructed to parade without delay at the City Chambers with three of their ward members, the chief constable having been asked to monitor the response time. It is recorded that this unique parade was indeed held, and the minute book of Ward III, Newington indicates that all wards reported within 35 minutes, Ward III being the first ward fully represented.

In 1924 the drill hall in Forrest Road was utilised as an alternative venue, but in the main drills were held in the Waverley Market, or the Industrial Hall in Annandale Street. In October 1932 there must have been a change of use of the Industrial Hall to a bus depot because all references thereafter are to "Central Garage, Annandale Street ".

Charity

Throughout the period in question the society was still involved in the event described as "the annual picnic for physically disabled and mentally deficient children". These children were pupils of the special schools which existed at the time and the picnics were organised through the auspices of the High Constables of Edinburgh and the Courant Fund. Both organisations provided funds to support the outing and the constables contributed approximately 6/- per head every year.

The outings were held at Norton Park, Ratho in June or July, and not only did the society contribute to the cost but they also attended and organised the picnic. In addition, certain members also supplied food and drinks and thanks were frequently recorded to John Dunbar of Ward I Calton for supplying aerated waters. In addition it is noted that in the late 1930s chocolates were provided by Vice-Moderator J M Cleugh.

A large number of children attended these events and the minutes of Ward XXI, Liberton report that in 1924 "there was a good turnout from the various wards of the constables and their ladies. The children spent a very enjoyable day and there were ample supplies of milk and food, and an abundance of prizes for the sports." In 1932 the picnic was attended by 1000 children, teachers, High Constables and their ladies. They set off from Waverley Station at 10.16 in the morning for a day in the country, and the train returned from Ratho at 5.22 pm. Testament to the success of the picnics is noted in the receipt of letters of thanks from teachers and pupils, and also by expressions of gratitude made by lord provosts and councillors at various functions throughout the period.

In similar vein the society assisted over this entire period with the Courant Fund Christmas Treat to children of the city. A donation in the order of 6/- per member was given towards this event and many members assisted by acting as stewards, the usual complement being office-bearers, captains and three or four members from each ward. In 1933 the treat took place over two days at various picture houses and on leaving, each child received a bag of cakes. The picture houses involved were :-
La Scala, TheTivoli, The Grand, The Palace, The Kinema, The Bungalow, The Springvalley Cinema, The Operetta, The New Coliseum, The Haymarket and The Picturedrome.

In January 1929 the society provided stewards at the King's Theatre on the occasion of Lord Provost Sir Alexander Stevenson's treat to school children. It is not clear whether or not 1929 was the start of this outing due to the paucity of records during the

1920s, but this very enjoyable outing to the pantomime continued for many years afterwards with the willing assistance of the High Constables.

A very full press report in "The Scotsman" in 1934 indicates that over 2000 children were present following special transport arrangements, and that members of the Edinburgh High Constables acted as stewards and general guardians. Prior to the pantomime, the theatre orchestra led some community singing, and when well known ditties such as "I'm happy when I'm hiking " and " Daisy Daisy " were sung, "the whole theatre broke loudly into song, filling the air with such a chorus of treble voices as threatened to send the roof sky-high". On leaving the theatre at the end of the afternoon each child was presented with an iced cake, after having sung "For he's a jolly good fellow" to Lord Provost Sir William Thomson.

During the 1920s and 1930s donations to charitable organisations had to be made either from contributions requested from all members of the society or as a result of the proceeds obtained from sweepstakes, tombolas, raffles etc at social functions such as the annual whist drive and dance or the annual excursion.

Special collections were made for the Queen Alexandria Memorial Fund in 1926, the miners' fund inaugurated by Lord Provost Sir Thomas Whitson in 1929, and the appeal fund for the dependants of those killed in the Gresford Colliery disaster in 1934. This latter appeal was made following a special meeting of committee and generally the contribution was 2/6d per member.

Funds raised at social functions were mainly directed to the Edinburgh Royal Infirmary, the Police Boot and Clothes Fund, and to Leith Hospital. In 1931, some funds from a whist drive and dance at the Palais de Danse were earmarked to prepare the room in the City Chambers set aside for the use of the society to house the panels for recording the names of all past-moderators, but generally fund raising was directed to outside charities. For example in 1933 money was given towards the occupational fund for unemployed men and also to the Grassmarket Mission, and in 1939 a sum was donated to Lord Provost Sir Henry Steele's Red Cross Appeal.

Total charitable donations in 1933 were recorded as £120 and this was about the average annual figure for that time. In 1935, a special collection was made among members and their friends for Edinburgh Royal Infirmary and for Leith Hospital to mark the celebrations for the Royal Semi-Jubilee of King George V.

A further event in connection with these celebrations was a treat for Leith children and the aged poor. Office-bearers and several wards assisted at a number of functions which appear to have been organised by the town council and took place at Waverley Market, Forrest Road Drill Hall and Dalmeny Street Drill Hall.

A similar celebration was held on the occasion of the coronation of King George VI in 1937 when some of the city's old people were entertained at the Waverley Market with members from all wards giving assistance.

Dinner

Accounts of dinners in the 1920s are scant, and in 1931 the failing economy in the country dictated that the guest list be substantially reduced in order to reduce the ticket price from 12/6d to 11/6d. Much press coverage was given to these events and very comprehensive reports of all speeches were included. For instance, in 1932 Lord Elphinstone deprecated the "retrograde movement" at that time to the calls for self government in Scotland, and said that he would very much deplore if he did not see the

High Constables of Edinburgh once again in the forefront as defenders of the Union. No doubt Interim Moderator John Davidson gave a suitably tactful response ensuring that the society maintained its impartial political stance.

The list of society guests generally numbered about 30 people, and typically, as in 1933, invitations would be extended to representatives from the Army, Navy and Air Force, the master of the Merchant Company, the chairman of Leith Dock Commission, the president of the Royal College of Surgeons, the president of the Royal College of Physicians, nine bailies, the city treasurer and four other city officials, one city councillor, the chief constable, the transport manager, the lord provost's secretary, the principal city officer, the moderators of the societies of the High Constables of Holyrood, Leith and Perth, four past-moderators and four press reporters.

Musical entertainment was a regular feature and a repertoire of some twelve pieces was usually given by two male soloists accompanied by a three piece orchestral accompaniment.

The printed programme varied little from that in use today and a copy of that from 1932 is reproduced at the end of this chapter. In order to assist with the seating arrangements and to assist in co-ordinating the service of food and drink, several society members were appointed to act as croupiers at each of the large tables. The event was held at the North British Station Hotel.

The dinner of 1933 seems to have been particularly successful with 391 attending and Sir Harry Lauder proved to be a very popular guest. He admitted to using a microphone for the first time that night, and after having delivered his toast to the society he sang verses of several of his best known songs. At the conclusion of the reply by Vice-Moderator Thomas Menzies, Sir Harry led the company in a hearty rendering of "keep right on to the end of the road ".

Social

As mentioned earlier, the society annual excursion was discontinued during the First World War, but once restarted in 1920 it continued uninterrupted until 1939 and was one of the highlights of the society's year, the only exception being1926 when it was cancelled because of the general strike and replaced with a charabanc outing.

In the main, these outings involved travelling by train to the west coast to enjoy a sail on the Clyde estuary and were of sufficient interest to generate substantial press coverage. In spite of repeated discussion in the 1920s at committee level over a number of years, the society did not feel it appropriate to invite wives or lady friends until 1928, but once started this practice continued thereafter. It is worth noting that no such restriction was ever placed on women attending the annual picnic for disabled children - in fact the opposite was the case and wives were encouraged to attend and assist.

The destinations of the outings in the 1930s are variously described as "Arran and Lochranza", "Whiting Bay - Arran ", " Brodick", " Tarbert ", and " Ardrishaig ". In order to stem dwindling numbers in 1934, the venue was changed for one year only to the Lake District.

Numbers attending in the 1930s were in the order of 300 to 400 and included a significant number of invited guests. A typical outing started about 9.00 am from Princes Street Station and travel was by train to Wemyss Bay where the party embarked on the steamer. Following a sail, luncheon was served on board and this was followed by a welcome speech from the moderator and a response from the council representative on behalf of the guests. Time restrictions made it difficult for the lord provost to attend, but several bailies, councillors and their wives were always present and frequently other guests included the principal city officer and other city officials, the moderators of Holyrood and Perth High Constables, the chief constable, the master of the Merchant Company and the traffic superintendent in Edinburgh of the LMS Railway.

An orchestra was also present on board, and following the short speeches there was dancing and community singing from distributed song sheets. The outing was normally held on Derby Day, and in addition to contributions towards prizes of chocolates etc. a Derby sweepstake was always held to raise funds for charity.

In addition to the on board entertainment, passengers usually disembarked for about an hour to view the countryside at close quarters.

The good citizens of Edinburgh must have been interested in such outings because detailed reports from up to four local newspapers -"The Scotsman", "The Evening News", "The Evening Dispatch", and " The Leith Observer"- are included with the minutes. One imagines that the outing was probably a good perk for the reporters involved, although press reports of many other society events are also filed.

The whist drive and dance in March 1931 referred to earlier was the first such event and over subsequent years this became a regular annual event and was well supported by members and friends.

Over the first few years numbers attending were between 300 and 400, and venues varied between the Palais de Danse and the Assembly Rooms and Music Hall in George Street. The function was dropped for a year in 1935 due to lack of support, but this was the exception to the rule and the following year saw a very successful function at the Palais de Danse. This was reported in the local press as "The High Constables' Ball where dances old and new alternated, the Palais Band was in great form, and a feature of the evening was the parade round the fountain led by the musicians" A photograph of some of the office-bearers and their wives is reproduced at the end of this chapter.

In March 1939 the venue was changed to the New Cavendish Ballroom in Tollcross, and this was the last whist drive and dance before the war.

Ceremonial

The ceremonial aspects of the life of the society regularly included escorting the lord provost and council to the opening service of the General Assembly of the Church of Scotland and also to their annual service at St. Giles Cathedral on Assembly Sunday. In addition, there was the annual church parade of the city police force in the early autumn, and the Armistice Day Service in November.

Other unique church parades included a service of commemoration and luncheon on the centenary of the death of Sir Walter Scott in September 1932, a jubilee commemoration service of the restoration of St Giles Cathedral in 1933, a commemoration service and lunch for the three hundred and fiftieth anniversary of the University of Edinburgh in 1933, rededication of the Kirk of The Greyfriars in 1934 following partial restoration, a memorial service in St. Giles Cathedral on the occasion of the death of King Albert of Belgium in 1934, a service of commemoration and thanksgiving in connection with 150 years of St Andrews' Church in George Street in

1934, a thanksgiving service at St Giles Cathedral in 1935 to celebrate the jubilee of King George V, and a memorial service following his death in January 1936.

As well as church parades, the High Constables attended the lord provost and council on several landmark occasions. In 1932 the office-bearers and the Leith wards were on duty at the opening of Leith Town Hall and Library, in 1935 they attended the laying of a foundation stone at the Royal Infirmary by the Duke and Duchess of Kent and in 1936 the High Constables were present and on duty at the proclamation of the new King Edward VIII at the Mercat Cross.

In the 1930s the City of Edinburgh bestowed the Freedom of the City on several occasions in the Usher Hall, and the society played a very useful and practical role by providing their services as stewards at the following ceremonies:-

In June 1934, 69 members attended the presentation ceremony for the Earl of Willington, Viceroy and Consul General of India and the Countess of Willington.

In May 1935, all office-bearers, captains and two members of each ward attended the presentation ceremony for the Duke of Kent.

In June 1935, the same complement of High Constables attended the presentation ceremony for The Rt. Hon. Joseph Aloysius Lyons, Prime Minister of Australia, The Rt. Hon. Lord Tweedsmuir, Governor General Designate of Canada, and for His Highness The Maharajah of Patiala.

On the first of these occasions the High Constables were required to maintain order during the ceremony and to persuade several protesters to leave the hall when Councillor John Cormack and his associates from the Protestant Action Society shouted slogans and protested vociferously against Mr. Lyons' catholic affiliation.

In December 1936, the usual arrangements were in place to attend the presentation ceremony for the Duchess of York, and at the conclusion of proceedings the assembly sang "will ye no come back again".

In April 1937, the High Constables acted as stewards at the presentation ceremony for the Duchess of Gloucester. As usual on such occasions there was great demand for tickets and a ballot was held to determine who would attend and which particular duty would be allocated.

In April 1938, members of the society attended the presentation ceremony for The Rt. Hon Walter Elliot and the Rt. Hon. Lord Macmillan.

In April 1939, the High Constables turned out for the presentation ceremony for the Hon. Joseph Patrick Kennedy, United States Ambassador to the Court of St. James and father of future US President John F Kennedy. No disturbances by the Protestant Action Society were reported on this occasion.

All office-bearers and 13 captains were invited to a Royal Command Performance at the Lyceum Theatre in July 1934, and it appears that this was purely to enjoy the entertainment and not to act in any official capacity,

In June 1937, King George VI and Queen Elizabeth attended the Rally of Scottish Youth at Murrayfield Football Field, and the High Constables took a very active and important role in carrying out stewarding duties. In June of the following year they also provided stewards for the Scottish Sheep Dog Trials.

Equipment
At the first committee meeting following the election of office-bearers and captains each year, instructions were given to the custodier for the ringing of batons to ensure

that the names and dates of all office-bearers were diligently recorded on new silver rings on the appropriate ceremonial batons.

During the annual dinner in 1936 some damage was caused to sports club trophies by staff at the North British Hotel. This was repaired at a cost of £3-10/- and the question of insurance cover for such items was investigated.

The council regularly granted a sum of money to the High Constables for the purpose of maintaining the equipment in good order and this grant was generally in the order of £50 per year.

Sport

The society Golf Club continued successfully and it is probable that the Society Bowling and Angling Clubs also continued unabated over this period but no records exist to substantiate this.

In April 1922 Moderator James Manclark felt it a suitable time to form a curling club because the increased number of members in the society would make more curlers available. Accordingly it was arranged that curling should take place every second Monday at Haymarket Ice Rink from 7.30 to 10.30 pm and that Councillor Welsh would see it through. Presumably this was to overcome difficulties in booking the ice, and all wards were asked to support this new venture.

The youngest of the society sports clubs, the Angling Club, was formed in 1926.

NOTES.

The attention of Members is directed to the following existing Bye-Laws.

23. Absence from Town, indisposition, or other necessary cause may exempt Members from attending meetings, provided they intimate in writing the reason of their inability to attend, to the Secretary, previous to the meeting being held. It shall be the Secretary's duty to submit these excuses to the Moderator, who shall decide whether they are to be accepted. Should the Moderator accept the excuse the same shall be marked in the roll, otherwise the Member shall be marked absent. In the event, however, of a Member failing to attend four out of the total number of Drills and General Meetings in any year, irrespective of excuses, his name may be struck off the Roll of Members, at any Committee Meeting held during the following year, at which the Captain of his Ward must be present.

30. Every motion affecting the Bye-Laws of the Society to be brought before the Society shall be intimated in writing to the Secretary at least fourteen days before the Meeting at which it is to be dealt with and notice thereof to be given in the circular calling the Meeting. If approved of at such Meeting by a majority of two-thirds of the Members present, the same shall, subject to the approval of the Lord Provost, Magistrates, and Council pass into law.

MOTION.

That Bye-Law 15 be amended to the effect of inserting after the word "Ward," occurring in the 7th line of said Bye-Law, the following words, viz. :—

"or they may be the director, manager, or secretary of a limited Company, having its registered office in the Ward, or of a limited liability Company having a place of business in the Ward."

Consider and deal with above Motion affecting Bye-Laws of the Society, as intimated by Haymarket Ward. (See item 8 of Agenda).

JAMES JACKSON,
Secretary.

The High Constables
of Edinburgh = =

Telephone: 26264.

75 LOTHIAN ROAD,
EDINBURGH, *22nd March* 1932.

DEAR SIR,
THE ANNUAL GENERAL MEETING OF THE SOCIETY, for the purpose of *nominating* Office-Bearers and Captains of Wards for the ensuing year, and transacting other business, will be held in the COUNCIL CHAMBERS, *on the evening of Monday, 28th curt., at 8 o'clock.*

The Order of Business will be as follows :—

1. Meeting to be constituted.
2. Roll to be called.
3. Minutes to be read.
4. Treasurer's Report.
5. Nominations of Office-Bearers and Captains of Wards.
6. Arrangements for Social Functions.
7. Presentation of Dunbar Trophy.
8. Motion (see p. 4).

The Committee, in terms of Bye-Law No. V., have prepared the following list of Gentlemen whom they recommend to the Society for nomination at this Meeting, viz. :—

Moderator	Mr ANDREW REID.
Vice-Moderator . . .	Mr ALEXANDER FULTON.
Treasurer	Mr JAMES JACKSON.
Secretary	Mr THOMAS MENZIES.

THE GENERAL MEETING for the *election* of the Office-Bearers and Captains of Wards will be held in the COUNCIL CHAMBERS, on *Monday, 4th April 1932, at 8 o'clock p.m.* in accordance with the Act of Council regulating the Constitution of the Society.

The High Constables Committee Room in the CITY CHAMBERS will be open at 7.30 p.m. on the above dates to give Members an opportunity of inspecting the room and the Moderators' Panels.

Yours faithfully,

JAMES JACKSON,
Secretary.

Billet calling Annual General Meeting 22 March 1932

Lady Gumley unveiling one stained glass window in the City Chambers on 15 March 1938. The Moderator's wife, Mrs Adams is on hand to unveil the second window, and the gentlemen are William Gillespie-Treasurer, George W Adams-Moderator, Lord Provost Sir Louis S Gumley and Bailie Coltart. (Courtesy of Scotsman Publications)

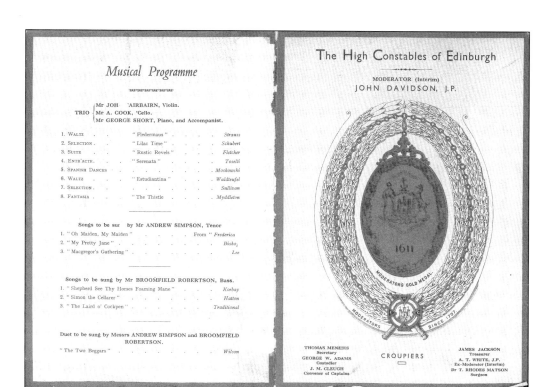

THE HIGH CONSTABLES OF EDINBURGH

ANNUAL DINNER

NORTH BRITISH STATION HOTEL
FRIDAY, 2nd DECEMBER 1932

Menu

Hors d'Œuvre
Grape Fruit Cocktail

—

Thick Lentil Soup

—

Fillets of Sole with Lobster Sauce

—

Loin of Mutton with Tomatoes
Roasted Potatoes
French Beans

—

Pheasant in Casserole with Truffles
Lettuce Salad

—

Pears with Cream Ice and Chocolate Sauce

—

Coffee

List of Toasts

THE KING   The Moderator

The Lord Provost, Magistrates and Town Council
of the City of Edinburgh   The Treasurer

Reply—The Rt. Hon. Lord Provost W. J. Thomson

Houses of Parliament   Major Andrew Wilson, O.B.E., D.L.,
Master of the Merchant Company

Reply—Ernest Brown, Esq., M.C., M.P.
Secretary to the Ministry of Mines

The High Constables of Edinburgh
Rt. Honourable Lord Elphinstone, K.T., LL.D.

Reply—The Moderator

The High Constables of
Holyrood, Leith and Perth   The Secretary

Reply—George E. Robertson, Esq.,
Moderator of High Constables of Holyrood

Our Guests   The Surgeon

Reply—Dr Robert Thin, M.B., F.R.C.P.,
President of the Royal College of Physicians

———

"Auld Lang Syne"

Dinner menu and toast list, 1932

S.S. "Duchess of Montrose"

MENU

LUNCHEON

Julienne   Kidney

Salmon Mayonnaise

Roast Sirloin of Beef   Roast Lamb, Mint Sauce
Pressed Beef   Ham and Tongue
Vegetables   Potatoes

Swiss Tart   Fruit Salad
Lemon Custard

Biscuits and Cheese

TEA

Filleted Fish   Grilled Herring

Cold Joints, Pickles, Salad

Teabread   Biscuits   Preserves

MEMBERS OF THE SOCIETY WILL WEAR
THEIR BADGES ON THIS OCCASION

ANNUAL EXCURSION

OF

THE HIGH CONSTABLES OF EDINBURGH

to LOCHRANZA

WEDNESDAY, 8th JUNE 1932

PLADDA

ANDREW REID   . .   MODERATOR
THOMAS MENZIES   .   SECRETARY

LOCH RIDDEN

ITINERARY

ON arrival at Wemyss Bay the party will embark on board the "Duchess of Montrose," and sail at 11 a.m., crossing the Firth of Clyde to the eastern shore of the Island of Bute, when a view will be obtained of the villages of Ascog and Kerrycroy, Mount Stewart House, the seat of the Marquis of Bute, and the village of Kilchattan Bay. The Greater and Lesser Cumbraes will be seen on the left. On leaving the Island of Bute the steamer crosses to the eastern shore of the Island of Arran sailing into Brodick Bay, thence Lamlash Bay, and a view of the villages of Brodick and Lamlash is obtained. When passing through Lamlash Bay the Holy Isle is on the steamer's left; proceeding onward the villages of King's Cross and Whiting Bay are passed, after which the steamer rounds Kildonan Point and passing Pladda Lighthouse, cruises along the southern shore of the Island before turning into Kilbrannan Sound. Passing through Kilbrannan Sound the Peninsula of Kintyre is on the left and the western shore of the Island of Bute on the right. Numerous and picturesque hamlets are to be seen on either shore. The "Duchess of Montrose" will arrive at Lochranza, which lies in the bay of that name at the north mouth of the Sound, at 2.45 p.m., when the party will disembark for fully one hour.

Leaving Lochranza at 4 p.m. the steamer sails through Inchmarnock water, passing the Island of Inchmarnock on the right, and enters the Kyles of Bute; proceeding through the Kyles of Bute the villages of Kames, Auchenlochan, and Tighnabruaich with their respective piers are on the left, and before reaching the Burnt Islands, Glen Caladh Castle is also seen on the left, and the "Maids of Bute" on the right. The steamer now sails into Loch Ridden and returning passes between the Burnt Islands. Continuing through the Kyles of Bute the village of Colintraive is passed on the left and shortly afterwards the cruise is continued up Loch Ridden. On leaving Loch Ridden and sailing through Rothesay Bay the steamer rounds Toward Point and the course is laid along the Cowal shore passing Toward, Innellan and Dunoon. On passing Dunoon the Cloch Lighthouse will be observed on the right, and the steamer thereafter crosses the river to Gourock, to arrive about 6.30 p.m., where the party will rejoin the train for Edinburgh.

TIME TABLE

8.35 a.m.	Special Train leaves Edinburgh (Princes St. Station).	
10.39 „	Arrive Wemyss Bay.	
10.50 „	Embark on S.S. "Duchess of Montrose."	
12 noon.	1st Luncheon.	
1 p.m.	2nd Luncheon.	
2.45 „	Arrive Lochranza.	
4 „	Leave Lochranza.	
4.30 „	1st Tea.	
5.15 „	2nd Tea.	
6.30 „	Arrive Gourock.	
6.40 „	Special Train leaves Gourock for Edinburgh.	
8.31 „	Arrive Edinburgh (Princes St. Station).	

Brochure for 1932 Annual Excursion

Office Bearers and wives at the High Constables Ball, Feb. 1936. Moderator Thomas Menzies with John Davidson, Ex-Moderator and George W Adam, Vice-Moderator in the front row. (Photograph by Scottish Pictorial Press)

High Constables leading a parade to the ceremonial Proclamation of the Accession of King Edward VIII to the Throne in 1936. George W Adams Moderator, William Gillespie Treasurer and James M Cleugh Secretary

20

CHAPTER 3

THE WAR YEARS 1939-1945

At the outbreak of the Second World War the society researched old minute books and ascertained that during the 1914-1918 war High Constable activities had been greatly curtailed, but nevertheless considerable funds had been raised by the society for war charities.

There had been no necessity in the 1914-1918 war for precautions against air-raid or the need for black out but in 1939 the society considered providing personnel to assist with air-raid precautions. In the event this did not transpire but Moderator William Laing reminded Lord Provost Sir Henry Steele, a former member of Ward XVI, Portobello that "the services of the society were at his disposal in any suitable capacity".

The activities of the High Constables during this period are perhaps best summarised by the comments of Secretary David Buchanan at the annual nomination meeting in March 1946 when he referred to the preceding year as having been one of - if not the most historic and memorable in the annals of the society. It had seen the victorious conclusion of the greatest war the world had ever known, and the society had the satisfaction of knowing that in addition to the many services the members had rendered individually to the nation - financially and otherwise - it had been the springboard for the establishment of the Garrison Theatre which had entertained approximately 570,000 members of H M services and their friends. Special mention was made of the valuable work done by the entertainers and by members undertaking stewarding duties, specific recognition being given to Dick Telfer, Campbell White and Fred Mitchell for their unstinting efforts throughout the period.

Constitution
In 1943 Lord Provost William Y Darling was keen that the High Constables should have their own premises in the vicinity of the High Street, and gave a personal contribution of £10-10/- to inaugurate a fund for this purpose. However nothing came of it and his contribution was ultimately returned to him. There appears to have been a particularly strong relationship between the society and Lord Provost Darling, and the office-bearers and captains held a special dinner for him in November 1943.

Drills
The winter drills of 1939 were cancelled because all halls were being used for wartime activities, and drilling of the High Constables did not recommence until after the war.

Charity
In May 1940 an extraordinary meeting was held and it was decided that the childrens' picnic outing should be held that year in Davidson's Mains public park, but that there

would be no annual excursion. A committee was formed to consider in principle some means of entertainment for the troops, and the outcome of this, the Garrison Theatre, proved to be the main activity of the society throughout the war years other than the routine business of committee and general meetings for nomination and election of office-bearers. No social functions involving the whole society were held at any time during this period.

In terms of assisting with the war effort, the society's energy was mainly directed towards setting up and running the Garrison Theatre, but in a separate effort they were able to raise by subscription a sum in the order of £30,000 towards Edinburgh Warship Week in 1942. This was a very large sum of money but should be considered in the context of the result of an eight week campaign throughout the city which resulted in raising £16.5 million of which £1.25 million was subscribed by "small savers".

Artistic direction of the Garrison Theatre was initially under the control of society member, Mr Jimmy Whitelaw who was known professionally as "The Edinburgh Entertainer". The shows were produced to provide "singing, dancing girls and a spot of real fun, all with an eye to a splash of brightness and jollity in the midst of these dark days ". The show was held every Sunday evening and it was hoped that stage artists appearing locally would participate free of charge, and that service men and women with appropriate flair and talent would also contribute. Initially, anyone wishing to audition was asked to apply to Moderator William Gillespie or to Jimmy Whitelaw.

The venue was the New Victoria Cinema in Clerk Street, the first performance was held on 23 June 1940 the cost being 6d per head, and the audience was composed mainly of men and women in the armed services. Civilians were only allowed in to accompany service personnel, and wounded men were transported to and from hospital and admitted free.

This was all carried out in spite of strong objections from many churches, not only those locally but from as far afield as the Southern Presbytery of the Free Presbyterian Church of Scotland in Tighnabruich.

The venture was an immediate success with 2000 people being entertained each week.

In order to fund the venture initially, in 1940 each member of the society subscribed a sum of 25/- towards the Garrison Theatre War Charities Fund . No subscription was taken from members on active service.

Such was the success of the theatre that regular letters of congratulation and encouragement were received from the service chiefs in Scotland, and on 22 June 1941, the first anniversary, the programme was broadcast on the forces wavelength, the main act that evening being George Formby. Reproduced extracts from the programme are included at the end of this chapter and give an indication of the appreciation expressed by a variety of service personnel of all ranks.

In subsequent years, well known guest performers included Sir Harry Lauder, Frank Titterton, George Graves and Will Fyffe.

A lasting feature of all performances was the hugely successful community singing led by L/Cpl Richard Telfer at the Wurlitzer organ. There are frequent references to the popularity of this item on the programme and a flavour of this can be seen from the following extract from a press report in April 1944 :

FOR THE SERVICES

Garrison Theatre's 230th Performance

Since June 1940 almost three million Service men and women from all the Allied countries, have been entertained at the Garrison Theatre, held on Sunday evenings, under the auspices of the High Constables of Edinburgh, in the New Victoria Cinema, and over £6,000 has been distributed to local and other war charities.

Full houses are the rule, and usually hundreds have to be turned away. Special arrangements have been made by the organisers for wounded men, and every week a number from hospitals in the district are admitted free of charge. An anonymous benefactor supplies the wounded with cigarettes. The theatre is stewarded by the High Constables.

Mr William Grant is the director of programmes, and, with a band of talented resident artists as a nucleus, he has maintained a high standard of performance throughout.

Last night's performance, the 230th, consisted in the main of a revue presented by Ralph Reader's R.A.F. Gang Show. A combination of song and dance with a generous quota of slapstick comedy, the show was warmly appreciated by the audience, which numbered 2000.

A notable feature was the community singing, led at the organ by Sergt. Richard Telfer, R.A.M.C., who included a number of request tunes accompanied by messages from members of the Forces."

[Note – The number of troops entertained by this time was more probably 300,000 rather than "three million" as reported]

Sufficient money to produce the shows was generated from entrance money and advertising. Indeed the turnover was such that monies were subscribed to various war charities - for example in 1942, £600 was contributed this way and similarly in 1943, £850 was contributed.

Initially, it had been intended to close the Garrison Theatre on 24 June 1945 after 262 performances, the three producers over the period having been Jimmy Whitelaw, Robert Borthwick and William Grant.

However, there was such a demand from service chiefs for it to continue that it re-opened on 28 October 1945 with Scottish Command providing "Stars in Battle Dress" for the occasion. The show ran throughout the winter until the final performance on 31 March 1946, and during this time the society presented a base drum to The Royal Scots Cadet Pipe Band who had been very supportive throughout. In total, the theatre ran for 5 years and 25 weeks, and over 500,000 people were entertained.

As the war proceeded it became apparent that the Garrison Theatre Fund donated by society members would not be needed to support the running costs. In addition to the donations of £1286 paid to war charities there remained at the end a surplus of £1050. This surplus was given to Lord Provost John L Falconer in order to build a cottage for disabled ex-servicemen as part of the scheme administered by the Scottish Veterans' Garden City Association. The cottage sponsored by the society was built at No 3 Salvesen Gardens and was initially occupied by a Cameron Highlander and his family, the soldier having lost his left arm in the war.

Due to various contractual and cost difficulties the house was not completed until November 1951 when it was inspected by the lord provost at a special ceremony. The house bears an inscription to the Edinburgh High Constables and is still in use today as part of the housing stock administered by SVGCA for occupation by ex-service personnel. Photographs of the cottage and associated plaque are included at the end of this chapter.

Following closure of the Garrison Theatre, the society recorded special thanks and accorded a presentation to the two members who had been most instrumental in ensuring the continuing operation and success of the venture, namely Hunter Smart who had acted as auditor and A Harris Horne, who had acted as treasurer throughout the whole period of existence of the theatre. It is remarkable to note that James A McArthur and Harris Horne were absent on only one Sunday out of the 249 performances up to March 1945, and special thanks were also accorded to James G Y Buchanan for his zeal throughout the venture.

Dinner
No formal dinners were held during the period of the war

Social
In 1945 following the end of hostilities the society were anxious to restart their social outings, but approaches made to L M S Railway and the North British Station Hotel showed that it was still too early to resume the annual excursion and the annual dinner.

Ceremonial
The High Constables gave moral encouragement and support to the government and service chiefs by sending telegrams at times of special victories or successes. In October 1942, they acted as stewards when the Freedom of the City was conferred on Prime Minister Winston Spencer Churchill. They also assisted as stewards at other functions in the Usher Hall such as the public meeting in February 1943 in connection with Lady Stafford Cripps' "Aid to China Fund", a public meeting in May 1945 in connection with Armistice Day, the "Victory in Europe Day" celebrations in May 1945 and the Freedom of the City awards on 14 March 1946 to Admiral of the Fleet, Lord Cunningham of Hyndhope, to Field Marshall Sir Rupert Alexander, and to Air Marshall Sir Arthur Tedder.

Routine church parades to St Giles Cathedral continued largely as before and following the Battle of Britain in the late summer of 1940 regular annual church services were introduced to commemorate the most important event in Royal Air Force history. The High Constables have been on duty at this service without interruption since that time. In 1943 office-bearers attended a special service to commemorate the 700th anniversary of the consecration of St Giles Cathedral. Additionally, there was a service to mark the 250th anniversary of the Mary Erskine School for Girls in June 1944.

In October 1943 the High Constables accompanied Lord Provost Sir William Y Darling and the council to Pontifical High Mass at St Mary's Roman Catholic Cathedral.

A newspaper cutting records that "there was an echo of the controversy about their attendance in some shouts and boos, but the councillors were cheered in the street as they entered the church".

The High Constables attended the lord provost and council in September 1944 in St Giles Cathedral for a service of prayer for Warsaw and also for a national day of prayer. In the same month there was a church parade and service with the 2nd Battalion Scots Guards. In April 1945 the office-bearers paraded with draped silver batons at the memorial service for President Franklin D Roosevelt and St Giles Cathedral was full to overflowing for this very moving service of tribute.

During the national celebrations for Victory in Europe Day on 8 May 1945, all office-bearers had attended the lord provost and council at the Mercat Cross. On the following Sunday they attended at the thanksgiving service at St Giles Cathedral and thereafter at the saluting base at the march past of His Majesty's Forces. Later in the same month, the High Constables attended their Majesties King George VI and Queen Elizabeth on their arrival at the Caledonian Station, and also at the subsequent service at St Giles Cathedral.

Equipment

Society equipment was augmented by the presentation of a mallet or gavel for use during meetings. This was gifted by Custodier David Wilkie in 1943 and was used regularly at the annual dinner. Generally the ringing of batons was carried out each year, but in 1942 this was deferred because of cost and the shortage of materials. No roll book was produced in 1943 but throughout this period the society still continued to contribute to the lord provosts' portraits.

In November 1943 Ex-Moderator William Gillespie submitted a design for a lady's brooch in the form of a High Constable's badge. It was agreed that this should be purchased at a cost of £5 and be given to the moderator's wife to be worn as appropriate. This brooch is still much appreciated and is worn regularly with pride on many occasions, and is a small but meaningful token of the great support given to moderators by their wives during their term of office.

Sport

Golf Club activities continued as usual in 1939, and until 1942 some of the outings continued as did the well established matches against the City Police and Perth High Constables. Thereafter there was no activity until the end of the war when three matches against other clubs were resumed in 1946. The lack of practice over the preceding years must have had a levelling effect since all these matches were drawn.

Little reference can be found to any other society sporting activities during the war, but it was agreed in July 1945 that the annual bowling match with Edinburgh Corporation should take place again after a gap of several years

THE HIGH CONSTABLES OF EDINBURGH

present

SCOTLAND'S GARRISON THEATRE

CLERK STREET   EDINBURGH

NEW VICTORIA

Every Sunday at 7.30 p.m. prompt

A Bright Musical Show with Smart Dancing and Snappy Comedy for the Uniformed Services of the Allies

Birthday Celebration Programme

Programme for Garrison Theatre performance 22 June 1941

DAVID H. M. JACK
Treasurer
High Constables of Edinburgh

ANGUS MILLAR
Surgeon
High Constables of Edinburgh

MARCUS W. WARD
Secretary
High Constables of Edinburgh

T. ROBERTSON MOSSMAN
Custodier
High Constables of Edinburgh

JAMES M. CLEUGH
Vice-Moderator
High Constables of Edinburgh

A. HARRIS HORNE
Treasurer
Garrison Theatre

A. MASTERTON BROWN
Convener, Artistes' Committee,
Garrison Theatre

JACK DUNBAR
A/Div. Superintendent
Gaumont-British Corpn. Ltd.

W. MARTIN HOBKIRK
Member, Artistes' Committee
Garrison Theatre

JAMES G. Y. BUCHANAN
Chief Steward
Garrison Theatre

DAVID SHARP
Member, Artistes' Committee
Garrison Theatre

Programme for Garrison Theatre performance 22 June 1941

27

BIRTHDAY GREETINGS

Message from LIEUT.-GENERAL A. F. A. N. THORNE
General Officer Commanding-in-Chief

It gives me great pleasure to extend my congratulations to the High Constables of Edinburgh on the occasion of the first anniversary of " Garrison Theatre."

Although I have only recently been appointed to this Command and have not had an opportunity of seeing the performances in person, I am well aware of the great work which has been done, and is still being done by " Garrison Theatre " in keeping members of the Services in good heart.

Unfortunately, I am unable to attend on 22nd June, but wish you, Mr Moderator and the High Constables of Edinburgh, the best of luck and good fortune in your future endeavours for the Services.

Message from LIEUT.-COMMANDER J. A. MACQUEEN, R.N.V.R.
Port Amenities Liaison Officer

I see you are having a Birthday Celebration night at the " Garrison Theatre," and I would like to take the opportunity of thanking you again for the tickets you have sent, and to let you know how keenly they have been sought after.

From different sources I have heard how much the shows have been enjoyed by men of Convoy Escort vessels, Minesweepers and other craft based here, and it is quite evident that the " Garrison Theatre " is filling a much needed want.

Good luck for the future.

Message from W. L. COULTHARD, C.F.

It gives me great pleasure to have the opportunity of saying a word or two in appreciation of " Garrison Theatre."

I had not long taken up my post on this island last August when I was asked could I not get a supply of " Garrison Theatre " tickets week by week as our men, with their brief leave ashore, sometimes found difficulty in gaining admission. My request was sympathetically received and speedily granted, and that arrangement has continued ever since.

From the eagerness with which the tickets are snapped up and from conversation with those who have attended, I know the programmes are greatly enjoyed, and that the theatre fills what would otherwise be an awkward gap in the leave of many men who are strangers to Edinburgh. This indeed, would seem to me to be its proper function, to give pleasure and refuge to men who are strangers in a strange city. I know it is doing this so far as this unit is concerned, and I have no doubt that is equally true of other troop formations. On behalf, therefore, of our troops here I would say, " Thanks to ' Garrison Theatre ' for the past and all good wishes for the future, and may all those who have worked so hard to make it the success it is, live to see and to celebrate the victorious conclusion of the present conflict."

Message from R.A.F. AND W.A.A.F. PERSONNEL

To-night " Garrison Theatre " celebrates its birthday, and we gladly take this opportunity on behalf of the R.A.F. and W.A.A.F. personnel, who have attended the concerts, to express our best thanks to the promoters for the splendid shows they have arranged each Sunday evening for the entertainment of the Troops. We offer them our congratulations at the end of a successful year, and our best wishes for the future. And may we thank also the many artistes who have appeared there, and assure them that we have greatly appreciated their shows. Here are some of our opinions :—

" I always reckon up when I am due to be out on a Sunday and book it for ' Garrison Theatre.' "

" What would we do in Edinburgh on Sunday evening without ' Garrison Theatre.' "

" We want more shows like this for the Forces—we feel it to be more personal than ordinary shows."

" We like the show—all of us—but I don't like the queue."

Such are the common reactions of the men and of the W.A.A.F. too, and there is great demand for such priority tickets as are available. The show is a favourite with all. Carry on " Garrison Theatre," and good luck ! You're doing a fine work.

RESIDENT ARTISTES — SCOTLAND'S GARRISON THEATRE

CISS M'LUCKIE, Soprano   MARIE FRIER, Soubrette
RICHARD TELFER, Organist   WILLIAM GRANT, Baritone and Entertainer
ROBERT BORTHWICK, Director of Programmes
BETTY GARDEN & KAY KIRKWOOD—Rhythm and Melody
FRED MITCHELL, Stage Manager   FRANK OLSEN, Pianist   KENNETH MACRAE, Tenor

22nd June 1941   *Programme*   **53rd Week**

TO BE BROADCAST ON "FORCES" WAVELENGTH from 10.08 p.m. till 10.50 p.m.

1. Reveille
   Light up your Face with a Smile   *Opening*
   Come Happy Day   *Ensemble*
2. THE THREE BRIGHT SPARKS
3. " Compassionate Leave "   BILL & BOB
4. KENNETH   " My Land "
5. MASSED ORCHESTRAS of the R.A.O.C. ; R.A. ; and 3rd A.A. Driver Trg. Regt., R.A.
   (By kind permission of their Commanding Officers)
   Conductors : F. OLSEN ; S. RAWLINGS ; G. REID
6. " Mother Machree "   MARIE & BILL
7. JACQUELYN & DREW—Your Sweethearts
8. A/B. FRED POWELL   Impressionist
9. MASSED ORCHESTRAS
10. BETTY & KAY with a " Tribute to London "
11. BILLIE & BOBBIE—another " Sister " Act
12. CISS   " The Sunshine of Your Smile "

13. MASSED ORCHESTRAS
14. A FEW REMARKS about a GREAT OCCASION
    Community Singing
    led by
    RICHARD TELFER at the Organ
15. " GO TO IT "   THE COMPANY
16. CISS   " Waltz of My Heart "
17. BILL & BOB
    " They Ought to Pin a Medal on his Chest "
18. BETTY & KAY   " Does he love me "
19. KENNETH   " The Road to the Isles "
20. MARIE   " Glamour "
21. CISS & BILL   " Yesterday "
    (Specially written by Bob)
22. GEORGE FORMBY
23. " AULD LANG SYNE "

Pipers from the 10th Battalion Royal Scots by kind permission of the Commanding Officer and Officers

The Society wish to gratefully acknowledge the Stage Furniture and Props lent free of charge by Capt. D. SHARP, St. Giles' Ward, No. 12

Programme for Garrison Theatre performance 22 June 1941

Garrison Theatre cottage and plaque provided by
Edinburgh High Constables at No 3 Salvesen Garden (courtesy of W R Ferguson)

*High Constables and the Town Council leaving St Mary's RC Cathedral, 31 October 1943
(Reproduced from unidentified newspaper cutting)*

CHAPTER 4

POST WAR – 1945 to 1960

Following the devastation and disruption of the war the society took some time to readjust to a peacetime routine. Changes in lifestyle heralded the end of the annual summer sail down the Clyde, and other changes over the period included renumbering of the wards and the relaxation of some rules regarding ward membership.

Constitution

The practice of renewing society membership every three years continued, and council representatives were always on hand at the annual election meeting to authorise the election and swearing in of members wishing to rejoin. Loyalty to the sovereign was also acknowledged regularly in the dispatch of telegrams to Buckingham Palace at times of special national events, the most significant being the death of King George VI on 6 February 1952 and the subsequent accession of Queen Elizabeth II.

The custom of imposing fines for failure to exhibit batons at meetings continued, and members continued to be struck off the roll for persistent non attendance. Ward captains were regularly reminded of their responsibilities in this respect. At various times it was proposed that honorary members should be appointed, but this did not find favour with the membership.

The time honoured custom of making contributions towards the cost of a portrait of the lord provost following retiral from office was continued, and in 1951 this was at the level of 5/- per member per annum.

At a special meeting in November 1946 T Robert Mossman was given the honorary office of ex-moderator when, as moderator, he "laid down his jewel of office" and resigned from the society on his election to the town council. This was possible because of an Act of Council of 3 December 1872 which specified that a moderator accepting the office of town councillor could hold the office of ex-moderator. In order to tide the society over until the next annual election meeting, Ex-Moderator David Jack assumed the role of moderator for six months.

A tragic rail disaster occurred on Sunday, 26 October 1947 on the 11.15 am train from Edinburgh to King's Cross. This was deeply felt by the society because many of the injured were known to members. One member, ex-captain Alwyn Frederick of Ward XVII lost his life in the accident, the society secretary James Dunbar and his wife were injured and ex-captain Masterton Brown of Ward XX lost his daughter and son-in-law. At the drill on 30 October members paid tribute to all who lost their lives at this time.

As a result of the Local Government [Scotland] [Edinburgh Wards] Order 1948 it was necessary to rename and renumber all wards in the society to accord with the reallocation of wards in the city. On 5 January 1950 the council approved the proposals submitted by the society for the allocation of existing High Constables to the wards for the city laid down in the new act. This re-arrangement aligned as far as possible the areas of the new and former wards, but there were cases where certain High Constables would no longer live or conduct business in the area of their own wards. However, in the course of time the position was restored to normal as new entrants were correctly appointed. The re-arrangement of wards was as follows:

New Wards		**Former Wards**	
I	St Giles	XII	St Giles
II	Holyrood	II	Canongate
III	George Square	XIV	George Square
IV	Newington	III	Newington
V	Liberton	XXI	Liberton
VI	Morningside	IV	Morningside
VII	Merchiston	V	Merchiston
VIII	Colinton	XXII	Colinton
IX	Sighthill	XIII	Dalry
X	Gorgie /Dalry	VI	Gorgie
XI	Corstorphine	XXIII	Corstorphine and Cramond
XII	Murrayfield Cramond	VII	Haymarket
XIII	Pilton	X	St Stephen's
XIV	St Bernards	VIII	St Bernards
XV	St Andrews	XI	St Andrews
XVI	Broughton	IX	Broughton
XVII	Calton	I	Calton
XVIII	West Leith	XIX	West Leith
XIX	Central Leith	XX	Central Leith
XX	South Leith	XVII	South Leith
XXI	Craigentinny	XVIII	North Leith
XXII	Portobello	XVI	Portobello
XXIII	Craigmillar	XV	St Leonards

It was obviously necessary to collect and redistribute most of the equipment held by members and this was successfully carried out in a single exercise at the City Chambers on 2 March 1950.

During the 1950s there was difficulty in identifying suitable candidates with appropriate residential or business qualifications in Wards IX, XXI and XXIII, Sighthill, Craigentinny and Craigmillar. Accordingly, dispensation was given to these wards to elect members outwith these particular geographical areas. It is recorded that at a meeting in 1950, Town Clerk John Storrar and Moderator James Buchanan had agreed that if any of these wards could not find a suitable nominee within their boundaries and if they could satisfy the moderator and executive of having made such an endeavour, they could seek a gentleman anywhere in the city. This agreement was further ratified in January 1959 by the Town Clerk William Borland who felt it was more essential to gain suitable persons from the city as a whole than to limit their acquisition in such cases to particular districts.

No roll books were printed during the war but they were restarted in 1946 and included both the society constitution, bye-laws and details of all members. However, in 1950 this system was altered in favour of two booklets, one containing the relatively permanent constitution and bye-laws with the roll of members being printed separately to comply with the re-arrangement of wards at that time and for ease of reproduction when necessitated by a large change in membership.

Over a period of some five years the use of a specially designed society tie was discussed, and although the idea was dropped in 1951, by 1955 the committee were overwhelmingly in favour. Ties for informal use were accordingly purchased from James How Ltd, George Street, at a cost of 19/6d each. These ties must have been of a very high quality because several were still in use 50 years later having been handed down by former members. The use of society ties was, however, not initially permitted in connection with formal functions, and in April 1957 it was reiterated that official dress for parades would be morning dress with black ties and white gloves with black points. The long held custom whereby office-bearers called on the lord provost at the City Chambers to celebrate the birthday of the sovereign seems to have stopped following the passing of King George VI in 1952.

Consideration was given to updating the society history in 1956 and Vice-Moderator J Norman H Steele prepared a short history for the use of members to distribute to interested parties. This short history was also published in the "Edinburgh Evening News" but the matter of a more detailed historical record was dropped.

The question of levying an annual subscription on members had been raised in 1934 and was debated again in the 1950s when the practice was to collect contributions from members for specific purposes as they arose. At the annual nomination meeting on 26 March 1956 a formal proposal that an annual subscription should be introduced was narrowly defeated, but other bye-laws were amended to introduce a four guinea entry fee for new members and to reduce the number of general meetings for drill from eight to six per annum.

Although the motion for the introduction of an annual levy did not receive constitutional approval of two thirds of those attending the meeting on 26 March 1956 it did receive 63% of the votes. This imposition of an annual levy was discussed over the next two years and it was finally agreed unanimously on 6 March 1958. Previous individual payments to a "contribution fund" had been solely for the purpose of meeting the expenses of social entertainment whereas the annual levy would in future also balance the general expenditure of the society. The accounts for the year ended 28 February 1958 show for the first time income from an annual levy amounting to £390. Previously, under the terms of the constitution, a levy could only be made on members at the end of the year once the books of the society had been balanced, but this was not a practical financial arrangement for the prevailing circumstances. In November 1959 it was agreed that new members joining the society after 30 September would not be required to pay the levy for that year.

Recorded comments from various lord provosts and councillors indicate the great regard in which the High Constables were held by the town council. At the annual election meeting in April 1957 Bailie Herbert Brechin is noted as stating that the magistrates and council held the society in high esteem and they were proud of the friendship and regard existing between them. He advised the society never to lower their standards because the High Constables at all functions, whether freedom ceremonies, garden parties or church assemblies were the envy and admiration of all, including the civic leaders of other Scottish towns.

Until 1955 all minutes were recorded in specially bound volumes, but it was decided then that it would be preferable to change to loose leaf folders when the bound volumes were complete. Consequently, the last minute of a general meeting contained in a bound volume is 3 April 1961, and the last bound committee minute is that of 7 March 1957.

In the late 1950s, the question of exhibiting society artefacts was considered with city officials, and in March 1959 the council confirmed that one display cabinet would be built in Committee Room "A" in the City Chambers later that year, and that a sum of money had been included in the council's budget. A display cabinet was thereafter provided in an alcove below the notice board displaying the names of past-moderators and this was used continuously for some 50 years. At meetings of the committee and prior to church parades this room was allocated by the council for use by the High Constables and was regarded by members as their base within the City Chambers.

Prior to 1857 the office-bearers of the society had consisted of moderator, treasurer, clerk or secretary, chaplain, surgeon and assistant surgeon, but following extension of the city in 1856 to make the boundaries coincide with the police boundaries and to transfer to the magistrates and council the powers of the Police Commissioners, re-organisation within the society was necessary. Accordingly the office of vice-moderator was established, the election of a chaplain as office-bearer was discontinued and the custodier of batons was made a regular officer of the society. In the 19th century, the office of chaplain was not necessarily held by an ordained minister of the church and indeed the last incumbents of that office in 1854, 1855 and 1856 were a builder, a plumber and a bookseller respectively. In 1932 the question of resurrecting the office of chaplain had been raised but not pursued.

In February 1959 Moderator J Norman H Steele suggested that an honorary chaplain should be appointed to the society in view of the close affinity and frequent visits to St Giles Cathedral. At the following committee meeting this was unanimously approved and Dr H C Whitley, the Minister of St Giles Cathedral, thereafter accepted the appointment as first honorary chaplain to the High Constables of Edinburgh.

To some extent therefore, the appointment of Dr Whitley as chaplain restored the position after a gap of some 100 years, and he was presented with his badge of office by Lord Provost Sir Ian Johnson-Gilbert at the spring inspection in 1959.

Drills

Because of the continued difficulty in finding suitable premises for parade purposes, the town council discussed the matter in 1947 and agreed that a portion of the garage at Annandale Street would be set aside for the use of the society at the appropriate times. The practice of drilling thereafter continued in the spring and autumn with parades on three separate evenings for drill followed by a separate parade for inspection at each season. Prior to each of the drill sessions, a committee meeting was held in an appropriate room at the same venue.

On assembling, the parade was formed into six platoons and a verbal roll call of the whole society was taken. Thereafter, platoon commanders ensured that the parade was correctly constituted by checking that each member was wearing his badge, carrying his large baton and was in possession of his small baton. The general level of attendance was somewhat less than 200, and fines were imposed for non attendance without excuse. Dress requirements were such that dark suits were necessary, hats of various shapes and sizes were worn and all members drilled with their large batons. Prior to October 1951, all members including office-bearers adopted the same form of dress, but it was agreed at that time that the moderator should wear full official dress and carry a silver baton at inspections as a token of respect to the lord provost. In 1957, the large baton drill was changed at the request of Drill Officer John Aitken, M.C, but no details of the change are recorded.

Following inspection by the lord provost or senior bailie, all platoons marched past the inspecting officer accompanied by a pipe band. The band was occasionally present at drills as well as inspections, and this not only gave a great boost to the quality of marching but also ensured a sense of occasion to the event. The band was provided by the city and initially this was the Edinburgh Tramway Pipe Band, subsequently renamed the Transport Welfare Association Pipe Band. All drills were held in the Central Garage, Annandale Street, with the exception of autumn1948 when the venue was the Waverley Market.

The number of members present at drills was carefully recorded, and prior to the drill the total aggregate number of points gained by each ward up to and including the event was calculated. This was then announced to the society in order that the leading contenders for the Dunbar Trophy should be known. Initially, the maximum number of points qualifying for the trophy was 120, this representing full attendance of all ward members at six drills, two inspections and two general meetings.

After all the changes to life style occasioned by the war, it was understandable that the society should consider the frequency of turnout for drilling practice. In 1949, a motion to have even more drills was heavily defeated, and in 1956 it was unanimously agreed at the annual general meeting that the number of parades in the spring and autumn should be reduced from four to three, i.e. two for drilling purposes and one for inspection by the lord provost. This suggestion had been under consideration since 1947.

It was felt by some in the society that elderly and infirm members should resign if they were unable to take part in drills, but this was not supported. It was accepted that such members had given long and devoted service and that they should attend drills and record their presence but be excused any part of the drilling.

There were several occasions when High Constables were required to resign from the society because of their election to the Town Council, and it was particularly gratifying for the society to have former member James Miller carrying out the inspections during his term of office as lord provost from 1951 to 1954.

Other regular guests were the chief constable and Her Majesty's Chief Inspector of Constabulary in Scotland, and in the spring of 1957 Lord Provost Sir John G Banks was accompanied by Lady Banks.

In 1959, the lax discipline of some members regarding the submission of meaningful excuses for absence was brought to the captains' attention by Moderator Norman Steele, and at the same time it was felt necessary to appoint a deputy drill officer.

Charity
Although the society was hopeful that the annual picnic for disabled children would recommence as soon as possible after the war, it was not practicable to do so until the summer of 1948. The venue for the picnic was Spylaw Park, Colinton, and it took very much the same form as the pre-war picnics with lunch and refreshments, sports, prizes

and music provided by pipers. The cost of the event was as usual funded by a contribution from all ward members and the essential assistance of members' wives and lady friends was greatly appreciated.

However, the form of entertainment for children was changing, as were concerns for their welfare, and prior to the 1951 picnic the director of education expressed concern because headmasters of the special schools had asked for a guarantee of covered accommodation for all the children. This followed problems experienced at the previous outing in 1950 when the weather had been particularly wet.

The society responded to this by supplying marquees and tents, and these were generously provided and erected free of charge by courtesy of Vice-Moderator Thomas Y Anderson. The picnics in 1951 and 1952 were a great success and the weatherman was kind. All the hard work put in by the society was greatly appreciated by successive lord provosts who generally paid a visit to the outings.

!953 was a busy year of society events as a result of the coronation of Queen Elizabeth II and accordingly the annual picnic was not held that year. Additionally, the director of education indicated that it was unlikely that the school meals department would be able to undertake the catering again, and in view of all the circumstances it was agreed to abandon future picnics and to concentrate society efforts on the crippled childrens' treat at Christmas, the war blinded at Newington House and aged old peoples' organisations.

Perhaps the success of the Garrison Theatre was still fresh in the minds of members, because it was agreed in 1954 that a special treat should be given to deserving old people at Christmas. As a result, a lunchtime event at the Music Hall in George Street was organised for old folks still resident in their own homes – many deserving individuals being specifically recommended by the city social services officer.

The first of these events took place on 14 December 1954 when some 500 old folks attended. During lunch, the party was treated to music and dancing by the band of the 1st Battalion Gordon Highlanders. Later, further entertainment was provided by the Scottish comedian Harry Gordon and also by Jack Holden. Lord Provost Sir John G Banks and the Lady Provost attended and took part, and the whole venture was deemed very worthwhile and successful.

In general, guests were not invited more than once, and gifts were given by the lord and lady provost - a packet of tea for each of the women and a packet of tobacco for the men.

This treat was repeated over three years in similar fashion, and in addition to the entertainment, the society provided motor transport for many of the guests. At that time relatively few people were car owners and the city welfare officer expressed the view that it would be a real thrill for the old folks if a car was provided for their transport..

By 1957 the numbers attending were dwindling, but reminders of the Garrison Theatre days were rekindled when part of the entertainment was given by Richard Telfer accompanying community singing at an electric organ - this being a far cry from Sunday evenings at the theatre organ in the New Victoria Cinema, but it was no less enthusiastically received.

In autumn 1958 it was agreed that the lunch event be dropped, and that parcels to deserving old people be delivered instead. Wards were asked to supply suitable names and ward members then uplifted and delivered the parcels personally. The first parcels were supplied at cost by society member Andrew Aikman and thus started a practice which has continued for some 50 years. The 18 items contained in the first parcels were as follows:

Two lbs.sugar, 8 oz. Stork margarine, 8 oz. New Zealand butter, 8 oz. tin of fruit, 8oz. of Christmas pudding, one jar apple/strawberry jam, one pkt. "Cresta", one pkt. salt, one tin Carnation milk, 8 oz. Ty-Phoo tea, 8 oz. Creamola, one jelly, one pkt. K.S. tomato soup, one 12 oz. tin of luncheon meat, one tin corned beef, one tin A1 processed peas, one tin Senovitch mixed vegetables and 6 Oxo cubes.

Following receipt of the parcels, many pensioners sent very warm letters of thanks. These demonstrable signs of appreciation have always indicated that that not only were the contents of the parcel helpful at Christmas time, but perhaps equally important were the personal visits.

The lord provost's Christmas treat for school children was reinstated in 1947, and the High Constables again provided stewards for matinee performances at the King's Theatre, the Gaiety Theatre in Leith and occasionally at the State Cinema, Leith. The events at the King's Theatre were under the supervision of ward captains and two members of each ward, and constables from the three Leith wards helped out at the Gaiety Theatre. These treats were repeated for a few years but the involvement of the society appears to have died out in the mid 1950s.

Following the death of the King, all members were invited to contribute voluntarily to the King George VI National Memorial Fund, and in March 1953 a sum of £90 was contributed by this means.

Dinner

In the immediate aftermath of war it was difficult to find suitable accommodation and catering capability to stage the society annual dinner. As an interim measure, the office- bearers and captains held a dinner at the North British Station Hotel in April 1947 at which Lord Provost Sir John Falconer and a few other guests were entertained. Costs were borne by the members attending and the timing coincided with the end of T Robertson Mossman's term as moderator. This set the precedent for the biennial moderator's dinner which is now a regular part of the society calendar although the funding arrangements have changed over the years to ensure that everyone attends as a non paying guest. Regular details of these dinners are not recorded for this period, but in 1951, when Moderator James G Y Buchanan had demitted office, the moderator's dinner was held in the Hamilton Lodge Hotel, Portobello.

Early in 1948 a government ban on functions for over 100 people was lifted and accordingly the society annual dinner was held in the North British Station Hotel on 10 December 1948 - this being the first since December 1938. As would be expected in the aftermath of a devastating war this dinner was a great success and was attended by about 300 people. The catering was not, however, of a very high standard and it was agreed that the subsequent dinner should be held at the Freemasons' Hall in George Street. This became the venue for the annual dinners in 1949,1950 and 1951, but by that time the popularity of the event was such that a new venue was necessary. Accordingly, it moved to the Music Hall in George Street for the next three years and ultimately returned to the North British Station Hotel in 1955. This was the only venue large enough to host this prestigious event and it became the traditional venue for many years thereafter.

The format of the dinner was the subject of much discussion in the early 1950s, the main criticisms by members relating to the amplification systems, the decoration of the hall, the number of toasts, the length and quality of speeches, the desirability of providing musical entertainment and the quality of the meal. It was agreed that the guest speaker should always be the choice of the moderator, and that instrumentalists and singers should continue to be a feature.

Guest speakers continued to be men of prominence and included the Hon. Lord Blades[1949], the Earl of Home[1952], His Grace the Duke of Buccleuch[1954], the Rt Hon Earl of Dundee[1955], Lord Normand of Aberlour[1956] and the Rt Hon Walter E Elliot, MP[1957]. In 1958 the invited guest speaker was unable to attend due to a change of dates and the Rev. Harry C Whitley stepped in to fill the breach.

The design on the front of the dinner menu remained unaltered and the motif continued to be up-dated with the names and dates of all moderators since 1707 engraved in leaves around the moderator's gold medal. A copy of the 1952 toast list is reproduced at the end of this chapter and illustrates the involvement of His Majesty's Forces, the city council and kindred societies. The principal speaker giving the toast to the society was the Rt. Hon the Earl of Home whose subsequent political career led to him becoming Prime Minister in 1963.

The menu at that time did not contain a full list of top table guests - this was to follow later.

Social

No annual excursion had taken place since 1939, and it was agreed that the Clyde cruise should be resumed in 1948 after a gap of eight years. Accordingly, on 26 May 1948 some 350 members, friends and guests travelled by train to the west and thoroughly enjoyed their sail "doon the watter".

Similar outings were undertaken over the following 4 years, the destinations being Lochranza [1949], Dunoon [1950], Campbeltown [1951] and Inveraray [1952]. The popularity of such excursions sadly decreased at that time, partly because of the difficulty in setting aside a whole day for the outing and also because ownership of private cars was becoming more prevalent and individual family outings or picnics to places outwith the city could be more easily arranged.

By 1952, the number attending the annual sail was down to 270. Of this number only 60 were High Constables and it was very difficult to justify the expenditure. This particular trip was almost cancelled because the original price quoted for chartering the "Duchess of Hamilton" was £360 –an increase of £100 on the previous year. After some hard bargaining a satisfactory price was negotiated, but by this time the writing appeared to be on the wall as far as future such outings were concerned.

In an attempt to boost numbers, invitations had been issued to members of the High Constables of the three kindred societies to join as paying guests, their moderators always having been invited as guests of the society, but this initiative did not find favour with the other organisations.

Nevertheless, the outings were still extremely good fun in spite of reducing numbers. The following extract from the regular column of the journalist "Macnib" of the "Edinburgh Evening News" gives a flavour of the atmosphere in 1951 :

"High Constables each year take flight, for one brief day their cares to banish ;
And yesterday they found delight in Campbeltown and Macrihanish.
While other Caledonian parts experienced weather not so Spanish,
The sun stayed out to cheer their hearts at Campbeltown and Macrihanish.

They say that Edinburgh folk are gey reserved and unco clannish,
But watch them as they laugh and joke in Campbeltown and Macrihanish.
Frae city big-wigs furrowed broos, the lines and signs of worry vanish,
When they take walks among the coos, 'twixt Campbeltown and Macrihanish."

In 1953, in view of the difficulty in getting sufficient support and also because it was going to be a particularly busy year as a result of extra ceremonials and functions occasioned by the coronation of Queen Elizabeth II, the outing was dropped. However, there was a body of opinion in the society that the annual excursion was a great event and after a gap of five years it was resumed in 1958 at a cost of 50/- per member. The guest list was severely curtailed to a maximum of ten including Lord Provost Sir Ian Johnson-Gilbert and the Lady Provost, and a very happy day was spent by the 276 people sailing to and from Brodick.

There was a feeling at that time that the outing could survive if held every two years, but on 8 June 1960 the last society annual excursion to the Clyde was held.

It is not clear whether the entertainment on board was as extensive in the post war years as in the 1920s and 1930s, but certainly the trips were always associated with fund raising by means of a raffle.

A popular feature of the new Edinburgh International Festival was the Military Tattoo held on the castle esplanade. This was first performed in 1950 and the High Constables frequently made this an annual social outing for society members and their ladies by arranging for a block booking in one of the stands to enjoy the various displays, the parades of the massed military and pipe bands and the floodlit conclusion with a lone piper on the castle ramparts.

The very popular society whist drive and dance was resumed in March 1948 with an attendance of 650 at the Music Hall and Assembly Rooms. Tickets were priced at 15/- per head, catering was carried out by the city catering department and music was provided by the Edinburgh Police Dance Band and the Royal Scots Regimental Band. Special transport arrangements were provided by the Corporation Transport Department with buses available on the various routes and many guests were invited including Lord Provost Sir Andrew Murray. As was customary on these occasions, a raffle was held and the sum of £54 was raised and donated to the Lord Provost's Flood Relief Fund.

The success of the whist drive and dance was such that it was repeated in November 1948, and thereafter became an annual event taking place generally in the autumn of each year. Throughout most of the 1950s, the numbers attending were generally in the order of 450 to 500, but towards the end of the decade the popularity declined somewhat with numbers falling significantly.

Ceremonial
1947 was a significant year in Edinburgh's cultural life when the Edinburgh International Festival of Music and Drama was inaugurated by Lord Provost Sir John Falconer. The High Constables were anxious to support this venture as much as

possible and have been involved in a ceremonial capacity with this event to a greater or lesser degree since its inception.

Other regular ceremonial duties resumed as before, and in addition to the Greeting and Kirking services for the council the annual round included the opening service of the General Assembly of the Church of Scotland, General Assembly Sunday, the Battle of Britain service, the Remembrance Day service and the annual service for seamen in South Leith Parish Church. In addition, there were special church services in 1954 to dedicate the Covenanters' Memorial in the Grassmarket, in 1957 to mark the opening of the Mass X-Ray Campaign, in 1958 to mark the rededication of the Edinburgh Hebrew Community and in 1959 for the bi-centenary of the birth of Robert Burns.

Presentation of the Freedom of the City was a relatively frequent occurrence at this time and the High Constables acted as stewards at all these events, starting with the award to General Dwight D Eisenhower at the Usher Hall in 1946. No invitation was extended to the High Constables to attend the civic luncheon following this event, and the society's disappointment was tactfully conveyed to Lord Provost Sir John Falconer.

In March 1949 the Freedom of the City was granted to the Duke of Edinburgh at the Usher Hall, and this was followed by a charity concert on the same day which was attended by 76 members of the society. In August of the same year, a similar ceremony was held, unusually, in Princes Street Gardens. The presentation on this occasion was to Sir Donald Cameron, Mayor of Dunedin, New Zealand, and some 70 High Constables were involved as stewards.

Other Freedom Ceremonies attended were in August 1950 for the presentation to the American Ambassador, Mr Lewis Williams Douglas; in January 1954 for the presentation to the Earl and Countess Mountbatten of Burma; and in February 1957 for Lord Rowallan, the Chief Scout.

1947 saw the start of the Edinburgh Highland Games at Murrayfield Rugby Ground and the popularity of this was such that it continued for many years. Throughout this period the society made a major commitment to support the event as much as possible. Generally, the games were held in August or September and upwards of 100 constables regularly acted as stewards for the whole duration of the event.

Stewarding facilities were also provided by the High Constables at a garden fete organised by the lady provost in the grounds of George Heriot's School in 1948 and in subsequent years at similar fund raising garden parties in the grounds of Lauriston Castle. In addition to these regular stewarding duties, the services of the High Constables were also provided at the clan gathering at Murrayfield in 1951 sponsored by the Festival of Britain, and at a youth rally also at Murrayfield in 1953.

The High Constables attended the proclamation of Queen Elizabeth at the Mercat Cross in February 1952, and Her Majesty visited Edinburgh on 29 June 1952 following her coronation earlier that month. She was presented with the keys of the city on arrival at Princes Street Station in the royal train, and the presentation was made by Lord Provost James Miller attended by the High Constables of Edinburgh. The ceremony was followed by divine service at St Giles Cathedral and this particular ceremony was to be repeated on subsequent official visits.

As a result of the change of sovereign several other civic events were held, and many were attended by the office-bearers and other constables in a ceremonial capacity. These included special celebrations at Murrayfield Rugby Ground and at the Mound in Princes Street, and a special service was held at St Giles Cathedral on the occasion of the presentation of the Honours of Scotland.

It appears that in 1954 or 1955 a technicolour film was produced to depict the traditions, customs and ceremonies of the City of Edinburgh. The office-bearers and the lord provost were portrayed in this film but there are no records in the city archive of such a film.

Not all civic turnouts required the society to give practical help, and office-bearers and other society members were often entertained socially by the lord provost and the council. As well as being present at the various receptions following church parades, in the early 1950s special receptions were held by the lord provost at New Year and during the period of the Edinburgh Festival. It is probable that the moderator would also have been involved as a personal guest of the lord provost at other social occasions as has been the custom in recent years, but no records of these occasions have been retained.

Equipment

During the war years when the energies of the society members were focused on matters of greater importance to the free world, strict control of the ceremonial equipment was not a high priority. Accordingly it is not surprising that in 1946 a significant number of items of equipment had been lost or mislaid and that the ringing of batons had not been carried out for a number of years.

Checks on members' equipment were carried out but it was some time before this equipment was brought up to date because of the relatively high cost involved. In 1950, members' missing equipment was replaced at a cost of £91, this expenditure being met from surplus monies in the badge and baton account.

The equipment was also in need of some overhaul, replacement and updating, and this was eventually completed in 1954 by Messrs Alex Kirkwood and Sons at a cost of £384. Prior to completion of this work, successful negotiations had been concluded with the council who were pleased to donate £250 to the cost. This delay was partly due to national legislation which precluded expenditure by local authorities on this type of work in the years immediately following the war. This special grant was over and above the normal annual grant which had been at a level of £50 for several years.

This expensive reinstatement of equipment caused the society to address the question of insurance for all the various items of equipment. Insurance cover had been in place for the regalia held in the City Chambers and for the office-bearers' equipment, and a valuation carried out in 1951 valued the moderator's gold medal and chain at £200 and the vice-moderator's badge and chain at £100. At that time there was no cover for equipment held by individual members so in 1955 the first steps were taken by obtaining a valuation for these items. Members' badges were valued at £4-10/-, their small batons at £7-15/- and the more ornate captains' batons were valued at £12-15/-. No assessment was given of the replacement cost of the large wooden batons.

In November 1955 the British General Insurance Co. offered to insure the members' equipment for an annual premium of £25-7/6d, and this was accepted on the basis that each ward should pay £1 towards the cost. However, payment for this insurance cover was short lived following Treasurer George M Bruce's suggestion in May 1958 that the premium be discontinued and that the society should build up its own fund for this purpose. This equipment fund was started in 1958/59 by transferring £25 from the finances for that year. About the same time the society purchased dies which enables future medals to be produced at a lower price.

41

A photograph showing the office-bearers and captains in the year 1947-48 was produced by photographers J Campbell Harper but unfortunately no copies of this were included with the minutes.

Some members were uncertain as to the protocol of wearing their badges at informal functions such as the whist drive and the annual dinner, and accordingly it was confirmed in November 1950 that the appropriate society badges should be worn at events involving all members. Some wards had previously acquired their own miniature ward badges for use at informal ward functions, and it was made clear that these were not acceptable while on parade.

Over the long period of existence of the High Constables several items had gone missing and in November 1957 two badges struck in 1887 were returned to the society by a firm of solicitors. One badge was that of the past-moderator in 1888 and the other was the vice-moderator's gold badge for the year 1887. This badge was one of a number which had been specially struck for members to commemorate the jubilee of Queen Victoria, and it included clasps dated 1887 and 1897.

Neither of these badges is now in the possession of the society but two other specially struck badges to commemorate Queen Victoria's Jubilee are included in the current inventory of equipment.

!948 saw the introduction of medals for past-moderators and past-surgeons and in April 1959 long service badges were first presented to members having served 25 years or more. At that time 21 such awards were made to serving members and 7 to recently retired members.

Sport

Not until 1947 did the society sports clubs restart their activities, the Golf Club being the first to resume play when they won their match against the Town Council Golf Club but lost against Perth High Constables at Rosemount. There does not appear to have been any difficulty in resuming the activities of the Golf Club, their annual whist drive, dinner and dance continuing to be an important date in the society calendar.

1948 saw the revival of the Bowling Club, and their matches against Edinburgh Corporation Bowling Club were occasionally attended by the lord provost.

Support for the Angling Club was not great in the early years following the war, and although some activity took place from 1948 onwards a special effort was made in 1956 to activate a revival and the club resumed with a competition against Perth High Constables at Loch Leven in May 1957.

It was hoped that the Curling and Rifle Clubs would follow shortly thereafter, but it was not until 1950 that curling resumed with 18 constables participating. Difficulties had occurred in booking Haymarket Ice Rink at a suitable time and it was also difficult in the mid 1950s to recruit enough members to make the club viable. However, a regular pattern was established, and the annual game against Perth High Constables, which had started in 1926, was also resumed.

Members of the Edinburgh society who participated in the match against Perth in 1951 (photograph included at the end of this chapter) were:

George Forrest (skip)	W. D. Lawson (skip)
J. B Alexander	Thomas Brown
J. Norman M. Steele	W. Roy
Thomas Anderson	John Horne

Office Bearers   1949 – 1950
D Cook-Custodier,   T Y Anderson-Secretary,   J G Y Buchanan-Moderator,
Lord Provost Sir A H A Murray,   J A McArthur-Vice Moderator,   D Wilkie-Ex Moderator,
J Dunbar-Treasurer,   W Murray-Society Officer,   Dr W S Dalgetty-Surgeon.
(Courtesy of Scotsman Publications)

Top Table at the Annual Dinner in the Music Hall, 4 December 1953
(Courtesy of Scotsman Publications)

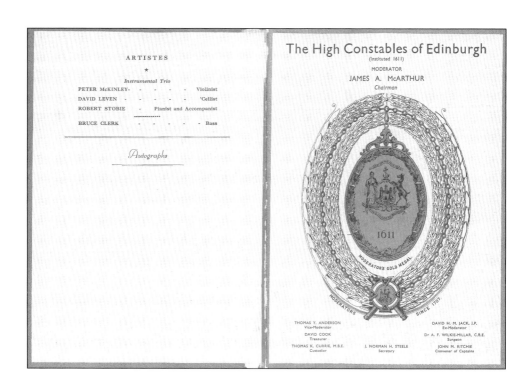

ARTISTES

*

Instrumental Trio

PETER McKINLEY - - - - - Violinist
DAVID LEVEN - - - - - 'Cellist
ROBERT STOBIE - Pianist and Accompanist

BRUCE CLERK - - - - - Bass

Autographs

The High Constables of Edinburgh
(Instituted 1611)

MODERATOR

JAMES A. McARTHUR
Chairman

1611

THOMAS Y. ANDERSON
Vice-Moderator

DAVID COOK
Treasurer

THOMAS K. CURRIE, M.B.E.
Custodier

J. NORMAN H. STEELE
Secretary

DAVID H. M. JACK, J.P.
Ex-Moderator

Dr A. F. WILKIE-MILLAR, C.B.E.
Surgeon

JOHN M. RITCHIE
Convener of Captains

THE HIGH CONSTABLES OF EDINBURGH

Annual Dinner

MUSIC HALL, GEORGE STREET
FRIDAY, 5th DECEMBER 1952

MENU

POTAGE PARISIAN

FILET DE SOLE JOINVILLE

DINDE ROTI FARCIE A L'ANGLAISE
CHOUX DE BRUXELLES AU BEURRE
POMMES FONDANTES

BOMBE DUC DE CORNOUAILLES
TIMBALE DE MACEDOINE DE FRUITS FRAIS

TARTELETTE IVANHOE

CAFE

TOAST LIST

THE QUEEN - - - - - The Moderator

The Duke of Edinburgh, Queen Elizabeth
the Queen Mother, Queen Mary, the
Duke of Rothesay, and the other
members of the Royal Family - - The Moderator

Her Majesty's Forces - - - - - The Treasurer

Reply—Rear-Admiral J. H. F. Crombie, C.B., C.B.E.

Lord Provost, Magistrates, and Town
Council of the City of Edinburgh - The Vice-Moderator

Reply—Bailie James Campbell.

The High Constables of Edinburgh   The Rt. Hon. The Earl of
Home, P.C., The Minister of State for Scotland

Reply—The Moderator.

The High Constables of Holyrood House,
Leith, and Perth - - - - - The Secretary

Reply—The Moderator of The High Constables and Guard of
Honour of Holyrood House, Mr J. Edwin Lamb.

Guests - - - - - - - The Custodier

Reply—Mr A. D. Mackie,
Editor of the *Evening Dispatch*.

The Moderator - - - - - The Surgeon

AULD LANG SYNE

GOD SAVE THE QUEEN

Dinner menu and toast list, 1952

Proclamation of H M Queen Elizabeth II, 8 February 1952
(Courtesy of Scotsman Publications)

Edinburgh High Constables v Perth High Constables, Feb 1951
(Courtesy of Scotsman Publications)

CHAPTER 5

1960 to LOCAL GOVERNMENT REORGANISATION IN 1975

Although life style in Great Britain as a whole is generally described at this time as being liberated, with much emphasis on drug-taking, rock-and-roll and "flower power", this change had little effect on the Society of Edinburgh High Constables.

The values and traditions of the society continued to be upheld and their 350th anniversary was celebrated in style in 1961.

Constitution

Procedure at general meetings continued as before, the roll being called out by the secretary or custodier at the start of each meeting and the minutes of the previous meeting being read out verbatim for approval. Following the election meeting in April, a photograph of all office-bearers with the lord provost was taken for press publication, and thereafter everyone gathered together in a function room in the City Chambers to enjoy the refreshments provided by the moderator and vice-moderator. Refreshment provided at this time consisted of hot pies washed down with beer or whisky, and this informal get-together was always eagerly anticipated.

Members still required to be re-elected every three years, and this task continued to be administered by a solicitor in the Town Clerk's department. Meetings continued to be held in the City Chambers, but due to their unavailability in spring 1974, the nomination meeting, election meeting and some committee meetings were held in the Minto Hotel, Newington. The cost of refreshments following the election meeting was considerably greater than when provided in the City Chambers, and on this occasion the society subsidised the expenses of the moderator and vice-moderator who traditionally bore the cost of this function.

Early on in this period there were discussions about the maximum term of office of the society secretary and treasurer, because there was a feeling that the society might be better served if the term of office for these two positions was not restricted to two years as with the other office-bearers. A proposal to this effect was submitted to the nomination meeting in March 1960 but was rejected by 130 votes to 60.

It had long been the custom that all office-bearers would automatically hold office for the specified maximum of two years, but the desirability of this practice was raised in 1963. Accordingly, it was remitted to the office-bearers to prepare a report on the period of service of all office-bearers. This report reminded members that the maximum period of service had been changed from one year to two in 1857 with provision for annual changes if necessary. No recommendations were given, but it was suggested that the length of service of each office-bearer could be restricted voluntarily to one year, thus avoiding any need for constitutional change.

The debate continued for a number of years and at the nomination meeting in March 1974 a motion was carried by 131 to 46 to voluntarily reduce the period of service in each office to one year. It appears that this was never put into practice but the matter continued to remain a somewhat contentious issue.

Certain wards still took great pride in competing for the Dunbar Trophy, and the rule of the competition precluding any ward from being presented with the trophy for more than two successive years seems to have been flouted on several occasions.

Ward VII, Merchiston, were awarded the trophy for the third year in succession in 1960, in 1972 Ward XVIII, West Leith, were given the trophy for the fifth year in succession and in 1976 Ward XVIII, West Leith, were presented with the trophy for the eighth time in nine years. Results of the competition from 1929 onwards are included as appendix 7.

Regarding the financial affairs of the society, the honorarium paid to the society officer was periodically reviewed and was gradually increased from 10 guineas in 1960 to £40 in 1975. Retiring moderators had been traditionally presented with a tangible gift in recognition of their services, but in view of the financial outlay now required of the moderator this was changed in 1962 to a monetary honorarium. This was paid every two years, the first honorarium of £70 being increased to £200 in 1968.

The happy and enjoyable custom of the moderator's dinner continued, this being held near the end of his period in office. Because of continually rising costs there was some concern about the financial responsibility placed on the moderator and as a result, in 1975 ward captains were not included and the dinner was confined to office-bearers, the moderator's own ward and a few special guests. Following this, the moderator's honorarium was substantially increased by 50% to £300 in order that all wards could be represented in future.

A continuing financial commitment was the contribution to the lord provost's portrait which was paid every third year at level of £70 per annum until 1974 when it was increased to £120.

The annual levy on members was £3.00 in 1960. This slowly increased to a figure of £3.10/- in the late 1960s and by 1975 the levy had risen to £6.00. It was reiterated in 1971 that new members joining the society after 30th September would be excused the levy for that year.

Anniversary celebrations were held in 1961 to mark 350 years since the election of the first constables in Edinburgh in 1611 on the command of King James I and the Privy Council. These celebrations comprised the following two significant events:

On Sunday 4 June 1961 a special service of dedication was held in St Giles Cathedral. This was attended by two thirds of the membership, and at the invitation of the society the lord provost also attended along with many magistrates and councillors. The council representatives turned out in their ermine and scarlet robes and joined in the procession from the City Chambers to St Giles preceded by Moderator George M Bruce and the High Constables. The sermon was given by the society chaplain, the Rev Dr H C Whitley, the text being the first verse of Psalm 127 "except the Lord keep the City the watchmen waketh but in vain". During the sermon, Dr Whitley maintained that "the High Constables of Edinburgh were not just a decorative relic, but a living reminder to all that the common life and good name of a city depended on the public service and sense of responsibility found among its citizens". Light refreshments were thereafter provided by the council for members and their ladies.

The highlight of the year was on 3 November 1961 when the lord provost, magistrates and council honoured the society by inviting members and their ladies to a reception and dance in the Assembly Rooms. This was attended by a record turnout of members and a very large number of magistrates and councillors in their ceremonial attire. Lord Provost J Greig Dunbar paid tribute to the society and referred to the happy relationship between the council and the society. In response, Moderator George M Bruce presented a cheque for £200 for the lord provost's personal benevolent fund to assist people in need, and he asked the lord provost to accept two memorial seats which had been placed that day on either side of the west door of St Giles Cathedral, this having served as a focal point for many society duties. The cost of the seats was £45.3/8d.and Edinburgh Corporation agreed to take responsibility for their maintenance.

The above mentioned civic reception was described as an outstanding event which would be recalled with pleasure for a long time by those participating.

A further event of note was the generous gift to the society by the Golf Club of a silver cigar and cigarette casket suitably inscribed. This was to be used regularly for members and guests at the top table during the annual dinner.

With respect to service to the society, a precedent was set in April 1961 when it was agreed that cumulative service should count towards the award of long service medals. This arose when a member, Ex-Captain David Pearson pointed out to the committee that he had given service to the society from 1934 until his departure for Australia in 1950 and on his return to Edinburgh had rejoined the society in December 1955.

However, several less enthusiastic members were still being struck from the roll of members for persistent failure to attend meetings as required or to respond to verbal or written approaches.

The arrangement referred to in Chapter 4 granting Ward IX Sighthill, Ward XXI Craigentinny, and Ward XXIII Craigmillar dispensation to allow them to elect members outwith their wards' geographical areas was a matter of regular debate and concern throughout the 1960s. Some other wards wished to have a similar dispensation, and in 1963 the committee agreed to apply this dispensation to a new member of Ward XVII Calton having heard that Ward XVI, in which area the nominee lived and worked, had no objections.

The whole question of such dispensation came to a head in April 1965 and by a vote of 25 to 2 the committee agreed to stick strictly to the dispensation agreed with the Town Clerk in 1959, thus ensuring that the moderator and office-bearers must be satisfied that the ward in question had made every endeavour to find a suitable candidate within their territorial area. It was also agreed about that time that the designation "Director" or "Managing Director" on nomination papers and in the roll book was insufficient, and that in future all such members should be designated by indicating his appointment and his trade or profession.

In 1969 the newly introduced postal codes were included in the roll books, and the introduction of decimal currency in 1972 required changes to the constitution to remove references to pounds, shillings and pence.

In order to co-ordinate the affairs of the society with the traditional dates of a normal society year, it was decided that the financial year should end on 31 January instead of 28 February as previously, and so in 1969 the treasurer's report covered only 11 months in order to introduce the new system.

During the latter part of the 1960s there was a feeling that the society should become somewhat more involved in civic affairs. However, after some initial investigation and discussion at ward level it became apparent that most wards were happy with the existing situation whereby the society should respond to requests from the council but should not actively seek additional duties. As part of this consultation, Vice-Moderator T N Miller met Lord Provost Sir James McKay in 1972 to discuss the possibility of more civic duties but there is no record of any specific response from the council. It is, however, recorded that earlier, in 1965, the council did not agree with Lord Provost Sir Duncan Weatherstone's suggestion that some High Constables should attend on him at council meetings.

In the late 1960s it was decided that 2 seats should be presented to the city and placed at the west door to St Giles Cathedral alongside those presented in 1961 as part of the anniversary celebrations. The reason for this generous gift is not recorded but 2 seats were purchased at £65 each and duly handed over at a small ceremony on 18 November 1969 to Lord Provost James W McKay and the minister of St Giles Cathedral.

In the early 1970s it was felt unnecessary to print the roll book every year, and since then the interval increased to two years, publication being timed to follow the traditional biennial change of office-bearers.

The position of honorary society chaplain became vacant in 1973 on retiral of the Very Rev. Dr. H C Whitley, but this position was filled shortly thereafter by the appointment of the new minister of St Giles Cathedral, the Rev. Gilleasbuig I Macmillan.. The chaplain's badge was presented to Mr. Macmillan at the annual general meeting in April 1975.

Reorganisation of local government in 1975 required a major change to the society's constitution, and in order to ensure a satisfactory transition the society set up a watching committee in 1972 to anticipate any necessary changes. The reorganisation involved ending the city of Edinburgh as an autonomous royal burgh and replacing it with one of four districts within the new Lothian Region. Many functions were retained by the district councils, but responsibility for strategic services with wide geographical implications were transferred to the Regional Council.

The number of wards in the city had remained at 23 since the Extension Act of 1920, but arrangements for the new Edinburgh City District provided for 60 wards within the former city area and added 4 other wards in an extended area to the west of the city. The extended area covered South Queensferry, Dalmeny, Kirkliston, Winchburgh, Newbridge, Ratho, Currie and Balerno.

Since the new wards were to be so diverse and unrelated to the former wards, the watching committee recommended that the society should continue to comprise 23 wards using the same names as previously. They also suggested that residential and business qualifications be dispensed with and that membership of any ward should be open to any gentleman on the voters' roll of the new extended area of Edinburgh City District.

It was also recommended that the opportunity be taken to bring the constitution up to date to reflect the current situation and the relationship between the society and the town council. Accordingly the duties to be performed were not specified, this being left for the new authority to arrange as required. The new constitution therefore consisted of two parts, a "given" part and a "domestic" part. The given part would be capable of alteration only by the City of Edinburgh District Council, and the domestic part would be modelled as closely as possible along the lines of the existing constitution. Any future amendments to the domestic part would require the approval of a two thirds majority of members present but no endorsement by the council would be necessary.

With these general principles in mind a further committee was formed in May 1973 to draw up specific proposals for necessary changes to the constitution, and after consultation with wards the committee agreed a final draft to be put to the society at a special general meeting. This meeting was held in the Annandale Street Garage on 3 October 1974 and Moderator T N Miller proposed blanket acceptance of the final draft without giving the meeting an opportunity for discussion on the individual changes. Following a very heated discussion the draft was not accepted and the moderator thereupon removed his chain of office, offered his resignation and vacated the chair. The meeting resumed under the chairmanship of Vice-Moderator John Christie and subsequently agreed a motion refusing to accept the moderator's proffered resignation and adjourning the meeting.

There was disquiet within the society that there had been no opportunity for individual members to make their views known at the special general meeting, and accordingly at a subsequent meeting on 21 November 1974 the opportunity was given to incorporate further amendments. At the conclusion, following "a lengthy and somewhat confused discussion", the meeting agreed a final document. Each clause of the final draft was considered in detail, but the main thrust of the changes was still in line with the previous recommendations. This document substantially revised the 1922 bye-laws which had survived with only minor amendments for over 50 years and a copy of the constitution of 1975 (incorporating amendments to 2008) is included as appendix 5.

This new constitution was subsequently approved by the newly formed Edinburgh District Council after they had agreed in March 1975, by the narrow margin of 32 votes to 26, to retain links with the Edinburgh High Constables

At the election meeting in spring1975, retiring Lord Provost Jack Kane highlighted the historic nature of the occasion as it was the last meeting to be held under the old system of local government. He referred to the great service rendered to the City and Royal Burgh of Edinburgh over a very long period of time and offered thanks for all the past service.

Drills

Drills and inspections continued to be held in the transport garage in Annandale Street although conditions there were anything but ideal for the purpose. By way of improvement, it was suggested by the transport manager that the transport garage at Marine Gardens, Seafield Road, might be more acceptable, and accordingly the society changed to this drill venue in spring 1963.

The Marine Gardens garage served as the drill hall for the society from 1963 till the autumn of 1967 when the committee voted 25 to 3 for a return to Annandale Street - the general feeling at that time being that the physical disadvantages at Annandale Street were outweighed by the advantage of its central position in the city. Over the next few years there was much discussion in committee about the unsuitability of Annandale Street garage, but the drills never returned to Seafield.

Since 1956 there had been 2 drills and 1 inspection in the spring and in the autumn, but throughout the 1960s there were occasional calls from individual wards for the number of drills in the year to be reduced from 4 to 2. No action was taken until 1975 when the major change to the society constitution gave the opportunity to curtail the parades to 2 drills and 2 inspections each year.

In the early 1960s, in order to cover for absences, a deputy drill officer and deputy platoon commanders were appointed. Around this time there was considerable dissatisfaction about the length of time members were required to stand on parade, and various suggestions were made with a view to minimising the long wait.

These long parades were not only due to the fact that a time-consuming verbal roll call of all members present was called once all platoons had fallen in, but also because of the need to collate the results of the Dunbar Trophy competition for the evening by analysis of this roll call before the moderator and office-bearers joined the parade.

In spite of these concerns being voiced throughout the 1960s, it was not until 1974 that a decision was taken to discontinue the verbal call-over on parade. Thereafter, platoon commanders were required to mark up the roll for their platoon and check their small batons as members arrived for the parade. These checks were carried out at small tables prior to the parade being called.

The dress code adopted by members was not entirely uniform, and indeed in the mid 1960s it was necessary to instruct several members to wear hats at drills and inspections. The question of haphazard dress was again raised in 1970 since some members were reported as parading in sports jackets, flannels, checked tweed hats and sometimes no headdress at all. It was remitted to the ward captains to emphasise the desirability of wearing a dark lounge suit, white shirt with society tie and bowler hat or Homburg soft hat. Progress in implementing this change was slow, and it was agreed to include a note about the appropriate dress on the billet calling the drills and inspections.

Perversely, although the society was attempting to introduce more formal and uniform dress for the members, intimation was received from Lord Provost Jack Kane in 1972 that in future he would not be wearing morning dress at society inspections.

Elderly and infirm members still attended the drills but were excused from taking part in the parades. Initially they rested in parked Edinburgh Corporation buses as the parade took place, but this was considered undignified and chairs were provided for them adjacent to the parade area. In 1970, there were some 12 to 14 members in this situation and they were always singled out by the inspecting officer for a brief chat.

Initially, drills and inspections continued to be accompanied by a pipe band, and although this was generally the Edinburgh City Police Pipe Band, for a short period in 1973 they were replaced by the Special Foot Constabulary Pipe Band.

This change was not satisfactory, the new band's reduced pace of 99 to the minute instead of the usual 120 causing problems with the march-past. Shortly thereafter the Edinburgh City Police Pipe Band resumed their duties, but demands on their time were such that they could only turn out twice a year for inspections. Accordingly, the spring and autumn drills proceeded thereafter without the assistance of a band.

As ever, the inspecting officer was the current lord provost or a senior bailie, but this pattern was broken in spring 1974 when the inspection was carried out by Chief Constable Sir John Inch because the lord provost and bailies were involved in the important election leading up to the reorganisation of local government.

Charity

The gift of parcels at Christmas to deserving people continued, although some wards had difficulty in finding suitable recipients. In such cases it was recommended that the parcels be taken to the warden of "The Margaret Tudor House" in the Grassmarket where true and worthy persons would be found.

Other wards had no such problem, and indeed some purchased additional parcels for local distribution. The traditional contents of the parcels were augmented for many years by the addition of sweets provided by ex-captain William Roy, Ward IV, at no cost to the society.

The cost of parcels remained at £1 until 1974 when it was increased to £1.20. All parcels included a card from the society secretary with Christmas greetings, and a considerable number of moving letters of thanks were always received, many of which still showed great appreciation for the personal visit of the High Constable as well as the parcel itself.

Some wards, however, considered that the parcels should be replaced by another form of charitable giving, and a proposal was made that they should be replaced by monetary contributions to non state-aided charities. Another specific suggestion was that a £100 donation should be given to the Cyrenians, but these alternatives did not find favour with the society as a whole.

Ad-hoc contributions continued to be made from society funds. In 1961, £200 was gifted to the Lord Provost's Benevolent Fund as part of the society's 350th anniversary activities: in 1965, £100 was given towards the Sir Winston Churchill Memorial Appeal and £150 went to the British Empire and Commonwealth Games Appeal in 1968.

A large proportion of members felt that apart from considering and responding to specific requests it was not appropriate for the society to make any special effort to raise money for charitable causes, but that this should not inhibit individual wards from doing so. In the late 1960s a questionnaire completed by members indicated that 95% were not in favour of the society participating in any additional events of a charitable nature.

Consideration was given to increasing the amount of the annual levy to support charities, and in 1964 when a request was received to help with the conversion of Dalry House into a day centre for elderly people, the whole question of the extent of the society's charitable giving was again discussed. The society auditor was asked to report on possible methods whereby individual members could enter into a covenant on behalf of society sponsored charities, greater sums thus being available by virtue of relief from income tax. The report indicated that a charter would have to be drafted, that this would require the approval of the Commissioners of Inland Revenue and that no financial advantage would be gained if a number of members declined to participate. It seemed likely that a significant number of members would not support such a scheme, and following a vote in committee with 13 wards against the proposal it was decided that no further action be taken.

Dinner

The ever popular annual dinner continued in much the same form as previously and continued to be held in the North British Hotel. In terms of attendance, the function was becoming a victim of its own success in that the hotel could only comfortably accommodate 310 and this number was sometimes exceeded. The lowest attendance was 278 in 1965. The list of guests invited by the society was extensive and it is recorded that there were 39 official guests in 1963, the balance being composed of 219 members and 52 guests of individual members. Included in the official guest list were journalists who subsequently reported the event in local newspapers.

To assist with the smooth running of the evening, wards were required to nominate croupiers who had to arrange an adequate but unobtrusive supply of drinks to their particular table and to ensure that good manners prevailed throughout the speeches. This was occasionally a problem if the loudspeaker system was inadequate and the table was not in close proximity to the top table. The official dress code was dinner suit with black bow tie with the exception of everyone at the top table and all croupiers who were required to wear evening dress with white tie. Towards the end of this period it was becoming increasingly difficult to appoint croupiers because the widespread use of evening dress for formal occasions was dying out. Musical entertainment continued to be a feature before and during the meal, and this was frequently provided by the Alex. Walker Trio and Orchestra who also accompanied the singing of "God save the Queen" at the conclusion of the evening.

The practice of sending a telegram of loyal greetings to the Queen continued, and all members were required to wear society badges. In 1957 it was agreed that members who had served over 40 years in the society should attend the annual dinner as guests of the society and that they should also be invited to join the reception following the annual inspections.

For the 350th anniversary in 1961, efforts to obtain an eminent figure of national standing as principal guest were met with disappointment. Several prominent speakers, including the Duke of Edinburgh, had initially signified their acceptance but all had withdrawn for one reason or another. In spite of the concerns being expressed beforehand, the dinner was a success, the principal speaker being J A Stoddart, M.P., and the reply on behalf of the guests was given by Earl Haig. The following telegram was sent to the Queen:-

"The Moderator, Executive and members of the Edinburgh High Constables send their loyal greetings to your Majesty on the occasion of their 350th anniversary dinner and their satisfaction on your safe return from your African tour".

In 1962 it was recorded that a collection during the annual dinner raised £43 for the "Freedom from Hunger Campaign". About this time a questionnaire was issued to all members and one very positive outcome was that the vast majority of members did not favour the collection of money for charitable causes at such functions.

By 1974, the cost of the dinner to members of the society had risen to £5.00, this figure being similar to the amount of the annual levy at that time.

Social

By now the days of society summer outings on the Clyde were over, the last such excursion being on 8 June 1960. The destination was Inverary and 223 members, friends and society guests enjoyed "an excellent occasion and a most pleasant day", but there were insufficient numbers to make the day a financial success.

The whist drive and dance continued into the early 1960s but this type of function was becoming less fashionable, and although the numbers attending remained in the order of 400 the last event of this nature was held in 1963. The rather formal music provided by the two bands in the late 1950s and early 1960s had been replaced by more up-to-date dance music provided by Cam Robbie's Band, but in spite of this, fewer and fewer people were participating in the whist, and these tended to be the older members. In addition, several function rooms were used instead of a large suite, and this inevitably led to segregation of official guests and office-bearers from the rest of the company.

30 October 1964 saw the first society dinner and dance, which also took place in the Assembly Rooms and Music Hall in George Street. A set dinner was substituted for the previous buffet type supper and this was served simultaneously in two rooms, the Supper Room and The Music Hall - the combined seating capacity being 450. Table plans were drawn up to ensure that members and guests of each ward sat together, and no speeches were made. Office-bearers and official guests were required to wear formal evening dress but others could opt for evening dress or dinner jacket. 54 invitations were issued to official society guests of whom38 attended. This first dinner dance was of limited success, problems again being experienced with the use of private rooms for official guests and poor catering. Accordingly, in the following year the function moved to the North British Hotel.

There is no record of fund-raising at these functions in the early 1960s, but in the 1970s a tombola was regularly provided with every ward being required to provide prizes.

Although the new form of dinner and dance was very enjoyable it only attracted a relatively small number of society members. In 1967 only 35% of members were present and in 1971, six of the wards were not represented at all. As a result, in 1972 a sub committee was formed under convener of captains Douglas J S Miller to formulate new ideas, and the dinner dance that year took on a new format with the introduction of Humphrey Littleton's famous jazz band, a cabaret and a tombola. This made for a very happy evening but still did not encourage enough people, and the proceeds of the tombola, amounting to £100, had to be used to offset the deficit on the evening.

In 1973, the venue was the Royal Scot Hotel in Corstorphine, but this proved to be too cramped and the dinner dance returned to the North British Hotel. The idea of the convener of captains forming a dance committee with other captains of his choice was felt worthwhile, and this continued for many years.

Attendance at the Edinburgh Military Tattoo continued to be a regular occurrence and reservation of a central section of the stand for High Constables and their ladies gave a further opportunity for members of all wards to socialise and enjoy a summer evening outing. The last reference to this outing is 1969 but no indication is given of the numbers attending.

Ceremonial

The High Constables were still required regularly by the town council to provide a ceremonial guard at several church parades throughout the year and on several occasions the lord provost of the day was accompanied to his own church for a special service.

Most services were attended only by the office-bearers accompanied by a few members, but the annual service to celebrate the Edinburgh International Festival of Music and Drama required each ward to provide two High Constables. Their duties continued to be rather more than ceremonial in that each ward was responsible for the safe conduct and proper seating of specific groups within the large representation of various academic, professional and other organisations who were invited to take part. All these representatives were appropriately robed, several groups were preceded by their mace bearers and all-in-all the procession was a very colourful occasion which attracted much interest from tourists. In 1970 the event was screened on the national television network as part of their news coverage.

Church parades to St Giles Cathedral in the early 1960s included special services for the BMA/CMA Congress, for the Congress of Christian Churches, for the 400th anniversary celebration of the Reformation and for a service attended by HM the Queen and the Duke of Edinburgh. The High Constables were also in attendance at the Synagogue for the induction of Rabbi Dr J Weinberg and at St Mary's Cathedral for the enthronement service for the new Bishop Gordon Gray.

Following the 1961 St Giles Cathedral service dedicated specifically to the society as part of the 350th anniversary celebrations and attended by many members, it was proposed that a similar biennial parade be held following the election of each moderator. Accordingly, the first such parade was held on 2 June 1963 with members parading in morning dress with top hats. Silver batons were carried by Moderator James W W Kemp and office-bearers but no wooden batons were carried by members.

This parade in 1963 was intimated by the society chaplain, the Rev Dr H C Whitley as "the kirking of the moderator", and created a precedent which has been followed ever since and forms an integral and important part of the society's calendar. Following the first service and parade, the lord provost, along with many magistrates and councillors, were pleased to give lavish entertainment to society members and their wives at a reception in the City Chambers, and this further cemented the links between the new moderator and the council.

After extended debate about the most appropriate dress for such occasions, it was agreed in 1965 that all members should wear white gloves with black points and society ties.

About this time, the lord provost requested that four additional High Constables should attend at church parades, and that they should bring up the rear of the procession. The society was very pleased to comply with this request which presented an opportunity for more members to exercise their ceremonial role.

The custom of accompanying the lord provost to greet H M the Queen in June and present her with the keys of the city on arrival at Princes Street Station in the royal train appears to have continued until 1963. There is no record of this ceremony thereafter and the station closed in September 1965 having been in operation for 95 years. Office-bearers also attended the lord provost and council at all services at St Giles Cathedral attended by the Queen.

An important civic event took place in October 1962 when Edinburgh hosted the state visit of His Majesty King Olaf of Norway. The King was awarded the Freedom of the City and some 50 High Constables were on duty at the colourful official procession and also at the presentation ceremony in the Usher Hall.

In the same year the society were also present at a routine Freedom of the City Ceremony for Professor Norman H Dott.

A further two similar ceremonies required the assistance of the society, the first being in 1965 when Yehudi Menuhin was honoured and again in 1968 when the recipient was Sir Alec Douglas-Home. Members also attended a United Nations Service in 1965 and a service in 1972 to commemorate the 400th anniversary of the death of John Knox. Both these services were held in St Giles Cathedral.

The provision of stewards to assist in running the Murrayfield Highland Games continued, but in 1963 doubts were expressed because the reduction in spectator numbers meant that some of the High Constables were largely superfluous. However, the society continued to give their support until 1966 when the games moved to Meadowbank Stadium

Equipment

It was agreed that no special badge such as that produced for members for the 300th anniversary in 1911 should be struck for the 350th anniversary, but long service stars for constables who had served 25 years continued to be presented. It was decided in 1971 that all such presentations should be made either at the annual election meeting or at one of the two inspections following the appropriate anniversary. The question of how to recognise service longer than 25 years was debated in the mid 1960s, and in 1967 it was decided that members having served 35 years would receive a small silver bar to add to their badge ribbon, and that after 40 years this would be exchanged for a gold bar. The first such presentation took place at the nomination meeting in 1968 when Ex-Captains Dugald Rose and W H Nisbet, both of Ward XX, received gold bars, and a silver bar for 35 years service became due to Past-Moderator James A McArthur.

About the same time it was agreed that all members who had served as convener of captains should also receive a personal ribbon attachment with appropriate inscription, and in March 1973 Moderator Thomas Baillie presented 10 gentlemen with such badges.

The gift to the society in 1965 of a High Constable's Queen Victoria Jubilee medal of 1887 prompted consideration of storage and public display of old equipment and momentos. The first display case provided in 1959 was inadequate to house all the artefacts apart from the silver batons, and accordingly in 1969 a second similar display case was installed in another alcove in Committee Room "A". The cost of the new case was £186 and the council contributed £100 towards the cost.

In view of the fact that many more items of equipment were to be on public display, the attention of the committee returned to the valuation and insurance of society equipment. In 1966 it was stressed that equipment in the hands of members was primarily their responsibility, and that they may wish to add an "all risks" item to their personal insurance.

It was agreed that all equipment should now be insured, and cover was undertaken by the Commercial Union Insurance Co. This increased level of cover now included all members' equipment, thus reverting to the position as it was in 1958.

A revaluation of equipment and trophies was undertaken and in September 1967 a value of £21,094.10/- was placed on all society equipment including that held by office-bearers, captains and members.

Missing equipment was occasionally seen for sale in antique shops, and in June 1968 it was agreed that the society secretary write to the principal salerooms and antique shop proprietors in the city requesting them to refrain from purchasing society equipment. Also, if they had any articles in their possession, they were asked to communicate immediately with the secretary because all such articles were legally the property of the society and not of any individual.

In an unfortunate incident at the annual dinner in 1973, the silver cigar and cigarette casket presented to the society by the Golf Club as part of the anniversary celebrations in 1961 went missing from the top table and was never recovered.

Dies for small batons were purchased in 1970 and three small batons were purchased in 1972. As the demise of the City and Royal Burgh of Edinburgh drew close, the City Archivist borrowed certain items from the society for an exhibition in May 1975 to mark the passing of the old Royal Burgh.

Sport

All four society sports clubs continued successfully throughout this period. The largest and most stable membership was still that of the Golf Club but the other clubs were always very keen to increase their membership and give the opportunity to other High Constables to enjoy the sport and the fellowship engendered by the clubs.

Golf

In the early 1960s Golf Club membership was around 60 but did not remain at this relatively high figure. Generally 4 or 5 afternoon outings took place at various courses throughout the Lothians where trophies and prizes were played for. In addition, matches were played against the golf clubs of Edinburgh Corporation, Edinburgh City Police and Perth High Constables. As ever, the club's dinner dance and presentation of prizes was very popular. In 1966 an additional foursome competition was played at Muirfield and this proved so successful it was repeated. Several outings were enhanced by the presence of Ken Buchanan, the former world lightweight boxing champion who donated a silver tankard as one of the prizes.

In 1975 Mr Douglas Miller presented a silver cup in memory of his father Lawrence Miller who had been captain and president of the club.

Bowling

The Bowling Club introduced an inter ward pairs competition in 1961 and regularly competed as a club against other bowling clubs from Coltbridge, Edinburgh Corporation and Perth High Constables. In order to enable some matches to be played on a weekday afternoon bowlers had to be recruited from outwith the society to make up the appropriate numbers, and on occasion it was necessary to play matches at Milton Street Indoor Stadium due to inclement weather. Another regular feature was a match with the directors and committee of the McBride Indoor Stadium at Milton Street. The level of membership in 1967 was 25 and an annual club dinner was held at the conclusion of the season. Until 1974 this dinner was often held as joint dinner with the Angling Club.

In 1969 the society Bowling Club became the first sports club to have a match against Glasgow Corporation but there is no record of why this started. Dugald Rose, Ward XX, the oldest member of the Edinburgh club, presented a silver rose bowl for this competition which is now an annual event. In 1972, following this game in Glasgow at Queen's Park Green, Edinburgh High Constables were taken to Glasgow City Chambers to be entertained at a civic reception and dinner, and this pattern has been regularly repeated.

Angling

In addition to club outings, the Angling Club also had meetings with Perth High Constables. These were often held on Loch Leven and were popular and very pleasant outings, the moderators of both societies attending the presentation of trophies after high tea at a local hotel. 1969 appears to have been the start of a difficult time for fishing because of the widespread distribution of algae on Loch Leven and also on Loch Lindores in Fife. In 1972 the outings against Perth High Constables were shifted to Loch Fitty in view of these problems.

In 1974 the club decided to reintroduce a dinner solely for the Angling Club, and this was very successful. The prize- giving included a new trophy, the Donald Kelso Tankard, and the Chief Constable Sir John R Inch was made honorary president of the Angling Club. This dinner was to become a regular event.

Curling

Regular curling matches were played at Haymarket Ice Rink between rinks within the club, and the winning rink received the "Wilkie Quaich" presented by Moderator J Ritchie Wilkie in 1969. In the same year, a short knock-out competition was introduced, and the prize for this was the "Sec's Stane" presented by Secretary T N Miller.

One match was regularly played against Perth High Constables. This was always a very enjoyable event and records indicate that the hospitality before and afterwards was often of a much higher and more memorable standard than the curling. In the post war years Perth High Constables produced a very strong team and accordingly there was much jubilation in 1966 when Edinburgh High Constables won back the trophy for the first time in 27 years. In 1974 several friendly fun games were played against local clubs.

High Constables parading at the first church service to mark the Kirking of the Moderator, June 1963. (Courtesy of Scotsman Publications)

Sir Alex Douglas Home receiving the Freedom of the City of Edinburgh, 3 April 1969
(*Photograph supplied by Scotsman Publications*)

Presentation of two seats at the west door of St Giles Cathedral, 18 November 1969
J Christie-Secretary, T Bailie-Vice Moderator, Rex de la Haye-Moderator,
Lord Provost Sir J W McKay, Chaplain the Rev Dr H C Whitley, Ex Moderator DSO Wilkie
(Courtesy of Scotsman Publications)

Lord Birsay speaking at Annual Dinner 1970 (Courtesy of Stephen Parry Donald)

CHAPTER 6

SERVING THE CITY OF EDINBURGH DISTRICT COUNCIL 1975 to 1996

Apart from the necessity to have the new constitution approved by Edinburgh District Council in order to continue the historic links with the High Constables, the major changes to the functions and responsibilities affecting local authorities in 1975 had little impact on the society. One of the constitutional changes removed the need for any internal changes to have the approval of the lord provost and council, and accordingly for the first time since 1611 organisation of society affairs was entirely within the control of the members.

At the first general meeting following the formation of the new authority Lord Provost John Millar expressed his pleasure at the continuing links with the society and was proud to announce that Edinburgh was the only city officially allowed to continue wearing their robes on ceremonial occasions.

The narrow margin of the council vote in 1975 meant that there was not wholehearted support at that time for continued association with the High Constables, and so over the next few years the society had to be particularly sensitive in its dealings with the council, especially with respect to allowances and grants payable.

In the first few years following local government reorganisation there was a distinct change in the political outlook of the council and there was a definite move away from formal ceremony. As a result, the society was put under some scrutiny by certain members of the council, and in 1980 the retiring Lord Provost Kenneth Borthwick expressed concern about the future, advising members to be watchful and to resist sudden change. This message was reiterated by Lord Provost Thomas Morgan in 1981 who counselled that the traditions of the city were very vulnerable, and there was adverse press comment regarding the role and function of Edinburgh High Constables.

In the early 1980s this uneasy relationship with the council was reflected in several ways. In May 1984, although the society paraded as usual at the kirking of the council they did not wear morning suits and top hats but paraded in dark lounge suits and bowler hats. The council had to be well satisfied about the functions of the High Constables before they were prepared to permit the use of the Council Chambers for their annual general meeting the same year, and at the kirking of Moderator George Dick the following year the hospitality offered was reduced to tea and biscuits. This policy was reversed two years later when drinks and a light buffet were the order of the day. A further indication of the austerity of this particular political administration was the cessation of the lord provost's traditional annual Christmas party which had been greatly enjoyed by those involved and regularly attended by moderators and their ladies over many years.

In spite of the tensions in dealing with the council as a whole during the initial years of this chapter in the society's history, relationships between the society and successive lord provosts continued to be very cordial and the longstanding custom of moderator and office-bearers meeting the new lord provost continued unhindered.

Some 12 months prior to the demise of the Regional Councils and re-formation of unitary authorities throughout Scotland in May 1996, elections to the new councils were held. During this lead-in period, when the society made informal representation to the Convener of the new City of Edinburgh Council, Eric Milligan, and to the Chief Executive, Tom Aitchison, it was indicated that there was no cause for undue alarm about continuation of the ancient links between the city and the High Constables. However, over previous years there had been positive moves by all public bodies to ensure that their policies could not be interpreted as displaying any discrimination on the grounds of religion, race or sex, and the society became very conscious that the tradition of all male membership could become a contentious issue.

Constitution

Introduction of the new constitution in 1975 brought about a change in the routine of general meetings. A meeting to nominate office-bearers was no longer required, and it was no longer necessary for members to be re-elected every three years. At the annual meeting for elections, now designated the annual general meeting, the Oath of Allegiance and Declaration de Fideli was reaffirmed by all members before the lord provost or a notary public. The oath and declaration was as follows:-

"I *do solemnly, sincerely, and truly declare and affirm, that I will be faithful and bear true allegiance to Her Majesty Queen Elizabeth and her heirs and successors according to law.*

I *hereby declare that I will be faithful and diligent in the discharge of my duties as a High Constable"*

At the conclusion of the annual general meeting in April, the moderator and vice-moderator continued to refresh the members with pies, beer and whisky.

Up until 1980 the society continued to request an annual grant from Edinburgh District Council, and this was regularly paid at the level of £200 to £250. The society was justified in requesting such a grant following an Act passed in 1967 which gave entitlement to an annual grant of £250, this having been subsequently increased by the Secretary of State to allow for the cost of inspections. In 1981, the local press commented adversely on the society's application and for the first time the city's director of finance requested a copy of the annual audited accounts.

The point was made by Treasurer George Dick that for £250 the society "was accountable to the ratepayers of Edinburgh and open to attack from political extremists on the council", and it was recommended that if the request for a grant was to continue, the accounts should be presented in such a way as to avoid the impression that this grant was being used to offset the cost of official guests at the annual dinner dance and the annual dinner. It was also noted that the council paid for the regular provision of the platform, flowers and loudspeaker system at the two inspections each year.

Grants of £200 were received in 1981-82 and in 1982-83, but in 1983-84 the committee decided that no grant should be requested and that Edinburgh District Council be advised accordingly. No further applications have been made since then although an item was included in the annual accounts with a nil entry until 1996 in order to take recognition of that element of the constitution which stated that "the council shall make such annual allowance to the society for defraying their necessary expenses as the council may from time to time decide".

As the cost of living increased, so also did the honorarium paid to the moderator. From a level of £300 per annum in 1976, it rose to £1200 per annum in 1996. In the main, this sum was to cover a substantial part of the cost of the moderator's dinner, and although it was included in the accounts as an annual sum, it was paid to the moderator at the end of his term of office. In order to assess the appropriate level of this honorarium, a small committee of past-moderators along with the society secretary was formed in the mid 1980s to make recommendations on any necessary increase. The annual honorarium to the society officer did not increase to the same extent, rising from £40 in 1976 to £100 in 1996.

The annual levy was set at £6.00 in 1975 and by 1996 this had risen to £35.00 per annum. The rise was generally gradual over the period, but in 1990 a long running debate about whether or not the cost of official guests at the annual dinner and at the annual dance should be borne only by those attending was addressed. As a result, the committee agreed to Treasurer Donald Semple's suggestion that the cost of these guests should clearly be a society cost, and accordingly the levy was substantially increased from £18.50 in1989-1990 to £23.50 the following year.

Over the 21 years covered by this period, the cost to members of a ticket to the annual dinner rose from £6.50 to £27.00.

A sum of money was still set aside each year to assist with production of the lord provost's portrait on completion of the term of office. In 1996, £250 was contributed for this purpose, Lord Provost Eleanor McLaughlin having opted for a stained glass window instead of the official portrait. This window is prominently displayed above the main staircase in the City Chambers on the floor above the windows gifted earlier by the society.

As a result of dissatisfaction with the management of the financial affairs of the society when they went into the red in 1977-1978, the office-bearers took a close look at the situation and the matter was resolved. However, this again highlighted the difficulty with the system of progressive office-bearing, the particular office of treasurer being one which, more than the others, required a considerable amount of specific professional training and expertise. The problem continued and was debated until 1983 when a sub -committee specifically appointed produced a detailed report which resulted in constitutional changes in 1984. These changes withdrew any restriction on the two year maximum term of office of the society treasurer and also empowered the committee, instead of the society as a whole, to alter the sum to be paid by new members on entry and to alter the level of fines to be imposed. The first treasurer to be appointed under this system in 1984 was W H G Mathison, Ward XX, who served for 5 years before standing down, at which time he was presented with a past treasurer's badge in recognition of his sterling service.

Apart from dealing with financial affairs, this constitutional change meant that the number of offices traditionally considered necessary before becoming moderator was reduced. Of the seven office-bearing posts, two now required to be filled by gentlemen of a specific profession, namely surgeon and treasurer. In spite of this, motions by Past Captain F A Ainslie, Ward VIII were brought forward at annual general meetings in the early 1990s in an effort to change the system of progression and to remove the two year maximum for other offices and although considerable support was indicated, it was insufficient to warrant constitutional change. In 1995, the traditional progression of custodier, secretary, vice-moderator and moderator was further changed when Custodier James G Banks did not stand for election as secretary, thus starting a trend whereby more members could enjoy the benefits of holding office for two years as custodier without this being taken as a wish to progress to other offices. The only posts which the society regarded as being necessarily progressive |subject, of course, to election| were those of secretary, vice-moderator and moderator. This system still allowed sufficient time to learn the complexities of the society before becoming moderator, but it did not commit the incumbent to more than 8 years in office, including that of ex-moderator. The first member for 80 years to serve as society secretary without having previously served as an office-bearer was Past Captain Kenneth Dunbar, Ward V.

On a more sombre note, in 1981 the committee discussed the appropriate dress to wear at funerals of members. The recommendation was that society ties should be worn and that office-bearers should attend as a group. At the funerals of office-bearers or past-moderators, it was recommended that office-bearers should attend in full morning dress with silver batons if this met with the approval of the bereaved family.

Modern methods were gradually being introduced for procedures at general meetings and committee meetings. In 1985, the roll call was called verbally at the annual general meeting in the City Chambers for the last time, and thereafter the system used at drills was adopted whereby platoon commanders checked attendance on arrival. Minutes of general meetings began to be circulated to ward captains in the early 1990s and shortly thereafter to all members, but in spite of this, members were still unwilling to give up the centuries old custom of the society secretary reading out verbatim the minutes of the previous general meeting.

This change from reading aloud previous minutes was accepted more readily at committee meetings when circulation of printed minutes to all committee members started in 1989. Previously it had been felt that copying and sending out the minutes would put too much additional work on the society secretary but once implemented, this substantially reduced the length of the meetings.

Considerable discussion took place in the late 1980s regarding the position of members unable to take part in drills due to long term illness or infirmity. It was again suggested that there may some merit in introducing some form of honorary membership but this was not accepted.

Events rare in the society annals took place during this period:-

In 1977, 50 years service to the society was celebrated by a member of Ward XX, Ex-Captain Herbert Nisbet. He had joined on 20th September 1927, and Lord Provost Kenneth W Borthwick made a special presentation at the City Chambers of an illuminated scroll testifying to his 50 years of loyal service.

In November 1983 at a gathering in the City Chambers, Lord Provost Tom Morgan made informal presentations from the District Council, from the society and from Ward XIX to Past Captain Sam Hall who joined the society in 1939 and who had now reached his 90th birthday.

Some years later at the 1993 annual general meeting, a 50 year gold bar was formally presented by Lord Provost Norman Irons to Past Captain George R Leggate of Ward

XVII, and he was also presented with a quaich from the ward by Captain Archie C McDiarmid to recognise this outstanding achievement.

In 1981, in order to improve communications throughout the society, Moderator W T Cavaye reported to the committee on the many functions which he attended on behalf of the society. This practice has continued ever since and the reports give a fascinating insight into the many civic and other events attended by moderators, invitations to such events frequently including the moderator's lady. Many of these social events were based on the activities of the society and of individual wards, but there were also many occasions when prestigious invitations were received from the lord provost, the chief constable, the service chiefs, the Merchant Company, kindred societies and many other organisations. A catalogue of moderators' activities since 1981 would require a chapter of its own, but this would certainly emphasise the prestige of the society and the extent to which it was recognised in the City of Edinburgh and elsewhere.

Since 1955 all members had been in possession of a society tie and following a request from Moderator I A T Gowans in 1984 this tie has been worn at all committee meetings since. Some wards also followed this practice at ward meetings. In 1992, Moderator Alan W Mowat was seen sporting this tie modified as a bow tie, and as several members wished to follow suit, 50 such bow ties were ordered for use with evening wear at formal society functions.

In 1985, the committee room in the City Chambers used by the society to house their equipment and to hold committee meetings was renamed the "Nelson Mandela Room".

To relieve the load on the society secretary, it was agreed in 1988 that responsibility for the organisation of church parades would be given to the vice-moderator, and that the surgeon would make all arrangements for the annual skittles competition. Both these duties had previously been carried out by the society secretary.

The pace of business life and the widespread travel requirements of many members caused some difficulty in complying with the terms of the constitution for attendance at general meetings and drills, and frequently last minute telephone calls would be received by the secretary or moderator. As a result, the number of fines increased, a few members who persistently failed to meet their obligations resigned and very occasionally members were removed from the roll.

Accordingly, in April 1990, the constitution was altered to emphasise that written excuses could be submitted after the event, thus obviating the need for last minute telephone calls. In addition, the moderator was given discretion to accept excuses rather than referring them to the full committee as previously. The opportunity was taken at the same time to tidy up several items in the constitution and to bring it fully up to date. A new booklet incorporating the updated constitution was produced in 1991 and the printing was generously undertaken by a member at no cost to the society.

Prior to1975 all drills had been preceded by a committee meeting at the drill venue. The reduction in drills resulting from the constitutional changes at that time was matched by a corresponding reduction in the number of committee meetings.

Reduction in the number of meetings for drills and inspections from six to four, and reduction of general meetings from two to one made a significant difference to the number of points to be awarded each year for the Dunbar Trophy, the number of counting events being reduced from eight to five. Accordingly, the committee suggested in 1977 that the rules be changed to include attendance not only at general meetings, drills and inspections but also at the kirking of the moderator. This was not accepted by the membership who wished to adhere to the rules laid down in 1912, and some concern was expressed that the proposed change might have brought an element of religious discrimination into society affairs. This would have been a retrograde step since the society had always been free of any such discrimination.

In September 1992, Past-Moderator William T Cavaye offered his services to update the society history in view of his impending retirement from work. This offer was readily accepted, but sadly his health deteriorated and he was unable to make much progress before his death in December 1995. Thereafter, this task was undertaken by Past-Moderator W R |Gus| Ferguson when he also retired from full-time employment.

The society's historical records, which had been stored for many years in a vault in the City Chambers, were passed to the City Archivist in 1993 for safe keeping under appropriate conditions. It was agreed that access would be granted to bona fide researchers subject to the approval of the society.

For many years the word "executive" had been used to describe the office-bearers of the society. Following a complaint that this word had been used incorrectly and gave the wrong impression of the function of the office-bearers, it was gradually dropped from official correspondence, invitations and minutes.

Drills

The change of drills and inspections from 6 to 4 per annum was first introduced in autumn 1975 with only one drill and one inspection taking place.

In general, inspections continued to be attended by the lord provost or a senior councillor, but in a unique departure in autumn 1983, Moderator I A T Gowans invited society member Adam Currie, ex-captain of Ward IV and Master of the Merchant Company to be the inspecting officer. Other inspecting officers included the Right Rev Professor Thos Torrance, Moderator of the General Assembly of the Church of Scotland in 1977, Depute Chief Constable Stanley Pringle in 1981, former Chief Constable Sir John Inch in 1984, W L Sleigh, Moderator of The High Constables of Holyrood House in 1985, Chief Constable Sir William Sutherland in 1989, Deputy Chief Constable Hector Clerk in 1991 and Deputy Chief Constable Graeme Powers in 1996.

Edinburgh's first woman Lord Provost, Mrs Eleanor McLaughlin regularly carried out inspections, the first being in April 1989. This was her first High Constable event and she lightened the occasion by remarking that the only time she had seen so many hats had been at the Townswomens' Guild.

The pattern of school life was changing, and it became common practice for schools to have a two week holiday in mid term in October, and many members with young children took advantage of this to go off on a family holiday. As a result, the timing of drills and inspections was revised and often a two or three week gap was necessary between these events. Consideration was even given to changing from April to May and from October to November

The standard of drilling and marching was not improving. Some older members had served in the forces in the war or during periods of national service after the war, but many of the newer, younger members had never experienced any form of drill instruction either as members of the forces, at school, or as members of any uniformed organisation.

Accordingly, special sessions were held prior to parades and on several occasions a police drill instructor was on hand. A booklet explaining the procedure was also produced but did not receive wide circulation. Infirm members who were unable to participate in the drill were still registered as present if they turned out.

Photographs of most inspections and medal presentations were recorded professionally, this work being undertaken initially by S Murray Donald and thereafter by his son Steven P Donald, both members of Ward X. For a period of some 50 years this firm has provided photographic services for most society events, and accordingly they have established a long photographic archive of society members and events.

Lothian and Borders Police now provided the pipe band at inspections, and in April 1988 a pipe tune, "The High Constables of Edinburgh" composed by Martin G Wilson, a member of the band, was presented to Moderator E Ian Adam by Chief Constable William Sutherland. In return, a presentation quaich was given to the composer, and this tune has been played during the march-past at all inspections since. An attempt was made to use a taped recording of the tune to assist with drilling, but this was not successful and much better results were achieved by the use of a sole drummer provided by the band. The services of the Police Pipe Band at inspections were greatly appreciated and the society reflected this by supplying pies, cans of beer and an honorarium on each occasion. The level of this honorarium was £50 in 1995.

In 1978, Moderator J Ritchie Wilkie introduced formal morning dress for office-bearers at inspections and invited distinguished guests from the forces and kindred societies to join the platform party.

The problems experienced with Annandale Street Garage as a drill venue continued, the joint use of an active bus garage with the drilling, inspection and march-past of 200 men accompanied by a pipe band never having been an ideal combination. Regular noise and air pollution was produced by buses entering and leaving the building, the loud speaker announcements to the bus crews were intrusive, there were usually several large patches of oil and sawdust on the floor, and on wet evenings leaks from the old roof usually fell where one of the platoons was standing at attention. Nevertheless, the association of the High Constables with the building in Annadale Street was a long one, and Edinburgh Corporation did as much as it reasonably could to minimise disruption and to provide floral and other decoration for the main platform in order to make a change from its normal appearance.

In 1986 an offer was received from Lothian and Borders Police to use their garage at Police Headquarters, Fettes Avenue. The offer also included facilities for meetings and hospitality and was readily accepted. This proved an excellent and entirely appropriate venue and greatly helped to augment the good relationship between the society and the police force. On the occasion of each of the two drills and two inspections every year, considerable effort was extended by the staff at Lothian and Borders Police in clearing the garage and arranging all the other facilities. The first drill was held in October 1986 and the High Constables considered themselves very fortunate to have the use these of these premises

In spite of the excellent relationship with the police this seemed to be of no avail to James and David Hall of Ward XII when they were caught speeding en route to an inspection in the late 1980s. Production of their small batons cut no ice with the traffic police, but when they realised that the pies for the police pipe band were on board the car, not only was the speeding offence disregarded but an escort was provided to the venue at Fettes Avenue. This was a fair outcome since Hall Brothers had generously supplied pies free of charge for many years.

The cost of drills and inspections came under review in this period, and in order to economise, a platform for society use was purchased in 1987. This was more economic than the recurring cost of platform hire.

Notwithstanding the 1975 constitutional reduction in the number of drills and inspections some members still wished to cut this down this even further and to combine the drill and inspection on the same evening, but this did not receive the support of the society. Long delays on parade waiting for the evening's Dunbar Trophy results to be collated became increasingly unpopular, and ultimately it was agreed in 1990 to omit announcement of up-to-date attendance figures and to report retrospectively on the position following the previous parade or general meeting.

In 1993 the format of the billet intimating the drill and inspection was modernised, the long standing arrangement of a small notice printed on both sides being superseded by a single sheet printed on one side only. The opportunity was taken at that time to make the wording less formal, and the use of personal computers with printing facilities significantly reduced the cost of this simple notice.

In 1994, Moderator W R Ferguson invited the moderators of all three kindred societies to join the platform party, and the ram's head snuff mull presented some100 years previously by the Edinburgh society to the Perth society was brought down specifically for the occasion. A photograph of all 4 moderators with the chief constable is included at the end of this chapter.

Charity
This period was quite significant in relation to the charitable activities of the society. Although Christmas parcels continued to be distributed and many sincere letters of appreciation were still received, the effectiveness of this practice was frequently questioned, many members feeling that some recipients were not in dire need and that the money spent could be directed to more deserving causes. The cost of parcels rose from £1.20 in 1975 to £10.00 in1995. From 1986 onwards the parcels were supplied by a Portobello firm run by Douglas M Spratt, a member of Ward VIII, and his personal involvement with the society was of enormous benefit because of the extra attention given to the content and presentation of the parcels.

A review of the contents of the parcels in 1989 highlighted a change in emphasis since they started in 1958. Cakes, biscuits and sweets were now being included instead of the original tins of luncheon meat, corned beef and vegetables. The contents were accordingly modified the following year to reflect a more healthy diet.

The Queen's Silver Jubilee Appeal in 1977 resulted in a direct contribution of £1,000 from the society, £500 of which was used to sponsor local sporting events for young people. During the national strike of firemen in late 1977, several wards visited fire depots in their area with gifts at Christmas for the army personnel who had been called in to control fires in the city by the use of the old and outdated "Green Goddess " fire engines.

At the annual dinner in 1978, Lord Provost Kenneth W Borthwick challenged the High Constables to raise £1,000 for the appeal fund for the restoration of St Giles Cathedral. Although there was some disquiet about the manner in which the challenge had been issued, because of its close links with the cathedral the society had a special collection among members and the sum of £1,150 was raised. £1,000 was given to the

St Giles Appeal and £150 to the Sir John Menzies Trust Appeal, this also being at the request of the lord provost.

1981 was designated the "year of the disabled" and all members paid an additional levy of £5.00 to support this cause at Christmas. Five cheques of £250 were presented to appropriate organisations in the presence of Lord Provost Tom Morgan at the City Chambers in December 1981.

In the mid 1980s there was a real desire for the society as a whole to increase their efforts to raise money for charity, and in 1987 a charitable account was set up with an initial, one-off contribution of £5 per member, disbursement of these funds being at the discretion of the committee. Over the next few years, proposals to form a charitable trust to accrue benefits from tax incentives were brought forward from time to time but did not find favour with the committee.

Following establishment of the charitable account, ad hoc gifts from society funds were donated as follows:-

1990   £320 to the Thistle Foundation to participate in the Paraplegic Games.
       £200 to the 133rd Haymarket Venture Scout Unit
1991   £100 to the Scottish Old Age Pensioners' Association for their AGM
       £250 to sponsor R K Sloan, Ward XIX, running for the 20th time in the London marathon in aid of RSSPCC
1992   £500 to the Bosnian Refugee Appeal
1993   £110 to assist pupils from Bosnia spending time at an Edinburgh school
1994   £300 to the Blackadder Trust
       £250 to the Citizens' Advice Bureaux

The recorded amounts raised at dinner dances in aid of specific charities were as follows:-

1983   £550 for the Leith Hospital Ultrasound Appeal
!984   £526 for the Cripple Aid Society
1985   £470 for the Western General Hospital Kidney Unit
1986   £660 for the Sick Children's Hospital
1987   £1,000 for the Western General Hospital Coronary Care Unit
1988   £1,000 for the City Hospital life support machine
1989   £650 for the Headway Group and
       £360 for the Western General Hospital Chiropody Department
1990   £1590 for the Fairmile Marie Curie Home
1991   £1600 for the Abbeyfield Edinburgh Society
1992   £1,300 for the Royal Scottish Society for the Prevention of Cruelty to Children
1993   £1500 for Challenger Children's Fund and £100 for refugee children
1994   No dinner dance held
1995   No funds were raised at the dinner dance

Although discussion had taken place over the early years of this period about organising a major fund raising event, it was not until the early 1990s that this happened. Between 1988 and 1992 Ward XIV had run three very successful evening events by using the facilities at Stockbridge House Day Centre and Donaldson's College for the Deaf to have informal, fun dances with tombola stalls and raffles. The sums raised at these events totalled some £9,000 and, encouraged by this, the society agreed to Moderator Alan W Mowat's proposal to have a bigger event for the whole society on similar lines. This was supported by 20 out of the 23 wards and by most office-bearers.

Nearly all wards participated in this first such event which took the form of an informal "Black and White Ball" held on a summer evening in 1992 in the school hall of George Watson's College. Everyone, including the lord and lady provost, entered into the spirit and theme of the function, and at the end of a very happy evening attended by over 300 guests the sum of £10,000 had been raised for charity. Many outside sponsors had contributed prizes, and in a significant departure members were asked to sell books of raffle tickets prior to the event. This was financially worthwhile, £5,000 of the total being raised by this means, but it was not universally popular with members. The proceeds were donated to Scotland Yard Adventure Centre in Eyre Place to provide indoor play facilities for children and young people with special needs. A room in the new building was named after the society and formal opening of the centre was carried out by the Princess Royal in November 1993.

A similar event was repeated in 1994 at the same venue, the theme on this occasion being a "Tartan Ball". In view of the unpopularity of the raffle this was not repeated, but a total of £5,500 was raised to assist with the administration and running costs of Scotland Yard Adventure Centre. These events both required a great deal of effort by many members and their wives in terms of organisation, sponsorship, acquisition of prizes for the tombola and decoration of the hall. As a result, in addition to raising money the activities added to the feeling of fellowship within the society, and although the principle of having such a function was not fully shared by all members, nevertheless many did participate and gave their wholehearted support.

Dinner

The pattern for the annual dinner continued as before and it was now established as one of the most prestigious regular dinners in the city. As its popularity increased, problems with the limited accommodation at the North British Hotel became even more acute. The maximum attendance at this hotel was 379 in 1984, but the size and layout of the function room was such that there was now considerable disruption to the toasts caused by members and guests unable to hear the speeches.

Construction of the Sheraton Grand Hotel adjacent to Lothian Road was completed in 1985, and this provided the option of a larger, more uniform conference or function room. Accordingly the society moved to this new venue in December 1985 and 396 members and guests were comfortably accommodated. The attendance rose to about 420 in the 1990s.

One of the advantages of the more spacious room was that each ward could be allocated its own table under the control of the captain, and accordingly there was no further need for croupiers. Over the previous few years there had been difficulty in appointing sufficient croupiers, even allowing for the fact that in 1975 the requirement for them to wear white tie and tails had been dispensed with, the alternative of full highland evening dress being considered appropriate. The move to the Sheraton Grand Hotel broke a very long and happy tradition of High Constables' dinners at the North British Hotel, the use of this venue stretching back almost unbroken to the start of the 20th century.

The musical introduction and interludes by the Alex Walker Trio and his successors had formed part of the programme for many years but this was discontinued. However, in 1983, pipers and drummers from the Daniel Stewarts' and Melville College Pipe Band played during the reception and piped in the members and guests at the top table after all others had assembled in the dining hall. This welcome addition to the programme continued until 1995 when this duty was taken over by Michael Gray, Ward XXI who was an experienced piper.

The choice of guest speakers continued to be the prerogative of the moderator, and during this period the number of speakers from outwith the society increased.

The toast to Her Majesty's Forces was almost invariably given by an office-bearer or society member, and the reply was given in rotation by the senior serving officer of one of the three armed forces. Until the mid 1980s, the toast to the City of Edinburgh was generally given by an office-bearer or ward captain, but thereafter, outside speakers noted for their wit and oratory were invited. In 1988, the Lord Provosts of Glasgow and Edinburgh were for the first time both women, and at the invitation of Moderator E Ian Adam, Lord Provost Eleanor McLaughlin responded to the toast to the City of Edinburgh given by Lord Provost Susan Baird of Glasgow.

The main toast of the evening to the Society of High Constables of Edinburgh continued to be given by prominent figures such as national politicians, writers, actors, entertainers and senior members of the legal profession. A list of principal speakers during this period is included as appendix 6.

The welcome and toast to kindred societies and guests was of course reserved for society members, but in the early 1980s the response to this toast, which had traditionally been the preserve of the moderator of one of the three kindred societies was given to an accomplished and experienced speaker specifically invited to entertain and amuse the company at the end of the evening.

No formal invitations were now given to journalists, but prominence was given in the press in 1977 to the controversial choice of Enoch Powell, MP, as principal speaker. This choice caused disquiet among some members because of his views on immigration and his infamous "rivers of blood" speech in Birmingham in April 1968 in connection with the Race Relations Bill. In the event his address concentrated on the use of future oil revenues from the resources recently discovered in the North Sea.

At the time of the 1978 annual dinner the New Zealand "All Blacks" rugby team were staying in the North British Hotel. A number of the players made an impromptu appearance at the top table and were introduced to the society. The result of the ensuing match at Murrayfield was Scotland 9, New Zealand 18 and the team were unbeaten on their UK tour.

The long established association with the three kindred societies continued, and the invitations to the moderators of Leith, Holyrood and Perth High Constables were always reciprocated. On many such occasions away from home, the moderator of the Edinburgh society was required to respond to the toast to "kindred societies and guests" and the speeches and toasts at these extremely enjoyable and lavish dinners often lasted into the small hours of the morning.

At the annual dinner in 1983, the society presented Lord Provost Tom Morgan with a £500 donation to the appeal fund for the City of Edinburgh Lifeboat, the lord provost being chairman of this fund. In the following year, £250 was donated to the appeal to assist with the Commonwealth Games to be held in Edinburgh in 1985.

In 1988, a collection was made during the evening for the Royal Scottish Society for the Prevention of Cruelty to Children, the secretary of this society having toasted the High Constables earlier in the evening. A sum of £613 was collected, but this form of collection for charity did not prove popular and was not repeated.

In 1991, in view of the possible danger to health by passive smoking, consideration was given to prohibiting all smoking during the function. However, the majority view was against such a course of action even although several hotels and restaurants were introducing such a ban. The dinner continued to be an occasion attended by men only with the exception of occasional invited speakers or female aides-de-camp to the service chiefs.

Periodically, criticism was voiced about the large number of official guests, the length of some speeches and the move away from using society members as speakers. In 1995, a small sub-committee produced suggestions about reducing the size of the top table and the number of speakers and recommended that the time for each toast be more rigorously controlled. In addition it advised that there should be a return to greater use of society members on the toast list.

Accordingly, at the 1995 annual dinner the number seated at the top table was reduced from 30 to 25 by cutting back on the number of official guests. The response to the final toast was given by a professional after-dinner entertainer to whom an appropriate fee was paid, this cost being included in the price of the ticket, and toasts were completed by 11.00 pm, thus allowing more time for fellowship among members and their guests.

Social

The main social function for members of all wards and their partners continued to be the annual dinner dance. As in previous years, a regular core of the membership continued to enjoy these occasions and the lord and lady provost were always included in the invitation list.

The dinner dance continued every year with the exception of 1994. Prizes for the tombola continued to be provided by the wards, and proceeds at the dinner dance in 1990 were boosted by auction of a signed print of the Scottish Grand Slam rugby team which raised £550.

In order to encourage good attendances, efforts were made to diversify the style of the function to make the event more attractive. This resulted in holding the dance at several different venues.

Until 1982, the dinner dance continued at the North British Hotel, and a change from a set menu to a buffet style meal was introduced for a year or two in the late 1970s. In 1977, the Queen's Jubilee Year, the numbers increased to 200 but this was still a relatively small proportion of the membership.

For three years in the early 1980s the venue chosen was Prestonfield House Hotel and this change encouraged a distinct increase in attendance. In 1985 the function was enjoyed by 280, but this larger number unfortunately highlighted limitations in the size of the dance floor. In 1986 the event moved to the Dragonara Hotel at Belford Bridge, but this proved too hot and crowded for the 258 attending, and for the following four years the new Sheraton Grand Hotel was the chosen venue.

By 1991, the "old faithful", the North British Hotel had been entirely refurbished under new ownership and was renamed the Balmoral Hotel. Happy memories were rekindled when the dinner dance returned here in 1991, 1992 and 1993.

By this time, numbers were again dropping to the disappointing levels of the late 1970s - in the order of 170 - and in 1994 the event was dropped in view of the Tartan Ball held earlier in the year as a major charitable event.

Another new venue, the Edinburgh International Conference Centre hosted the dinner dance in 1995, and this excellent facility encouraged an increase in attendance to 260 with no fund-raising being carried out.

Other social events for society members and partners included block bookings for a musical event at Holyrood in 1980 to celebrate the Queen Mother's 80th birthday, ceremonies on the Castle Esplanade for the installation of new Governors of Edinburgh Castle and a visit in 1988 to the unique "Gold of the Pharoes" exhibition at the City Art Centre in Market Street.

In 1979, Moderator J Ritchie Wilkie introduced a new social event for office-bearers, ward captains and their wives. This took the form of a cocktail party in the New Club, Princes Street, and over succeeding years moderators have returned the generous hospitality of the wards in different ways. The last such moderator's party during the term of Edinburgh District Council was held in 1994 by Moderator W R Ferguson on board m v Gardyloo, the ship used to dump Lothian's sewage sludge at sea. The ship was berthed in Leith Docks at the time, and this somewhat unusual but very happy event was attended by Lord Provost Norman Irons, the last lord provost to serve during the 21 years of this particular regime of local government.

On several occasions in the mid 1990s, following performances at the Edinburgh International Festival of Music and Drama, Lord Provost Irons invited office-bearers and some members to provide a guard of honour at civic receptions in the City Chambers. Guests at these receptions comprised visitors and artists from all corners of the globe, and after having paraded outside the City Chambers in full morning dress with silver batons the duty constables enjoyed mixing with the musicians and actors.

Ceremonial

Routine ceremonial duties requested by Edinurgh District Council continued as before with the exception of attendance at the mid week official opening of the General Assembly of the Church of Scotland in May. However, a regular feature of the society calendar was now a service to celebrate St. Andrew's Day on 30 November.

In the main, these ceremonies were attended by the office-bearers and six constables. At parades which included representatives of all the academic and professional bodies, two members from each of the 23 wards were still required to direct and escort these groups to and from St Giles Cathedral.

This chapter of the society's history coincided with several special anniversaries of organisations based in Edinburgh and further afield and the High Constables paraded on many such occasions including the following:-

1975

75th anniversary of the Boys' Brigade, Leith Battalion at North Leith and Bonnington Parish Church

1977

25th anniversary luncheon to celebrate Queen Elizabeth's accession to the throne. This was preceded by attendance at the Keys Ceremony at the City Chambers on the Queen's arrival in the city.

1978

50th anniversary of the Boys' Club at Canongate Kirk.

850th anniversary of the Royal High School at St Giles Cathedral. At this event, four of the office-bearers were replaced by four ward members who were also former pupils.

800th anniversary of Holyrood Abbey at Canongate Kirk.

75th anniversary of the Royal Navy Reserve, Forth Division at St George's West Church.

150th anniversary of St Stephen's Parish Church

1979

650th anniversary of charter being granted to the City of Edinburgh. This service was held at St Giles Cathedral in the presence of the Queen and the Duke of Edinburgh and many High Constables were invited to the subsequent civic lunch.

250th anniversary of the Royal Infirmary and 100th anniversary of the Simpson Maternity Pavilion at St Giles Cathedral.

1983

500th anniversary of South Leith Parish Church

100th anniversary of the Boys' Brigade at North Leith Church.

400th anniversary of the University of Edinburgh at St Giles Cathedral

200th anniversary of the Solicitors of the Supreme Courts at St Giles Cathedral

350th anniversary of The Royal Scots Regiment at St Giles Cathedral and subsequent March Past

1987

Tercentenary Service for former Lord Provost John Drummond at Canongate Church

1990

70th anniversary of Lodge Solomon at the Synagogue

1993

75th anniversary of the Royal Air Force at St Giles Cathedral

1995

75th anniversary of Lodge Solomon at the Synagogue

200th anniversary service for James Craig at St Andrew's and St George's Church.

In 1975, following extension of the city boundary, a special service was held in South Queensferry Church. High Constables paraded on this occasion which represented the first official visit of Edinburgh's lord provost to South Queensferry since 1593.

In 1976, some 16 High Constables paraded with Lord Provost John Millar at the Royal Scottish Academy on the Mound to welcome the Queen and Duke of Edinburgh accompanied by French President Giscard d'Estaing and his wife to a reception and civic lunch.

The society was also on duty at the request of Lord Provost Kenneth W Borthwick in 1977 at civic luncheons for the Mayor of Vancouver and also for the Lord Mayor of London.

In September 1978 the society were on duty at a service in Greyfriars Kirk for the Burma Star Association which was followed by an impressive march from the Stone of Remembrance at the City Chambers to Princes Street where the salute was taken by Viscount Slim and Lord Provost Kenneth W Borthwick.

Other ceremonials included annual services in connection with the Commonwealth in the late 1970s, and also the Commonwealth Games Flag Ceremony on the Castle Esplanade in July 1986 when the flag was handed over to Lord Provost John McKay by the Mayoress of Brisbane.

The service for Moderator Ian M Crosbie's kirking in 1989 was shared with the Royal

Navy when HMS Edinburgh was berthed in Leith Docks. This service was attended by the Duke and Duchess of York.

Further regular annual turnouts were started in the early 1990s with attendance at the service at St Giles Cathedral for the recently introduced Edinburgh International Festival of Science and Technology, and at the Synagogue when the Edinburgh Hebrew Congregation marked the Edinburgh International Festival of Music and Drama.

The European Economic Community held a summit conference in Edinburgh in 1992 amid high security and the High Constables were in attendance to assist at a reception in the Assembly Rooms.

The appointment in 1995 of Cardinal Thomas Winning to the College of Cardinals was marked by a mass in St Mary's Metropolitan Cathedral and Lord Provost Irons was attended at this service by the office-bearers of the society.

Equipment

Following dissolution of the City and Royal Burgh of Edinburgh in 1975 it was felt that there should be some permanent record of the service given to Edinburgh Corporation, and although it was agreed with the council that an appropriate note be added to the notice board in the City Chambers listing society moderators no action appears to have been taken.

Throughout the period covered by this chapter, regular equipment checks were made by successive custodiers. These checks were generally carried out physically by ward captains at an appropriate drill meeting, and a completed check list returned to the custodier.

In 1977 the insured value of all regalia and equipment was £60,995, the items in the City Chambers showcases representing £14,340 and the equipment held by members and office-bearers representing £46,655. The cost of insuring items in the showcases was met by Edinburgh District Council and the annual cost to the society of insuring members' equipment at that time was £233. The large wooden batons held by each constable were given a value of £100, small silver ringed batons £15 and whistles were entered at a nominal value.

A further detailed valuation in 1984 by Hamilton and Inches, Jewellers, George Street indicated the value of regalia and equipment to be substantially greater than previously assumed, items in the City Chambers being assessed at £42,400 and those retained by members and office-bearers at £113,000. This valuation listed long wooden batons at £200, small batons at £60 and badges at £50 with a higher figure of £150 to £180 being put on special badges for captains and office-bearers. In 1988 further enquiries indicated the replacement cost of a single large wooden baton might be as high as £800.

The cost of insuring members' equipment again gave cause for concern in 1988 because the extent of damage or loss was small and the cost of insurance cover for such equipment was then in the order of £500 per annum. It was therefore recommended that members should be asked to forfeit their returnable equipment deposits and that these monies be transferred to a new "equipment replacement fund" which would be used to pay for any damage or replacement, thus avoiding the need to carry insurance. In addition, new members would pay a sum directly into this account on entry. This further change to the constitution was agreed at the annual general meeting in 1991 and the fund gradually rose to a level of £3,200 in 1990, the ultimate aim being £3,500.

In order to ensure a sufficient stock of equipment, 12 small batons, 6 large wooden batons and 25 whistles were acquired in 1977, the whistles being provided by the Chief Constable and suitably engraved. The cost of each wooden baton was £100, and these were individually crafted by a firm of heraldic wood carvers in Blairgowrie.

In 1978 a suitable cigar box to replace that stolen at the annual dinner in 1973 was identified and approved by the Golf Club. This was subsequently purchased and put to use again at the annual dinner of the society.

A pair of High Constable cuff links from the estate of Past-Moderator T N Wilkie was given to the society in 1980. These cuff links passed from moderator to moderator as part of the official equipment and gave pleasure and a sense of occasion at many functions.

At most official ceremonial parades the seven office-bearers were accompanied by six constables. Eleven ceremonial batons fully decorated with silver rings were used along with one partially decorated moderator's baton and one wooden baton. The practice of making and presenting these ceremonial batons started around 1820 with new silver rings being added each year, each ring being appropriately inscribed with the name of the respective office-bearer. Over the years, these batons required renewal and replacement, and accordingly the society was in possession of 380 loose silver rings inscribed with office-bearers from 1821 to 1942.

In 1987 the moderator's incomplete ebony and silver baton was fully ringed by the addition of 30 old rings, and a completely new baton was manufactured using hardwood with new silver end rings and caps similar to those on the existing treasurer's, secretary's and surgeon's batons and incorporating 54 old rings.

The cost of this work was in the order of £750 and it ensured a greater degree of dignity and uniformity at official parades with all the office-bearers and six constables carrying silver batons.

At the annual dinner in 1987 the enthusiasm of the society officer was such that the society gavel was broken. The repair was undertaken by a member of Ward XIII who formed a new handle using hazel wood from Cramond.

From time to time, items of equipment still turned up for sale in antique shops. In 1993 a wooden baton numbered 31 was purchased in Fife by a member's wife for the sum of £30 and this was subsequently bought back by the society at the same cost, this being insignificant in relation to the cost of a new baton. The condition of the baton was such that it was issued to member no. 31 in place of his original issue which was taken into stock for future use.

The society's oldest artefact, the splendid treasurer's box which had been presented in 1698 was brought back to its original use in1993 when it was regularly removed from the display cabinet and used at committee meetings for the collection of fines.

Sport

In the early 1980s it was quite feasible for firms to produce a small number of ties with specific designs at relatively low cost, and in 1981 the society commissioned and purchased 50 ties specifically designed to include motifs comprising symbols of all four sports clubs with the High Constable crest in the centre above the initials "EHCSC". These ties proved popular with many members of the clubs. The popularity of the ties was such that these were followed in 1985 by the purchase of sports club sweaters in a variety of colours, these sweaters also bearing the appropriate crest and initials on the left breast. These also proved popular and were of rather more practical use during competitions than the ties.

In view of the relatively small number of members in each sports club the cost per head of participating and of entertaining guest teams was quite significant. Accordingly, in 1988 it was agreed that the society would assist the sports club by bearing the full cost of insuring and engraving all the various sports club trophies.

Although the clubs catered for the limited number of members who had an interest in these particular sports, there was no such organised activity which might include players from all wards and would generate greater interaction throughout the whole membership. Accordingly, in 1977 an inter-ward skittles competition was proposed and sufficient wards expressed interest to make a knock-out competition viable, the office-bearers also undertaking to provide a team.

Between January and March 1978 the first such competition took place at the Sheep Heid Inn in Duddingston, each team comprising 8 players with friends being allowed to substitute up to 3 places if the number of ward members was insufficient. The evening was lubricated with a plentiful supply of beer and it included a welcome break for hot pies. The performance on the skittle alley was usually inversely proportional to the number of pies and the quantity of beer consumed.

After a year or two some members expressed disquiet when it became apparent that several outside substitutes were being invited because of their renown on the skittle alley rather than their companionship, and this was felt to give an unfair bias to the competition. As a result the rules were changed to admit only constables from other wards as substitutes.

However, the event became a regular and popular event and two trophies were awarded - the Moderator's Shield, presented in 1978 by Moderator J Ritchie Wilkie for the winning ward and the Treasurer's Cup presented in 1979 by Treasurer W T Cavaye for the highest individual score. For the first years of the competition "ball boys" were engaged to re-erect the skittles after each play, but this was discontinued in 1980 following introduction of the Employment of Youth Act. As a result, the evening became very energetic with the participating players constantly replacing skittles, hopefully for their team mates to knock down.

In the early 1980s, refurbishment of the Sheep Heid Inn meant that other alleys had to be used, and after short spells at the Carousel public house in Leith and at the indoor sports stadium at Murrayfield, the competition moved in 1985 to good facilities at the Ship Inn, Musselburgh. This venue continued to serve the society well until 1995 and the obligatory pies continued to form an important social part of the evening. In 1996, following cancellation of the booking by the Ship Inn, the competition was re-arranged at the Right Wing in Willowbrae Road.

Certain wards always had difficulty in providing sufficient able bodied members to participate and accordingly the number of players per team was quickly reduced from eight to six and then to four. In 1991-92 it was felt that perhaps ten-pin bowling requiring only a one arm action would be a less strenuous alternative, and a trial inter ward competition was held at the indoor stadium at Murrayfield. This knockout tournament was won by the office-bearers, but the form of the evening was not conducive to socialising between wards and the experiment was not repeated.

Administration of the skittles competition was initially the responsibility of the society secretary, but in view of all the other duties required of him organisation of the competition was transferred to the surgeon in 1989. A list of winners of the skittles competition is included as appendix 7.

In 1986 a proposal was again mooted for the reintroduction of a rifle club, but insufficient interest was generated and the proposal was dropped.

Golf

The club continued to comprise the largest number of society members with numbers varying from 45 to 60. The usual routine included 5 monthly club outings in the summer with several trophies being awarded, and the outings took place at various courses throughout the area such as Kilspindie, Longniddry, Broomieknowe, Royal Musselburgh, Baberton, Prestonfield and Royal Burgess.

Club trophies added during this period included the "Sir John Orr Putter" presented in 1979 by the Chief Constable and "The Moderator's Putter" presented by Moderator George Dick in 1985.

In the early 1990s, business commitments made it increasingly difficult for many members to attend outings during working hours and accordingly afternoon outings were reduced from 5 to 3, one of these being a pairs competition between wards.

The long established matches against the Police [now Lothian and Borders Police], the "Old Edinburgh Corporation" [now Edinburgh District Council] and Perth High Constables continued to provide excellent sport and equally good fellowship, and in 1978 a new match was introduced against the Royal Air Force. A new cup for this event was gifted by the moderator and was known as the Ritchie Wilkie Cup.

In 1989, the match against Edinburgh District Council was memorable in that one of the council's guest players was Alan Shepherd, the American astronaut, the only man to have "golfed" on the surface of the moon.

In 1995 a match was also played against the Edinburgh Merchant Company Golf Club, and this was to become a regular annual event.

In 1990, the "Old Corporation Golf Club" celebrated its centenary and the High Constables attended the celebrations and presented them with a "Willie Park" putter for competition within their club. Willie Park had been an outstanding Midlothian golfer in former years and had also been winner of the Open Championship in the 1860s. About the same time the High Constables entered a team for the centenary year of the "Dispatch Trophy" competition but regrettably did not proceed further than the second round.

The enjoyable Golf Club dinner dance and prize-giving continued every year in February, and special celebration of the centenary of the club comprised a golf day at Royal Burgess golf course in May 1995 involving teams of three drawn from society members. The day started with snow on the course and finished splendidly at a centenary dinner in the Merchants' Hall with some 80 people present in the company of Lord Provost Norman Irons and representatives of the four clubs against whom regular matches were played.

Bowling

Membership of the society Bowling Club dropped somewhat during the period, but a core of dedicated members worked hard to ensure that the club was a force to be reckoned with. The inter-ward pairs competition continued until the 1980s, but when there were insufficient wards represented to make this viable it was changed to a club pairs competition, the prize for which was the Dunbar Trophy. The Dugald Rose bowl was competed for against Glasgow District Council, and the Manclark Trophy against Edinburgh District Council.

In 1979 a bowling trophy was discovered in the safe of Past-Moderator David Cook and this had been originally presented in 1919 by the High Constables of Perth to be competed for annually. The first game in 1919 was won by Perth. The trophy was valued at £450 and had last been competed for in 1937

Perth High Constables appear to have been served by some expert bowlers during this period, and the Perth trophy stayed in Perth for 17 years before being finally wrested from their grasp by a win for Edinburgh High Constables in 1995.

Throughout, all home games were played at Coltbridge Bowling Club where the staff and members were always unfailingly helpful in providing the necessary facilities. The annual competition between the High Constables and the Coltbridge Club was discontinued in the 1980s, but a new fixture was arranged against the Whitehouse and Grange Bowling Club shortly thereafter and this became established as an annual event.

Angling

The Angling Club continued their matches against Perth High Constables and these generally took place over two legs at different lochs. The trophy for this event -the King Cup - continued to be awarded to the winning team by the moderator of either the Edinburgh or Perth Society at the Bridgend Hotel, Kinross, at the meal following the second day of fishing.

Membership varied between 20 and 30, and latterly many of these were fishing friends of High Constables who were admitted as associate members. In the mid 1970s and early 1980s there were as many as 6 to 8 outings, but latterly these were reduced to 3 or 4 per annum, the angler with the biggest aggregate catch being awarded the Donald Kelso Tankard. Loch Leven was a very regular fishing venue with the exception of 1992 when a severe infestation of algal bloom again occurred. Other venues included Cobbinshaw Loch, Coldingham Loch, Butterstone Loch, Lake of Menteith and Loch Fitty.

1975 -76 was the 50th jubilee of the club and a special dinner was held at the Royal Burgess Golfing Society to celebrate the event.

Donald Kelso, Ward V, was presented by the club with an automatic reel in 1976 after serving 21 years as secretary and treasurer.

1978 saw the presentation of a new trophy by Past-Moderator Christie - the John Christie Quaich - for the member with the best basket on any of the club competitions held on Loch Leven, and in 1987 a tankard was also presented by John Kyles, Ward XI.

For several years in the 1980s and 1990s the High Constables were invited to send a representative to take part in the Edinburgh and Leith United Clubs competition, the inter city competition between Glasgow, Edinburgh and Dundee, and the Loch Leven championship competition.

The social highlight of the Angling Club's year continued to be their annual dinner and prize-giving which was generally attended by the moderator. For many years the venue for this was the members' house at Edinburgh Zoo.

Curling

The activities of the High Constables' Curling Club were disrupted in 1978 when the season was shortened by the closure, after many years, of the Edinburgh Ice Rink at Haymarket. The following year saw no regular play, but this was rectified in season 1979 - 80 when play was resumed at the new Murrayfield Curling Club adjacent to the existing ice rink and rugby stadium. New facilities were also available at Gogar Park Curling Club on the outskirts of the city, and this ice rink was used for the final meeting of the season.

Membership varied between 20 and 35, and the league competition for the "Wilkie Quaich" and the knock-out competition for the "Sec's Stane" continued. A pairs competition for the "Surgeon's Quaich", presented by Surgeon W Govan, was introduced in 1977, and in 1983 Andrew S Hepburn, Ward XIII presented the "Hepburn Salver" for a points competition. However, in 1995, because of falling membership, the format of internal club competitions changed with cessation of the pairs and the knock-out competition. Two separate league competitions were introduced - a winter league and a spring league - and the season ended with an individual points competition at Gogar Park, all other games being played at Murrayfield. The "Sec's Stane" became the prize for the winter league, the Wilkie Quaich for the spring league, and the winner of the final play-off between the two winning leagues was awarded the Surgeon's Quaich.

The main competition with other clubs continued to be against Perth High Constables. The venue alternated between Perth and Edinburgh and old friendships continued to be cemented. In addition, friendly games were played in the late 1970s against Edinburgh Rotary Club, the Bank of Scotland, and Boswell and Duddingston Clubs. The society also entered a rink in the King George IV Trophy competition and the RAF provided opposition for a match at an ice rink in Kinross in 1979.

In 1978-79 the weather in Scotland was sufficiently cold for an outdoor "Grand Match" on the Lake of Menteith, and a rink from the club took part in this somewhat rare event. The members participating were Bertie Howe,Ward I - Murray Donald, Ward X – Jim Banks, Ward VI and Andrew Hepburn, Ward XIII.

The new curling rinks built in the late 1970s provided excellent dining facilities, and a custom was quickly established of holding the club's annual general meeting and prize-giving at the conclusion of the season following the points competition.

Office Bearers 1975/76.
BACK ROW : *Philip Brown, Surgeon - W A W Sivewright, Drill Officer - H Forbes Murphy,*
Auditor - Douglas J S Miller, Secretary - W T Cavaye, Custodier - R M Woods, Society Officer
FRONT ROW : *J Ritchie Wilkie, Vice-Moderator - John Christie,*
Moderator - Lord Provost Jack Kane - T N Miller, Ex-Moderator - James W Coulthard, Treasurer.
(*Courtesy of Stephen Parry Donald*)

Presentation of cheque to the Lord Provost in response to the Queen's Silver Jubilee Appeal,1977.
W T Cavaye, Secretary – D J S Miller, Treasurer – Lord Provost Kenneth W Borthwick – T P L
McGlashen, Surgeon – J Ritchie Wilkie, Moderator – I A T Gowans, Custodier.
(*Photograph supplied by Scotsman Publications*)

Parade for the opening of the Edinburgh International Festival of Music and Drama, 1978.
(*Courtesy of Scotsman Publications*)

Autumn Inspection in Annandale Street Garage, 1978
(*Courtesy of Stephen Parry Donald*)

Dinner Dance at Prestonfield House Hotel, December 1983, Moderator I A T Gowans
(Courtesy of Stephen Parry Donald)

First Inspection at Police Garage, Fettes Avenue in October, 1986
with Lord Provost Dr John McKay and Moderator George Dick.
(Courtesy of Stephen Parry Donald)

Top Table representation at the Annual Dinner, 1988.   Moderator E Ian Adam with Edinburgh
Lord Provost Eleanor McLaughlin and Glasgow Lord Provost Susan Baird.
(Courtesy of Stephen Parry Donald)

Kindred Societies at Spring Inspection, 21 April 1994
Derek Mowat, Moderator Perth High Constables-Chief Constable Sir William Sutherland-Lord
Provost Norman Irons-Moderator Gus Ferguson-Oliver Balfour, Moderator of the High Constables
of Holyrood House-Robin Salvesen, Moderator Leith High Constables.
The Ram's Head Snuff Mull presented by Edinburgh High Constables to Perth High Constables
in 1873.
(Courtesy of Stephen Parry Donald)

CHAPTER 7

INTO THE TWENTY FIRST CENTURY
1996 to 2003

As a result of the Local Government [Scotland] Act 1994, administration of the city was transferred on 1 April 1996 from the shared responsibility of the City of Edinburgh District and Lothian Regional Council to a new, all purpose, City of Edinburgh Council.

This resulted in the re-arrangement of many local authority services, and the new council's insistence that women should not be excluded from membership of the High Constables of Edinburgh resulted in a major upset within the ranks of the society and threatened their links with the new council.

Constitution
The new City of Edinburgh Council had been elected in 1995 to run in parallel with the last year of the old district council, and preliminary discussions between society office-bearers and senior members of the new administration indicated that future involvement with the council might well hinge on the society's willingness to change its constitution to admit women as members. For many years, local authorities had been implementing and encouraging equal opportunity policies wherever possible, and over preceding years council grants had been withheld from clubs and organisations which refused to adopt such practices.

In June 1996 it was made clear by Lord Provost Eric Milligan that the new council wished High Constable membership to be open to men and women. This policy was supported by all political parties and it was hoped that this could be achieved by constitutional change at the 1997 annual general meeting. The council was also concerned that some areas of the city were excluded from membership of the society because the names of the 23 wards did not match the existing 58 wards in the city. This was a result of constitutional change in 1975 when the city boundary was extended and it had been decided for convenience to retain the old ward numbers and names while extending possible membership to any registered elector within the new city boundary.

In view of the antiquity of the society and enjoyment of the particular type of fellowship engendered by a male only organisation, it was understandable that the initial reaction of many office-bearers and members was to resist the introduction of women. In order, therefore, to give a measured response to the city's wishes, a sub committee set up to look at the implications of such a change produced a comprehensive report in January 1997 along with a résumé of the society history.

These papers were sent to all members, and discussion within the committee highlighted many reservations within the wards and raised questions about the powers of the council to disband the society. Historical records indicated that legal opinion sought by both the council and by former society members following the major schism in 1857 made it clear that:

"the society of constables, or high constables as they were allowed to be called in 1810, was not an incorporation, but was merely the aggregate body of the constables deriving their office from the magistrates of the city, but had no independent or permanent existence as a separate society."

Following circulation of this report a special meeting of the society was held on 26 February 1997 within the Signet Library to allow a full and frank discussion. This sounding board concluded with a summary of members' views, those at the meeting completing voting slips following the discussion, those unable to attend having posted their completed slips to the secretary beforehand.

The meeting was poorly attended with only 97 members showing up, and some 70 members neither attended nor submitted their views. The outcome of this straw poll was that 53% of those attending the meeting were in favour of the change, but this figure was reduced to 44% when the postal votes were included.

At a subsequent meeting with Moderator Brian C A Short, Lord Provost Milligan emphasised that the council stance had hardened and that failure to change would mean exclusion from civic functions and church parades, would threaten relationships with Lothian and Borders Police and might also threaten use of the City Chambers. The lord provost also stressed that the council applied the same considerations to all bodies with which it was linked by funding or the use of facilities. On the other hand, the meeting was very cordial and Lord Provost Milligan indicated that if women were admitted to the society the council would not impose quotas and that he would consider how the role of the High Constables could be expanded.

This message was also conveyed to all members by Lord Provost Milligan at the annual general meeting on 7 April 1997, and at a special meeting of the society within the City Chambers on 13 May attended by 194 members the society agreed by a 76% majority |148 to 46| to the proposal to change. This was in excess of the two thirds majority required for constitutional change, and accordingly the constitution would be altered to read "persons" instead of "gentlemen", thus removing any impediment to women joining the society. This change was formally implemented at the annual general meeting in April 1999.

During this period the society was the subject of much press comment, some of which implied that the High Constables were elitist and sexist. Moderators at this time were required to comment and discuss the issue in newspaper, radio and television interviews, and at the 1997 special general meeting Moderator Simon Bolam commented: "There can be few issues in recent times - indeed across the 386 years of our proud history - that have been more important. It is not surprising, therefore, that the subject has been debated across the society with such intense interest and passion. The debate has ranged from views that the change should be totally and uncompromisingly rejected to very significant anger as to what the fuss is all about, and that the alteration is totally correct and proper for the times we live in."

Once the issue had been settled, the style of dress to be worn by women also caused much debate, with some wards even producing their own designs. A small sub committee recommended that a leading Scottish designer of corporate and ceremonial dress be appointed to design the new uniform, and in spite of the relatively high cost of such an appointment the society agreed that a totally independent view was essential because there could be no satisfactory compromise to the widely differing views expressed by the membership.

The resulting design was compatible with the dress for male High Constables and comprised a black jacket with black box pleat skirt finishing 10 inches from floor level, black hose, black shoes with maximum one and a quarter inch heels and white gloves with black top stitching. The jacket was designed with scarlet sleeves and medal strip, and a black tricorne hat trimmed with a scarlet and black cockade was to be worn for formal inspections and parades. A black bowler type head helmet was proposed for less formal drills.

In 1998, Ward XXI Craigentinny had two vacancies, and the members felt that if both vacancies were to be filled by women it would be a less daunting prospect and would assist in recruiting the first women to the society. Accordingly, Margaret Williamson and Deirdre A Kinloch Anderson were elected as Edinburgh High Constables on 15 October 1998. Election of more women was a relatively slow process, the next such election not taking place until June 2002. This election was again to Ward XXI. A photograph of the first women High Constables in parade dress is included at the end of this chapter.

Following the upheaval caused by this major constitutional change, it was felt appropriate to review all aspects of the role of the High Constables with a view to modernising the society in a rapidly changing world environment. A questionnaire issued to all members in 1998 and discussed fully by all wards resulted in some 19 recommendations being made by the sub committee appointed to review the role and function of the society. Many related to improvements in the administration of society affairs, including the provision of information and drill instruction for new members, and the procedure and format of the annual general meeting. Accordingly, the practice which had existed throughout the life of the society of reading aloud the minutes of the previous general meeting was stopped, and these minutes were printed and circulated with the notice calling the meeting. This was first implemented for the annual general meeting in April 1999.

The questionnaire also revealed that most members considered the charitable aspects of the society to be a small part of their expected role, but it was accepted that Christmas parcels should continue.

Some of the recommendations required changes to the constitution, and at the 1999 annual general meeting the constitution was amended to formalise the relationship with the City of Edinburgh Council and to include women as members. In addition, a proposal to establish a post of honorary historian was accepted, this post not to be considered as an office-bearing position. The first society historian, Past-Moderator W R Ferguson, was appointed at the same meeting. A further proposal to restrict the age for election to persons between 25 and 60 years of age was voted on by a show of hands and rejected by a majority of members.

Notwithstanding the reluctance of the society to participate in events specifically aimed at raising funds for charity, a proposal at the April 2000 annual general meeting to include a specific sum in the annual levy as a contribution to the charitable fund was accepted by an overall majority of 98 to 61. This did not require any change to the constitution and accordingly a two thirds majority was not required. This sum was fixed initially at £5, and at the same meeting it was agreed to alter the constitution to arrange for the levy for each following year to be fixed by all members at the annual general meeting and not, as previously, by the committee at the first meeting following the annual general meeting.

This theme of regular annual giving developed further over the following year, and in April 2001 the membership agreed by a 149 to 38 majority that a charitable trust be established on behalf of the society. This proposal had been mooted several times in the latter half of the 20th century, and its eventual acceptance meant that although charities would benefit as a result of reclaiming tax on all donations, contributions to the general charitable fund |including the cost of Christmas parcels| would have to be by voluntary donation, separate from the levy. In addition, control of the fund would not remain with the society but would pass to the appointed trustees. Following this decision, the levy for the forthcoming year was set at £26, with an additional voluntary donation of £17 being anticipated. This donation would comprise £12 for Christmas parcels and £5 for other charitable works.

One further outcome of the detailed appraisal was the need to produce a concise summary of recent decisions made in respect of the administration of society affairs, other than those covered by the constitution. Changes in policy and procedures were decided by the committee, and traditionally reliance on new procedures depended on the reliability of the knowledge and memory of past committee members and office-bearers. Changes in the system of progressive office-bearing in 1995 when the new secretary took office without previously having served as an office-bearer exacerbated this problem and emphasised the need to have a readily available reference guide. Accordingly, in March 1999, a useful secretary's guide was produced by Past-Moderator Simon Bolam, and this included all appropriate decisions taken by committee since 1972.

Throughout this period members were still required to maintain the required level of attendance, and these who consistently failed to attend meetings were contacted by the moderator to remind them of their obligations.

In June 1999, the committee reviewed the level of fines and agreed to alter them to a uniform amount of £1. This resulted in increased fines for absence without permission at meetings, failure to exhibit small baton when called upon by the moderator and neglecting to bring large baton when required.

The informal gathering of all members for refreshments in the European Room in the City Chambers following the annual general meetings in April still continued, but from the start of this period the traditional pies were replaced by sandwiches and other bites. Also, the cost of this was now borne by the society and not by the moderator and vice- moderator as had been the case for many decades. This change took place when it was decided that the moderator should not be paid an honorarium as such, but that the cost of the moderator's dinner and other entertainment would be set against the general expenditure of the society.

Significant long service to the society was recognised when Past-Moderator John Christie resigned in 1996 after more than 40 years enthusiastic service. In April 1998, Fred Wilson Horne of Ward XIX received his 50 year gold bar and a specially engraved quaich from Lord Provost Milligan, and later that year at the annual dinner the Very Reverend Gilleasbuig Macmillan was presented with a silver paper knife to mark 25 years as society Chaplain.

Notable national and world events were recognised in September 1997 when the society sent a letter of condolence to the Prince of Wales on the death of Diana, Princess of Wales, and in September 2001 when Moderator J Richard Allan added the name of the society to a book of condolences opened at the City Chambers to mark the tragedy resulting from the attack on the twin towers of the World Trade Centre in New York on 11 September 2001.

In 2000 the question of public liability was considered. Throughout its history the society had never carried insurance cover for this type of liability, but in view of the increasing incidence of claims by members of the public for compensation in respect of injury or loss it was considered prudent for the society to take out appropriate insurance cover. The first premium for such a policy was £105 per annum. During the same year it was felt appropriate to increase the honorarium paid to the society officer from £100 to £150.

A constitutional issue which had been raised some 10 years previously was again considered at the 2001 annual general meeting. A motion to reduce the number of turn outs for drills and inspections from 4 to 2 per annum by combining the drill and inspection into one evening was defeated, only 92 of the 210 members present being in favour of the proposal.

As the use of computers in offices and homes became more widespread, the society took advantage of this new technology. At the turn of the century, the council agreed to information about the High Constables being linked to their web site, and in 2001 a specific High Constable web site was set up. This included a brief history, photographs of the moderator in parade dress, photographs of society regalia and a current programme of events. The initial web site was www.edinburghhighconstables.org.uk and a copy of the brief history displayed on the web site is included as appendix 1.

Communication by e-mail became increasingly common between office-bearers and many members although no official roll of e-mail addresses was published. In 2002, e-mail excuses for non attendance at drills were accepted as a substitute for written excuses although this did not comply fully with the requirements of the constitution.

At the same time it became apparent that the badge reproduced on society stationery was of poor quality and definition. This was in the form which had been used for the best part of 100 years and did not therefore accurately reflect the current matriculated arms of the City of Edinburgh Council. Accordingly, a new society logo was designed in computer format with the assistance of the council's graphic design team and the approval of the Lyon Clerk. The greatest use of the logo was black on white for all society and ward stationery with a gold embossed version being reserved for use on the letterheads of moderators and vice-moderators. A version with coloured arms was reserved for special events and invitations at the discretion of the moderator.

Improvements to the front page of the menu for the annual dinner were made at the same time, continuing reproduction over the years having resulted in so much deterioration that the names of many of the moderators listed were illegible. The new page was again produced in computer format so that clarity would be maintained.

The possibility of bestowing honorary membership on some older retiring members who wished to continue their links with the society was yet again raised in 2002, but support for such an idea was not sufficient to warrant any consideration of constitutional change. Informal involvement at ward level was left as a matter for individual wards to decide, and it was conceded that retired constables would still be entitled to wear the society tie.

Although celebration of the 400th anniversary of the institution of the society in 1611 was not due till some 9 years hence, it was decided in 2002 that it would be prudent to have early discussion on the form that such celebrations should take. Accordingly, a small sub committee brought forward five concepts for consideration as follows:

1. Presentation of a standard to the city
2 Award of a civic medal or clasp to each High Constable
3. A quatercentenary ball
4. A special charitable effort
5. A new edition of the society history.

In order to provide the necessary funds for any of the agreed concepts, it was agreed at the annual general meeting in 2003 that until 2011 an additional annual charge of £5 per annum would be levied on members.

Drills

The routine of drills and inspections continued as before with the usual facilities being provided at the police garage in Fettes Avenue. As ever, the courteous and cheerful assistance of the staff at police headquarters was greatly appreciated and a drummer from the Lothian and Borders Police Pipe Band continued to beat out the marching rhythm during drills. Lord Provost Milligan attended as many inspections as possible, and in his absence other senior councillors deputised. As a result of the police involvement in security arrangements for the Commonwealth Heads of Government Conference in October 1997, the drill and inspection were postponed until November, and at the invitation of Moderator Brian C. A. Short the salute at the inspection was taken by Air Commodore J H Haines, Air Officer Scotland and Northern Ireland.

In order to introduce some variety to the traditional routine Moderators J R Allan and L Wallace asked the Society Historian to give very brief talks at the spring drills in 2001,2002 and 2003, and an RSM from the Scots Guards attended the autumn drill in 2001 to give useful assistance in the basic skills of drilling and marching. On this occasion the office-bearers abandoned the platform to join their platoons. The moderator of the High Constables of Perth was a guest at the autumn 2002 Inspection.

Modernisation of parade dress was also discussed in the early part of this period, and the introduction of tartan, possibly in the form of a handkerchief of Edinburgh tartan being worn in the breast pocket, was suggested but not implemented. Infirm members who attended the parades but were unable to march continued to be marked present for purposes of the Dunbar Trophy.

Charity

Although the major fund raising events of the early 1990s had not been supported by all members, they were effective in raising significant sums for charity, and accordingly in 1997 Moderator Brian Short arranged an informal jazz band ball in the Royal High School. Only a small number of wards were represented but the event attracted some 140 members and guests, and the £3000 raised went to assisting the development of 3 promising youngsters who would not otherwise have had any opportunity for further education on leaving school.

In 1999 the society charitable fund was able to support donations of £1000 to an appeal for restoration of St Giles Cathedral and £500 to Maggie's Centre, an organisation devoted to caring for cancer patients. Although doubts were expressed by several wards about the continued purchase and delivery of Christmas parcels this practice continued alongside the other charitable givings. The parcels continued to be supplied under the care of Douglas M Spratt, Ward VIII, and many moving letters of appreciation continued to be received by the society secretary.

In response to a request from Lothian and Borders Police for financial support for their benevolent fund, the society donated a sum of £500 in 1996. This donation was in appreciation of the close links with the police over many years and the free use of their premises when required.

On 21 June 2001 the charitable trust was legally established, and the first disbursement of funds in 2002 comprised 276 Christmas parcels, £750 to the Ark Trust and £750 to National Childrens' Homes Scotland. Charitable givings administered and distributed by the trust for the following year comprised £1,250 to Fresh Start [Edinburgh churches], £1,250 to the Multiple Sclerosis Therapy Centre, £500 to St Giles Cathedral Renewal Appeal, £280 to the Commonwealth Ex-Services League and the regular purchase of Christmas parcels.

As ever, some wards continued with their own charitable activities either by entertaining old folks at the theatre, visiting ex-service men or raising funds by organising "race nights" with betting on filmed horse races for fun and participation by members of their own ward, other wards and friends.

Dinner
The annual dinner continued to be as successful and enjoyable as ever and the altered format with fewer official guests, shorter speeches and paid speakers as necessary proved popular. Efforts still had to be made, however, to ensure that speakers kept within their time limits. The cost of the dinner to members in 2000 was £34.

The dress code for the annual dinner came under scrutiny in 1997 when the requirement for official guests to wear white tie and tails was dropped. This form of evening wear was seldom in the personal wardrobe of such guests, it was expensive to hire, and over previous years this requirement had been largely ignored by guests and speakers. The wearing of badges by members other than office-bearers was left to the discretion of wards, but the standard of dress code was however emphasised in 1999 when it was agreed, following an incident, that jackets should be kept on throughout the whole of the function.

Although the use of the Sheraton Grand Hotel was questioned in 2000, this venue remained unchanged. Numbers attending the dinner remained in excess of 400, a maximum of 429 being achieved in 1997.

Principal speakers at the dinner are listed as appendix 6, and the change in religious tolerance over the years of the society's existence was illustrated in 2002 when the principal speaker, Archbishop Keith O'Brien gently chastised Moderator Richard Allan with the lord provost's baton while alluding to one of the initial injunctions to constables in 1611 to " search and seek out Jesuits, Priests and Trafficking Papists."

Social
As indicated by falling numbers in the mid 1990s, functions such as the formal dinner dance were much less in vogue, and the last such event took place in October 1997 at

the new Murrayfield Rugby Stadium. Although this event was enjoyed by those present, they numbered only 116 and comprised members and their partners from only 10 wards.

While detailed consideration was being given to the society's role in the 21st century, a variety of different functions were arranged in an effort to encourage more interaction between wards.

In 1997 an interesting visit to Tulliallan Police Training College took place, and in the summer of 1998 an enjoyable afternoon was held in Inverleith Park with 85 members and partners participating. The focus was a petanque competition which took place in torrential rain, but the inner man was well satisfied by the use of a large roasting spit under the protection of a marquee.

A proposal for a quiz night for members only was well received and the first of these was held in Myreside Pavilion in spring 2000. All wards participated with teams of up to 6 people, and a trophy, the Quiz Tazza, was presented by Captain David Cavanagh on behalf of Ward III. The first competition, attended by 100 constables, was closely fought and eventually won by means of a tie-break when Moderator Kenneth Dunbar's detailed knowledge of the "Broons" in the cartoon pages of the "Sunday Post" won the day.

The quiz night was run by a professional quiz master, beer and sandwiches were on hand, and any surplus funds were contributed to the society charitable fund. This simple but popular form of entertainment proved successful and with minor changes came to be an annual event and winners are listed in appendix 7.

Another departure was a Burns Supper for society members and partners in January 2002. This very enjoyable formal event was held in the Royal Scots Hotel, Corstorphine, and revealed a wealth of literary and musical talent within the society, the only external participant being Moderator Richard Allan's wife. It was attended by some 100 people and rekindled some of the spirit of dinner dances of the past.

Following this, a new format of smaller gatherings was tried in 2002/2003. These events were run for groups of approximately 25 members and partners and provided the following range of options:

1   A concert promenade at Caroline Park House.
2   A night at the opera at the Festival Theatre.
3   How to listen to the pipes.

The evening at Caroline Park proved a great success but there was insufficient support to allow the other evenings evening to proceed.

Ceremonial

Notwithstanding difficulties encountered in the initial months of the formation of the City of Edinburgh Council there was no reduction in the number of church parades for the society. Indeed, true to his word, Lord Provost Milligan was very enthusiastic about the useful ceremonial role played by the High Constables in emphasising historical links with the past, particularly in view of the fact that Edinburgh was continuing to develop as a major tourist centre with events such as the International Festival of Music and Drama, the Military Tattoo, the huge Hogmanay Party and many other attractions being promoted worldwide. The association between the council and the society was further cemented in May 1999 when Eric Milligan was appointed to serve a second consecutive term as lord provost. This re-election of a lord provost was unprecedented since the 18th century and heralded a very busy period for the society office-bearers and other members in terms of ceremonial duties.

Regular annual church parades to St Giles Cathedral continued for the International Science Festival, the Kirking of the Council and the General Assembly service in May, the Edinburgh International Festival of Music and Drama in August, the Battle of Britain service in September, the Remembrance Day service in November and the Festival of St Andrew in December. In 2002, the role of the High Constables at the Remembrance Day parade was extended to include escorting parties other than the lord provost and councillors. In general, these services were attended by the seven office-bearers and six other High Constables, but at the services inaugurating the Science Festival and the Festival of Music and Drama, all 23 wards were still required to provide two constables to carry out important stewarding duties.

For many years Edinburgh University, and latterly the newer universities in the city, had marked the beginning of each academic year with a service in St Giles Cathedral. In the early 1990s, this service was extended to include representation from schools in the area, and following transfer of the local authority education function to the City of Edinburgh Council in 1996 this special service has been supported by the lord provost and council. Accordingly, Edinburgh High Constables have taken part in this procession since 1996.

The society also accompanied the lord provost and council to additional services to celebrate the International Festival of Music and Drama. These took place in the Synagogue in Salisbury Road and at St Mary's Roman Catholic Cathedral in York Place.

Outwith the city centre, the long standing custom of attending the annual service for seamen at South Leith Church in November continued, with the usual generous hospitality being provided after the service in Trinity House, adjacent to the church.

Throughout his term of office Lord Provost Milligan invited the office-bearers to join him in December to switch on the outdoor Christmas tree lights at Leith, and occasionally at Gorgie. In 2001 and 2002 the Leith ceremony was attended by members of the Leith wards.

The service for the kirking of the moderator had generally been kept separate from other special services at St Giles Cathedral. However, this changed in 1997 when Moderator Simon Bolam's kirking was combined with the annual service for the kirking of the council, and this entirely appropriate combined service continued thereafter. At this service only, office-bearers, past-moderators and the six constables on official duty wore morning dress with top hats, the other constables being less formally attired in dark suits and bowler hats - the normal dress for drills and inspections. At subsequent moderators' kirkings, members were permitted to wear either form of dress in an effort to encourage greater participation.

The society was pleased to be in attendance at a civic service in St Giles Cathedral followed by a reception for the Commonwealth Heads of Government in October 1997

In May 1998 the Heart of Midlothian Football Club were worthy winners of the Scottish Cup, and the lord provost showed his delight by including the office-bearers in a hastily arranged civic reception. This was held amidst much jubilation, albeit that the High Constables ceremonial uniform looked somewhat out of place among the ecstatic fans in Parliament Square. A photograph of the celebrations is included at the end of this chapter.

At the official opening of the new Museum of Scotland on St Andrew's Day 1998, the High Constables led a large procession from Chambers Street through the Grassmarket to a service at St Giles Cathedral. This procession comprised some 350 people from throughout Scotland, and the lord provosts of Edinburgh, Glasgow, Aberdeen and

Dundee were in attendance as well as High Constables from Leith and Perth. A photograph of the High Constables leading the procession is included at the end of this chapter.

Ceremonial use of the High Constables during the summer visits of the monarch to the city was reintroduced by Lord Provost Milligan in 1998 and in 2001. Office-bearers formed a guard of honour at the City Chambers, and on both occasions they were inspected by Her Majesty Queen Elizabeth. The 1998 presentation of office-bearers to the Queen was recorded as "a significant event in the history of the society" and a photograph of the occasion was used as the centrepiece of the official Christmas card used by the lord and lady provost later that year.

In May 2002, the High Constables accompanied the lord provost during the Ceremony of the Keys at Holyrood House, and the society took a prominent role leading the parade. Office-bearers were introduced to the Queen, and the Duke of Edinburgh expressed interest in the silver batons. This was one of the rare occasions when Edinburgh High Constables have had any such role within the normal area of jurisdiction of the Guard of Honour and High Constables of Holyrood House.

The most significant political event in Scotland for some 300 years was devolution of power from Westminster to the new Scottish Parliament in 1999. The society felt honoured and privileged to be invited to form a guard of honour on the High Street adjacent to St Giles Cathedral during the procession from Holyrood Palace which preceded the historic State Opening of Parliament by her Majesty the Queen Elizabeth II within the Assembly Hall on 1 July 1999. A photograph of this procession is included at the end of this chapter.

In 2002, the Lord Provost Milligan was invited to participate in the 5th annual Tartan Day celebrations in New York City. These celebrations were concerned with widening the links and relationships between Scotland and the US, and his unexpected and unique request to be accompanied by a guard of High Constables was readily accepted by the society. Accordingly, Moderator Richard Allan along with three other office-bearers and one past-moderator flew to New York at their own expense, and on 6 April 2002 marched down 6th Avenue [the Avenue of the Americans] in full ceremonial dress with silver batons. The High Constables preceded the lord provost's party and the Lothian and Borders' Police Pipe Band at the "Tunes of Glory" parade which comprised some 10,000 pipers and was led by the Edinburgh born film star Sean Connery who was also a Freeman of the City of Edinburgh. The High Constables were at the front of this parade, and to enter into the theme of the occasion they all sported handkerchiefs of Edinburgh tartan in their top pockets.

Although New York was still recovering from the catastrophic attack on the World Trade Centre on 11 September 2001 this did not dampen spirits, and all the participants returned with memorable stories of both formal and informal experiences. On the day following the parade the party visited the "Scottish Church" on West 96th Street in the company of the lord provost.

Office-bearers and members subsequently participated with the lord provost's party in similar "Tunes of Glory" parades to Murrayfield Stadium in November 2002 prior to a friendly rugby match between Scotland and South Africa. They also paraded along the Champs de Mars and through Montmartre in Paris as part of the Montmartre-Ecosse Alliance Parade at the time of a 6 nations France v Scotland rugby match in February 2003. Moderator Richard Allan and constable Ian Muir, Ward VI also participated in the Chicago Tartan Day Parade in March 2003.

These events were all associated with charity collections for Marie Curie Cancer Care and involved the society in virtually no expense. Most of the visits abroad were undertaken by the office-bearers, but in the event of insufficient support from office bearers a ballot for places was held for other members who expressed interest.

As part of the Queen's Golden Jubilee celebrations in June 2002, the High Constables provided an escort to the lord provost and council at special church services in St Andrew's and St George's Church in George Street, and also in St Mary's Roman Catholic Cathedral in York Place. Other services attended included one in 1998 to commemorate the 50th anniversary of the Leonard Cheshire Foundation, a special service attended by the Princess Royal on 2nd January 2000 in St Giles Cathedral to mark the new millenium, the 80th anniversary of Lodge Solomon at the Synagogue in February 2000, and a parade in April 2002 from the Castle to St Giles Cathedral for a service with the Salvation Army. Services at St Cuthbert's Roman Catholic Church and Gorgie Parish Church in the lord provost's own ward were attended in October 2002 and January 2003.

In the last year of Lord Provost Milligan's term of office the society attended a total of 20 different ceremonial events, this being approximately twice the number in previous years.

The lord provost's High Constable baton had lain in a display cabinet for many years and it was perhaps significant that Lord Provost Milligan was pleased to accept this baton at the start of his term of office, and that it lay symbolically on his desk thereafter. His unique period of office extended throughout the full seven years of this chapter of the society's history, and members greatly appreciated his strong support and the innovations that he introduced to their ceremonial life. Following introduction of the overseas trips, Lord Provost Milligan established a close bond of friendship with moderators and office bearers.

At the conclusion of his term of office Moderator Richard Allan recorded that he had attended 150 events over 2 years including 50 dinners. Office-bearers had been presented to the Queen at a number of special events and had attended ceremonial event in New York, Paris and Chicago – those being the first ever occasions at which the society had particpated in such events aboard.

In spite of the somewhat tenuous relationship with the City of Edinburgh Council at the start of this period the strength of individual wards continued to flourish, and the friendship and fellowship essential to such vitality continued to be one of the most important features of life as a High Constable of Edinburgh.

Equipment

The society's silver batons continued to be updated every two years with the names and dates of office-bearers, and the equipment held by individual members was checked regularly during this period. These checks indicated the extent of loss or damage to be extremely low. In 2001 it was made clear that individual members' equipment was valued between £1,000 and £2,000 and that the prime responsibility for its safe keeping rested with the members. The equipment fund set up in 1991 had grown to a value of £3,000, but members were reminded that they could not rely on this fund to cover the cost of replacement in all circumstances. It was also pointed out that the considerable assets of the society in terms of regalia and equipment were not recorded in the annual accounts, but Treasurer Douglas Walker considered that this would not be appropriate.

In 2000, it was noted that the benches in Parliament Square which had been presented to the city by the society in the 1960s were in poor repair. These seats were very popular with tourists, and when their condition was pointed out to the council they readily undertook the necessary repair work.

In the same year the society successfully recovered a small baton which was catalogued for sale at an auction in England. The baton, numbered 48, made reference to Edinburgh High Constables and to King George IV, and was recovered by the society at no cost following an assertion by the committee that it was still rightfully in the ownership of the society. In this connection the world wide web proved very useful in identifying other similar items of society equipment listed on various web sites throughout the world. One such item was a copy of James Marwick's history and this was offered for sale in California at a cost of $150 [approximately equivalent to £100 at the time]. In 2002 some miniature cups were presented to the society by descendants of James Cruikshanks.

David Robertson's history lists the insignia of the society in 1924, and a check in 2001 of the artefacts held in the display cases in the Mandela Room in the City Chambers revealed that several items had gone missing in the intervening period. The major losses were a small silver baton presented by George Beattie, Moderator 1851, a silver boatswain whistle dated 1831, a silver mounted snuff horn or mull presented by James Dallas, Moderator 1820, a Moderator's flask presented by James Crichton, Moderator 1880, and a silver loving cup presented by the High Constables of Perth in 1894.

In order to avoid a recurrence of this gradual loss, the society historian recommended that a detailed inventory of all equipment held in the City Chambers be prepared, and that this should be checked every two years in addition to checking the equipment held by members and office-bearers. Such inventories were carried out by Custodier Colin Cargill in 2002 and an updated version of this appears as appendix 2 and appendix 3.

A suggestion to the effect that society cufflinks should be supplied to interested members was pursued in 2002, and later that year members representing nine wards agreed to purchase cufflinks at a cost of £22 each. The cufflinks were to be made in a form similar to members' badges incorporating the society crest. They were also produced with the option of a silver or gold background.

Sport

The annual skittles competition continued to be held in January and February, and all the work of organising the wards and arranging venues still fell to the surgeon - this being a much greater task than tending to any constable who might fall ill while on duty.

As a venue, the "Right Wing" in Willowbrae did not prove very satisfactory, and after a spell at Corstorphine Inn in 1998 and 1999 the competition moved back to a renovated Sheep Heid Inn in Duddingston. It was good to return to the alleys where the competition had started in 1978, and although there was regret that moves towards healthier eating meant that there were no hot, greasy pies to lend sustenance, there was no restriction on the consumption of beer other than the effect it might have on one's ability and legality to drive home.

Competition was keen, and Ward XVI Broughton had a particularly good run when they won the Moderator's Shield for 4 successive years from 1994 to 1997. There were also several tense and exciting moments as the last bowl was thrown by those in contention for the Treasurer's Cup for the highest individual score.

However, the increasing age profile of members meant that some wards found it difficult to raise a team although, on the whole, the society still preferred skittles to 10-pin bowling. Accordingly in 1999 the number of players in each team was reduced from 6 to 4 and the length of each match was restricted to only two ends. This revised and less energetic format encouraged 18 teams to agree to participate, and the reduction in the number of shots played meant a closer result - the final play-off for the Moderator's Shield being won by Ward XIII by only one point.

The number of ends the following year was increased from 2 to 3, but in spite of these changes there were still some doubts about the long term future of the competition with a significant number of wards calling off at the last minute. However, the position began to look more hopeful in 2003 with the influx of some new, younger members into the wards.

The society sports clubs continued in very much the same vein as previously with no major changes, and in response to a request from new members more ties were manufactured in 1999. It was also agreed that the now defunct Rifle Club trophies could be used for prizes by the other sports clubs.

Golf

Monthly summer venues were varied by visits to the courses at Newbattle, Gullane and a new course at King's Acre [Lasswade]. Several annual matches continued throughout this period, opposition being provided by the golf clubs of Perth High Constables, Lothian and Borders Police, the Edinburgh Merchant Company and the old "Edinburgh Corporation". In 1999 and 2001 opposition was also provided by golfers from the Royal Air Force. On every occasion many friendships continued to be nurtured at the nineteenth hole. As usual, the level of skills varied but seasons 1996 and 2001 were notable in that no defeats were suffered by Edinburgh High Constables.

The Golf Club dinner dance and prize-giving continued to be the annual social focus for the club, and to mark the new millennium in 2000 special medals were struck for the winners of the knock-out competition. The strength of the club remained fairly steady at around 50 although this was slightly increased in 2001 and 2002.

The Henderson Handicap Medal [1895] was mislaid for a period in 1999, and because this caused some concern it again focused the attention of all sports clubs on the adequacy of arrangements for insurance cover on their trophies. The Golf Club had 16 trophies out of a total of 29 held by all four clubs, and it was agreed that the society would provide cover up to £500 with the clubs taking responsibility for any shortfall. The most valuable trophy was the Golf Club's "Cuthbertson Trophy" which was valued at £7,900 having been presented in 1904 for annual competition.

Bowling

The Bowling Club continued to start their season with the invitation pairs competition at Coltbridge Bowling Club and this was followed by the annual general meeting of the club. Generally, four matches were played against other clubs throughout the season, but sadly in 1997 the club's oldest fixture against a team from Edinburgh Council was cancelled because the club had been disbanded. However, this slot was filled in 1999 with the new opponents being a team from the Bank of Scotland. This was a particularly successful year with the club recording wins in all their matches.

Membership of the club was not high numerically, but loyal support from friendly bowlers outwith the society still helped to fulfil the regular fixtures against clubs from Perth High Constables, the City of Glasgow Council, Whitehouse and Grange and the Bank of Scotland. The biennial away match against the City of Glasgow Council continued to be rounded off with a generous reception at the City Chambers. In 1998, the weather was so bad that the Glasgow match was transferred to an indoor rink, but the subsequent reception was attended by Lord Provost Pat Lally and several councillors.

Home fixtures continued mainly at Coltbridge Bowling Club with the occasional match being held at Whitehouse and Grange Bowling Club. On occasion, the club was also represented at the Lynch McQueen Triples Competition at Whitehouse and Grange, but there is no record of the High Constables ever winning this competition.

Angling

Membership of the Angling Club continued to be boosted by the welcome addition of associate members from outwith the society, and throughout this period membership remained fairly static at about 30, with some 8 or 9 of these being associate members.

Normally there would be 5 outings each summer, the main venues being Loch Leven, Loch Fitty, Portmore reservoir and Coldingham Loch, with occasional visits to Linlithgow Loch and Morton reservoir. In 2000, the outing to Coldingham Loch was particularly successful with one of the associate members setting a new club record with an 8 pound 7 ounce rainbow trout.

The match against Perth High Constables for the King Cup continued as before over two legs, but in 2000 the favoured venues of Butterstone Loch and Loch Fitty were replaced by Morton reservoir and Lindores. The results of the competition were fairly even and friendships were rekindled both during the competition and afterwards over high tea at a local hotel.

The number of trophies played for within the club was boosted to 4 in 2000 by presentation of the David Cavanagh Plate for the heaviest fish caught throughout the season.

Up until 1998 the club continued to be represented at the Edinburgh and Leith United Angling Clubs Competition, and on one occasion [1998] they also competed in the Inter Cities Competition.

Curling

The altered format of competition within the Curling Club continued, the winners of the winter and spring leagues meeting for a play-off at the end of the season to win the Surgeon's Quaich. All league games were played at Murrayfield Curling Club, but the points competition at the end of the season continued to be held at Gogar Park Curling Club with the annual prize-giving and annual general meeting following.

The only match undertaken by the club was the annual home or away fixture against Perth High Constables for the splendid trophy which was first presented in 1924. Edinburgh won this competition from 1996 to 1998, but Perth wrested the cup back in 1999 and retained it thereafter.

The popularity of curling in Scotland was increasing and in the latter part of this period membership of the club rose steadily to the point in 2002 when there were 30 playing members - the highest for many years. This interest was greatly boosted by the magnificent gold medal victory by the Scottish Womens' Curling Team in 2002 during the Winter Olympics at Salt lake City, and it was very gratifying that one of the stalwarts of the High Constables Curling Club, Andrew Hepburn, Ward XIII, was President of the Royal Caledonian Curling Club at that time.

Celebrations to mark the victory by Heart of Midlothian in the Scottish Cup, May 1998.
(*Courtesy of Scotsman Publications*)

Cartoon from the "Edinburgh Evening News", May 1997.

The first women High Constables in their official uniform, Margaret Williamson and
Deirdre Kinloch Anderson, both Ward XXI, October 1998. (photograph supplied by "Newsflash")

High Constables leading the procession at the opening of the new Museum of Scotland,
St Andrew's Day 1998. (Courtesy of W. R. Ferguson)

Moderator Richard Allan and his team taking time out in Paris, February 2003.
(Courtesy of Richard Allan)

High Constables parading at the New York Tartan Day celebrations, 6 April 2002
F Owen George, Surgeon – Colin Cargil, Custodier – J Richard Allan,
Moderator – David Rutherford, Secretary – Simon Bolam, Past Moderator
(Courtesy of Richard Allan)

Her Majesty the Queen inspecting Society Office Bearers in July 1998 with
Lord Provost Eric Milligan and Moderator Simon Bolam.
(Courtesy of City of Edinburgh Council)

Official Opening of the Scottish Parliament, 1 July 1999
(Courtesy of City of Edinburgh Council)

CHAPTER 8

TOWARDS THE QUATERCENTENARY 2003 – 2008

It was perhaps inevitable that increasing pressure of business commitments would lead to a move by members to reduce the time spent attending society meetings and parades.

A decision in 2005 to reduce the number of committee meetings and official parades proved popular with many members and did not appear to have any adverse effect on the basic longstanding traditions and principles of the society. Likewise, this did not reduce enthusiasm for the planning of events to celebrate the society's quatercentenary celebrations in 2011 or lead to any diminution of activity at ward level or in the various sports clubs.

In May 2003 Lesley Hinds was appointed as Edinburgh's second woman lord provost. A strong relationship was established by successive moderators and office-bearers and this association was cemented at several significant events such as the official opening by Queen Elizabeth II of the new Scottish Parliament building at Holyrood in October 2004 and Tartan Day in New York in April 2005.

Constitution

A new system of proportional representation was adopted for council elections in May 2007 and this resulted in the administration of the Edinburgh Council being controlled by a coalition of different political parties, none of which commanded an overall majority. This was a difficult situation in respect of achieving political objectives but the new Lord Provost, George Grubb, was assured that the society would support the council with its usual impartiality and enthusiasm. Lord Provost Grubb responded to these assurances by showing great support and enthusiasm for all aspects of society activities.

In 2003 two copies of Marwick's 1865 History of the High Constables of Edinburgh were acquired – one purchased at a cost of £90 and one donated by the widow of a former member. These rare volumes were not often offered for sale and it was good for the society to have some in stock for reference purposes. In order to further good relations with the council, one copy was rebound and presented to Chief Executive Tom Aitchison for use by him and by succeeding officers. Mr. Aitchison indicated that the volume would be very useful in relation to his induction course for new councillors when reference to the role of the society was made.

A motion to dispense with the two meetings specifically held for drilling purposes in spring and autumn was put to the annual general meeting in 2005, the proposal being that any necessary drilling could be carried out on the same evening as the inspection. A similar motion had been defeated 4 years previously with only 92 members in favour at that time, but in 2005 the motion was carried with the support of 141 members. This decision was first implemented in autumn 2005.

This change had implications in respect of points to be awarded for the Dunbar Trophy, but after discussion it was agreed that no other events should be introduced to the competition and that the trophy should be awarded solely on the basis of attendance at the annual general meeting, the spring inspection and the autumn inspection. Accordingly the maximum points possible to any ward would be 36, a total far removed from the 120 points possible when the trophy was first presented in 1912 with two general meetings being held in addition to six drills and two inspections.

An overview of the activities of individual wards in 2005 revealed that on average most wards had meetings 7 times per year with some meeting more frequently and with one ward meeting together on only two occasions. The venues and styles of ward meetings were extremely diverse and similar variations were clear in the pattern of social activities which were understandably geared to the inclinations of the ward members. Formats and locations for ward dinners varied considerably and some wards still continued with regular dinners for ward members only without spouses or partners being invited. Many wards expressed a wish for more events including all members of the society and cited the 2004 Moderator's Reception in the Playfair Library as a good example.

Throughout the period the society website was regularly updated and by 2008 the comprehensive information collated by Past-Moderator Leonard Wallace included the following:

A calendar of forthcoming events.
Photograph and details of the Moderator's Gold Medal.
Information on the Annual Dinner.
List of past-moderators, details of wards and a list of current office-bearers.
Brief history of the society and the text of Marwick's history.
Information on and purpose of the charitable trust.
Description and photographs of society uniform.
Photo gallery.
Secure area for use by members only.

In 2005 the style of uniform for women in the society was discussed, the original uniforms having been in use for six years. The supplier of the original uniforms was no longer able to continue and accordingly a small sub-committee comprising four women members and an ex-moderator was formed to consider the position. Having experienced the limitations of the original uniform in terms of cost, availability and practicality for other use, the women were able to recommend simpler forms of dress. For drills and inspections, a change to a black or dark navy suit with straight skirt or dark navy trouser suit was suggested along with a black bowler hat suitable for women. For ceremonials, the recommendation was a skirt in pinstripe black or grey cloth with a single pleat at the back. A long line black jacket falling away at the front from the waist, with a collar and a single vent at the back was also suggested and this was to be closed by three silver celtic buttons and embellished with three smaller celtic buttons at each cuff. A dressage hat decorated with a flash in the material of the society's tie secured by a celtic button was to replace the original tricorne hat. These recommendations were readily accepted by the committee.

In 2006 a further milestone was reached when Deirdre Kinloch Anderson was elected captain of Ward XXI Craigentinny. This was the first time a woman constable had been elected to this position and was some 7 years after her admission as one of the first two women in the society.

The annual general meeting in 2006 was a special one for Past Captain Adam Currie, Ward IV who received his 50 year service star from Lord Provost Lesley Hinds. He had joined the society on 15 December 1955, and as a special mark of appreciation was invited to act as inspecting officer at the following inspection. This was no new experience for Past Captain Currie who had also carried out an inspection in autumn 1983 when Master of the Merchant Company.

In late 2006 it was suggested that members might wish to attend a presentation in respect of the U K Armed Forces Regular Reserve. This presentation had been proposed by the Army who felt this was part of their role to keep the general public better informed, but after the matter had been considered by wards it was apparent that there was little enthusiasm for this presentation. Many regular and volunteer forces were still involved on active service in Iraq and Afghanistan and the conflicts in these countries were not universally supported in Scotland.

When it was agreed to establish a charitable trust in 2001 the levy was set at £26 and an additional voluntary sum of £17 was recommended for charitable purposes giving a total payment of £43 for the year. By 2007 this payment had increased to £55, but the cost of running society affairs was largely contained during this period. This was partly due to low inflation and partly due to savings made by photocopying formal notices to members instead of having them printed, and by using electronic means to communicate with office-bearers and captains.

The cost increase was mainly caused by the additional payment of £5 levied annually from 2003 for the quatercentenary celebrations and an increase in the recommended charitable donation from £17 to £22.50. By 2008 a substantial sum in the order of £6,600 had accrued in the Quatercentenary Fund and the sub-committee set up in 2002 was reconstituted to produce the detailed planning necessary for such an event.

Over the years the duties falling to certain office-bearers had changed, and in 2007 it was agreed that the biennial task of compiling the roll book should be undertaken by the vice-moderator. This change, in addition to the reduction in the number of drills each year would ease pressure on the secretary's considerable workload.

At the same time requirements for the office of society surgeon were considered, and although the constitution did not specify any qualification other than membership of the society, this office had traditionally been reserved for a member with a medical qualification. Over the previous 25 years, five members had served two terms of duty as surgeon and it was felt that if the society dispensed with the need for a medical qualification more opportunity would be given to other members to serve as office-bearers. Accordingly, it was agreed that the title be retained but that there would be no need for a specific medical qualification.

For many years nine committee meetings had been held each year although the constitutional requirement was for a minimum of eight. In 2005 the society committee felt that nine meetings was excessive and it was agreed that this should be reduced to eight by ceasing to hold the traditional December meeting.

This reduction appeared to have no detrimental effect on the business to be transacted, and in order to accord with a more modern approach to the administration of the society's needs the committee proposed that the constitutional requirement be reduced from eight to six meetings each year. This was approved at the annual general meeting in April 2008.

A further proposal to remove the constitutional requirement for prospective new members to provide details of their number on the Register of Electors for the City of Edinburgh was defeated at the same meeting.

In early 2007 the committee considered publication of the updated history which had been prepared by Past-Moderator W R Ferguson. The City of Edinburgh Council had made a generous offer to undertake printing and production of the document and to bear half the cost. Accordingly it was agreed that publication of 500 copies should proceed on the understanding that the contents would be brought fully up to date before final printing. It was anticipated that much of the society's outlay would be recovered by sale of the books to members.

A great deal of friendship, camaraderie and fun had always been generated within wards, but none of this would have been possible without the overarching disciplines and responsibilities of membership of the society. Members failing to attend the requisite parades were still being called to account by Moderator Robert Forman in 2008 and the council expected the High Constables to carry out all duties as requested.

Drills
In continuation of efforts to improve the standard of drill, in 2004 the drill officer and platoon commanders attended the T A Centre at Redford for advice in the basic techniques of drilling. At the subsequent autumn drill the society was given 25 minutes instruction in static drill and on this occasion there was no platform party or march-past rehearsal, office-bearers being requested to join the ranks. In 2008 a sub committee was set up to review drilling procedures and dress code and to produce a booklet with words and pictures.

A major change occurred in the autumn of 2005 when, for the first time, no separate meeting for drill was carried out prior to the inspection. The concept of a combined drill and inspection on the same evening worked well and Drill Officer John Henderson arranged that new constables attended early for instruction. With the assistance of platoon commanders he ensured that the practice drilling was completed in good time before arrival of the inspecting officer and the total time spent on the parade ground was only some 15-20 minutes greater than previously.

As usual, the marching was greatly assisted by the pipes and drums of the Lothian and Borders Police Pipe Band and cancellation of the drill only evening was welcomed by the police officers who were relieved of the substantial task of clearing the garage of vehicles.

Lord Provost Lesley Hinds was pleased to attend as inspecting officer whenever possible. Past Captain Currie, Ward IV, was uniquely invited to inspect the parade on 27 April 2006, and other inspections were carried out by Chief Constable Paddy Hopkins, Councillor Steve Cardownie and Chief Constable David Strang.

Lord Provost George Grubb carried out his first inspection of the society in autumn 2007 and in a departure from tradition he asked Moderator Robert Forman to call forward 6 constables identified during his detailed inspection. The fears of these constables regarding failure to dress properly were quickly allayed when the lord provost presented each of them a miniature bottle of whisky.

Charity
With the society's charitable trust now firmly established, few events specifically aimed at fund raising were promoted. However, surplus income from social functions was transferred to the fund, and it is noted that in June 2004 Wards XIV and XXI raised a sum of £2,000 for Maggie's Cancer Caring Centre as the result of an informal race night.

Approximately half the trust's funds distributed in 2004 were in respect of the usual quota of Christmas parcels and a further £3,000 was variously distributed to the Scout Council [for the Bonaly Outdoor Centre], the Scottish Storytelling Centre, the Ark Trust, Maggie's Cancer Caring Centre and Bfriends.

Some wards continued to have difficulty in distributing their 12 parcels to appropriate recipients at Christmas and felt that this expenditure could be directed to more deserving causes. The Salvation Army offered to help but it became apparent that to find a suitable alternative with a Christmas meaning would be difficult and hence there was no change to the usual quota of 276 parcels in 2004.

In the following year members were given the option of using their donations for the purchase of parcels or allowing their donations to be distributed as the members of the charitable trust saw fit. Approximately 100 members chose the latter option, thus introducing a change to a tradition which had been started in 1958.

This change increased the funds available for general distribution, and in 2005 some £7,500 was spent on deserving causes in addition to the reduced gift of parcels. The recipients of this distribution were the Chernobyl Life Line, a former Castlebrae High School student, Fresh Start, One City Trust, Artlink, Richmond's Hope, Children's Holiday Venture, the Rock Trust and St Columba's Hospice. Many recipients of Christmas parcels continued to write to express their sincere appreciation. Past Captain Douglas Spratt, Ward VIII continued to give excellent service in supplying and wrapping the contents and Christmas 2007 saw the 21st year of this tradition. Following their distribution in 2006 interest was expressed regarding the contents and no report on this had been given since 1989.

The allocation process adopted by the charitable trust was based on identifying causes with an Edinburgh connection and weighting donations towards charities where the money was likely to have the greatest impact. In 2006, £6,250 was distributed and the following charities benefited:- Fresh Start, Police Aided Clothing Scheme, Cystic Fybrosis Trust, Primary Biliary Care Foundation, Cunningham House, Scotland Yard Adventure Centre and Bethany Trust, the last three being awarded £1,500 each. The following beneficiaries each received £1,500 in 2007:– The Samaritans of Edinburgh and the Lothians, Erskine Edinburgh Home, 6 VT Youth Café and the Grassmarket Mission.

In the summer of 2004 Moderator Leonard Wallace's formal role was set aside when he participated with the lord provost in the Sports Relief Scottish Mile at Murrayfield.

Likewise, the society's participation with a three man team in 2005 in an "It's a Knockout" competition at Meadowbank Stadium was equally informal. This event was promoted specifically to raise money for victims of the Asian tsunami in December 2004 and donations to this cause were also contributed by some wards and by individual members.

Dinner
The Sheraton Grand Hotel continued as the venue for the annual dinner although serious doubts were raised following the November 2006 event when disappointment was expressed at the standard of catering. Criticisms of this type had been raised regularly but there had also been concern that year about suspected fraudulent use of a member's plastic credit card in connection with the purchase of wine for his ward.

Questions were raised again early in 2007 regarding the cost of entertaining the significant number of official guests and it was suggested that this cost should be spread among all society members and not only those attending the function. This point had been a matter for concern for many years although steps had been taken in 1990 to spread the costs equitably throughout the society. In addition all past-moderators had traditionally been formally invited to the function and entertained at the society's expense, but the position on this had become inconsistent. In view of these doubts and inconsistencies, steps were taken to review the suitability of the Sheraton Hotel, the number of officially invited guests and clarity of the budget for the event.

Guest speakers continued to be at the invitation of the moderator and the principal toasts were given by men and women of distinction in public life as indicated in appendix 6.

Social
As indicated in Chapter 7 interest was gradually waning for the type of society-wide social events which had been a feature during much of the 20th century.

Innovative plans to hold a "McGonagall Evening" in early 2004 failed to come to fruition due to lack of support, but in the same year a novel event held at the former Edinburgh University Union was supported by 76 people. This was a masked ceilidh dance and at £30 a head enough money was generated to pass on £100 to the charitable trust.

In addressing the need for a social function to include all members and friends of the society, Moderator Leonard Wallace held an informal "Moderator's Reception" in the Playfair Library of Edinburgh University on 8 October 2004. Wine and canapés were served to 168 people and the beauty and ambience of the hall was conducive to a very relaxed and enjoyable evening. Background music was provided by a musical quartet under the direction of Surgeon R Dennison and this set the seal on the evening's fun. The success of the event was such that it was repeated by Moderator David Rutherford in October 2006 in anticipation that it would become a biennial event.

In 2004 Lothian and Borders Police invited members to participate in a presentation of police work in their area. Although the initial response was encouraging a relatively small proportion of members attended the event which nevertheless proved to be a very worthwhile and entertaining evening.

The format of the successful quiz night for society members continued to remain very popular with up to 20 teams participating. The results of this hard fought competition are indicated in appendix 7 and as previously all surplus funds were passed to the charitable trust for distribution.

In contrast to the diminution of informal events for the whole society, social activities at grass roots level within wards continued to flourish as ever and thereby maintained the friendships and camaraderie essential to such an organisation. Likewise, the high esteem in which the society was held was indicated in the reports of successive moderators who continued to represent the society at many prestigious functions throughout Edinburgh and the East of Scotland.

Ceremonial

The society readily accepted a proposal in 2003 to join with kindred societies to arrange a fund-raising cocktail party at Edinburgh Castle. The gathering was in support of the Jubilee Appeal for Commonwealth Veterans and the guest of honour was HRH the Duke of Edinburgh. A limited number of tickets for this unique occasion to be held on 4 July were sold at £25 each and the substantial organisation and co-ordination work was undertaken by Ex-Moderator Richard Allan.

The Duke of Edinburgh was met on arrival by Lord Provost Lesley Hinds and the moderators of all four societies. A guard of honour comprising members of all the societies paraded outside the Great Hall of the Castle, and having inspected the parade the Duke joined the champagne reception in the Great Hall. He spent a very relaxed time chatting with those present and showed great interest in the regalia, particularly the silver batons worn by the Edinburgh society office-bearers. At the conclusion of the evening the Duke made an appeal on behalf of the Commonwealth Veterans and the total sum raised by this very happy social occasion was £6,400.

The society was honoured when Lord Provost Lesley Hinds asked for the provision of an escort for the Queen to and from the City Chambers on the occasion of the formal opening of the new Scottish Parliament building at Holyrood on 9 October 2004. The office-bearers and members involved were present throughout the duration of the festive parade down the Royal Mile.

Regular parades with office-bearers and six constables escorting the lord provost and councillors continued as before in addition to celebration of the usual festivals in the city which required representation from all 23 wards for stewarding purposes. In view of the somewhat complicated arrangements required for the service to celebrate the start of the Edinburgh International Festival in August each year, a rehearsal involving all wards had for many years been carried out on the preceding Friday. In October 2004, this rehearsal was discontinued in response to a request by the wards, and a change to the briefing arrangements on the day of the parade ensured that the services took place in the usual orderly fashion.

In addition to regular parades the society was also on duty in November 2003 at a national Mass of Thanksgiving to celebrate the elevation of the Most Reverend K P O'Brien to Cardinal. In April 2004 the 10th anniversary of democracy in South Africa was marked by a service in St Giles Cathedral and a special service to commemorate the 500th anniversary of the Royal College of Surgeons was attended in July 2005. On 16 June 2005 office-bearers officiated at a meaningful and moving event when the Burmese pro-democracy leader Suu Kyi was awarded the Freedom of the City of Edinburgh. Suu Kyi was unable to accept the honour in person as she had been under house arrest in Burma for many years, but she was represented at a ceremony in the City Chambers and thereafter at a tree planting in Princes Street Gardens.

2005 marked the 200th anniversary of the enactment of the Edinburgh Police Act and two former office-bearers joined members of the police force to meet and talk with the public in the High Street. The High Constable uniforms and silver batons proved to be a source of great interest with the citizens of Edinburgh and with tourists.

In response to an invitation from the Merchant Company the society helped to officiate at the Kirking of the Master in October 2003 and 2005.

A sporting celebration took place in May 2006 when Heart of Midlothian won the Scottish Cup. The society had the good fortune to join in the celebrations when on parade at their previous win in 1998 and Lord Provost Hinds was delighted to include the society again at the reception in honour of the club on the day following their victory.

Despite the successful visit to the USA in 2002 to participate in the Tartan Day celebrations in New York there was no enthusiasm for this event in the following two years. However, in April 2005, at the invitation of the lord provost a party consisting of Moderator Leonard Wallace, Vice-Moderator David Rutherford, Secretary Robert Forman, Past Captain Iain Scott Ward VII and constable Deirdre Kinloch Anderson, Ward XXI accompanied Lord Provost Lesley Hinds and her party to the Tartan Day events. The duties again included providing a guard of honour in the Tartan Day Parade along the Avenue of the Americas and in addition the High Constables helped to ensure the safe transportation of the Wallace Sword into Grand Central Station where it was to be displayed. This was the first time in 700 years that the sword had left its home in Scotland. Several other functions were also greatly enjoyed and members officiated at the 10 kilometre Scotland Run in Central Park. The cost of the trip was again borne by the members attending.

Equipment

In early 2004 the council indicated that refurbishment of the City Chambers would result in the Mandela Room no longer being available to the society for committee meetings. This refurbishment also resulted in removal of the notice boards listing past-moderators and of the two equipment display cases which had been in place for some 50 years.

For a period alternative rooms within the City Chambers were used for meetings and ultimately in 2006 it was found that the Dean of Guild Court Room proved to be a very acceptable option. This room was lined with wooden panels listing all former Deans of Guild and the council had generously undertaken the inscription in gold leaf of dates and names of all former moderators on an adjacent set of panels. In addition, a new display case to house some historic society equipment including all the large silver ceremonial batons was provided outside the door to the room. Much of the equipment listed in appendix 2 was held in these cases, the remaining items being stored in the vaults of the City Chambers.

Regular use of the silver ceremonial batons resulted in maintenance being required, and a substantial overhaul of the batons was carried out in 2004. In addition to this work the batons continued to be inscribed regularly with the names of successive office-bearers.

For many years the supply of new and replacement equipment had been carried out by Alex Kirkwood and Son, Albany Street, and in September 2003 they completed the first bulk supply of society cufflinks, some with silver and some with gold background depending on the preference of individual members.

In 2005 the Scottish Executive's initiative on knife crime included proposals to prohibit carrying certain weapons including truncheons or batons. The society sought to have an exemption made to any future legislation to permit the carrying of batons for ceremonial purposes.

An audit of all equipment held in trust by office-bearers and members was undertaken in 2006-07 and all equipment was generally found to be in good order although not every member was in possession of a whistle and several whistles were inappropriately marked. The audit also revealed that the loss of individual items continued to be very small.

In 2007, reapprasial of insurance cover on all society equipment was carried out by Treasurer Alistair Beattie. Following this review it was confirmed that insurance for all items normally held under lock and key in the City Chambers, including silver batons, was covered as part of a policy held by Edinburgh Council. The premium for the society's own All Risks policy had increased substantially to £525 per annum but this would now include not only the Moderator's gold badge and equipment held by successive office-bearers but would also provide cover up to £10,000 for trophies owned by the society and by the various sports clubs.

In the event that the replacement cost of loss or damage to members' equipment could not be recovered from the members' own personal insurance cover, then this cost would be taken from the society's equipment fund.

In order to have proof of value in the event of any claim, the custodier undertook to arrange for valuation of the equipment and trophies held in the City Chambers.

Sport

In continuation of efforts to make participation in the annual skittles competition as easy as possible for older members, the format was again changed to shorten the game to only two ends. The competition at the Sheep Heid Inn in 2004 was supported by only 14 teams of which 2 withdrew, and a major rethink was necessary.

The experiment with ten-pin bowling in 1991-92 had not been wholeheartedly welcomed, but by February 2005 Surgeon Richard Dennison had persuaded 16 teams of 4 members to participate in a new ten-pin bowling competition at the Edinburgh Corn Exchange in Gorgie. Occupation of the hall was given over entirely to the society and the format adopted resulted in a happy and enjoyable evening for many society members with the competition being won by Ward XIV by a margin of 23 points. The success of the evening was such that the format and venue was continued over the following years, and trophies for the Moderator's Shield and the Treasurer's Cup continued to be awarded to the winning team and the highest individual score respectively. 2008 was the first occasion when a woman constable not only participated but formed part of the winning team.

Golf

Membership remained steady around 60 and the three summer outings were usually supported by some 15 constables. Venues for these outings were varied from year to year with competition taking place in 2006 at courses at Gullane, Liberton, Kilspindie and Ratho.

The usual regular fixtures proved as enjoyable as ever, opposition being provided by the old "Edinburgh Corporation Club", the Edinburgh Merchant Company, the Royal Air Force Leuchars, Perth High Constables and Lothian and Borders Police. In 2006 an additional annual match was introduced against the High Constables of the Port of Leith

In 2004 a Tri-Am competition within the club was promoted and the response was such that in order to encourage this initiative the society agreed to subsidise the cost of the initial competition to the extent of £80. The event, held at King's Acre Golf Club in July 2004 was very successful with 20 teams participating. The competition was won by a team from Ward I and the outing proved so popular it was repeated annually thereafter.

As with other areas in the life of the society the club's formal dinner and dance had become outdated and out of fashion and in April 2004 the last such function was held at the Royal Burgess Golf Club. This event, which included the annual prize-giving, was replaced in subsequent years by a dinner for members and partners held at Mortonhall Golf Club.

Bowling

The club membership remained fairly static but in order to ensure that all obligations for matches were met the club decided in 2004 to appoint official "Associate Members" who were not members of the society. By so doing, a membership of around 16 was established with 5 of these being High Constables.

Following the initial invitation pairs competition at Coltbridge Bowling Club regular fixtures continued as before, with three rinks of four competing in the match against Glasgow City Council. As ever, this match continued to be memorable, not least because of the lavish hospitality following games played at Riddrie Bowling Club, these civic receptions and dinners being attended by the depute lord provost of Glasgow, bailies and other councillors.

Other matches were played against Perth High Constables, Whitehouse and Grange Bowling Club and the Bank of Scotland.

In an unusual turn of events Perth High Constables won the match in 2005 but failed to retain the trophy in the following two years.

Curling

With membership remaining steady there was little change in the enjoyable routine competitions between the 4 teams comprising the leagues throughout the winter months. Membership of 24-27 ensured that the selected league teams of 4 curlers could play against each other as and when required with a final play off being keenly contested in March each year.

Despite careful team selection the club was unable to win back the trophy from Perth High Constables although the margin in 2005 was only 2 shots overall.

As a result of the closure of Gogar Park Curling Club due to construction of the head office of the Royal Bank of Scotland, all games had to be played at Murrayfield Curling Club.

Over eighty years of tradition was broken when the club welcomed constable Jacqueline Easson, Ward X as a playing member in 2005. Constable Easson was the first women to join any of the society's sports clubs and it was a singular honour for the club when Ross Hepburn, Ward XX was selected to represent Scotland in the World Curling Championship in Canada in 2008.

Moderator Leonard Wallace on parade at Edinburgh Castle with Moderators from the High Constables of Perth, Leith and Holyrood House, July, 2003. (Courtesy of Stephen Parry Donald)

All 4 Societies of High Constables in Scotland on parade for the Duke of Edinburgh at Edinburgh Castle, July, 2003. (Courtesy of Stephen Parry Donald)

The Duke of Edinburgh in conversation with Past Captain Douglas Spratt, Ward VIII at Edinburgh Castle, July, 2003. (Courtesy of Stephen Parry Donald)

The Duke of Edinburgh inspecting silver batons with Custodier James Gray at Edinburgh Castle, July, 2003. (Courtesy of Stephen Parry Donald)

Ceremonial bodyguard for the Lord Provosts of Edinburgh and Glasgow escorting the
Wallace Sword to Grand Central Station, New York, April 2005.
Past Captain Iain Scott, Constable Deirdre Kinloch Anderson, Lord Provost Lesley Hinds,
Vice-Moderator David Rutherford, Lord Provost Liz Cameron, Moderator Leonard Wallace,
Secretary Robert Forman. (Courtesy of Iain Scott)

Moderator Leonard Wallace, Secretary Robert Forman and Past-Captain Iain Scott ready to lead
the New York Tartan Day Parade, 2 April 2005. (Courtesy of Iain Scott)

Moderator David Rutherford and Vice Moderator Robert Forman leading Lord Provost
Lesley Hinds in the parade to Princes Street Gardens, following presentation of the
Freedom of the City to Suu Kyi, July 2005.
(Courtesy of City of Edinburgh Council)

Guard of Honour led by Ex-Moderator David Rutherford (extreme left) and Vice-Moderator Gerrad Clark (extreme right) to celebrate the Edinburgh International Festival 2007. (Courtesy of Paul McSherry Photography)

APPENDIX 1

A BRIEF HISTORY OF THE SOCIETY OF HIGH CONSTABLES OF EDINBURGH

In the late 16th century Edinburgh was the recognised capital of Scotland and as such was the home of the Scottish Parliament and the Courts of Justice. As a result, the city attracted many people of different religious and political persuasions who were constantly at odds with each other and who frequently resorted to fighting and rioting. The difficult task of maintaining law and order fell on the magistrates of the town council and on the bailies, who, in addition to their normal civic duties, had special responsibility for the various quarters or districts into which the town was divided. Extensive powers were given to them to organise burgesses to keep watch and ward over the various districts to ensure that householders and their families were generally safe and were specifically protected from "nightwalkers and vagabonds".

This state of unrest and lawlessness did not improve following the Union of the Crowns of Scotland and England in 1603, and in 1611 the Privy Council of James I passed an act to suppress disorders in the city of Edinburgh. In August, following an instruction to the magistrates and council, constables were elected to serve throughout the burgh and in September of that year 16 "Orders and Injunctions for Constables" were printed. These orders were mainly directed at keeping and preserving the King's Majesty`s peace, and the constables were given powers to enlist the support of neighbours to prevent disorder and to arrest suspected criminals.

Edinburgh council records indicate that the constables were closely involved with municipal activities during the 17th century and their duties at that time included collecting levies from citizens to assist them to keep the streets clean and to engage paid soldiers to form the Town Guard. The orders and injunctions were amended from time to time and in 1700 following a request from the constables the council agreed that short batons for their pockets should be provided as long as the constables paid for the batons from their fines. The procedure at that time of fining members for non attendance without a valid excuse and of inspecting the batons at the election of new constables is similar to current practice.

The first reference to the title of moderator is in 1689, and in 1722 four persons in addition to a treasurer and a clerk were elected to attend the moderator. This arrangement has evolved over the years and the 7 posts holding office in the current society are : moderator, ex-moderator, vice-moderator, treasurer, secretary, surgeon and custodier. The early system of geographical division of the city into quarters and districts was replaced in the middle of the 19th century when municipal wards were created, but throughout its existence society membership has always been associated with particular areas of the city. Currently there are 23 wards of 12 members in the society, giving a total membership of 276. Each ward bears the name and number of the equivalent municipal ward as they existed prior to 1975, extension of the city at that time having made it impractical to rename the wards of the society. All registered electors within the extended city area are now eligible for election.

Initially, all new constables were elected by the magistrates and council without reference to the existing body of constables, and the normal period of service was three years. However, following a major change in the status of the society early in the l9th century this custom changed, and the council began to accept a long leet of nominations from the society from which they then elected the required number of constables. This practice of election by the town council was phased out early in the 20th century when it was replaced by the current system whereby the society elects its own members. The three year restriction on the period of service was retained until as recently as 1975 although most members were happy to make themselves available for immediate re-election, this practice having been acceptable for the previous 100 years. There is now no restriction on the maximum period of service and recently one member completed 50 years with the society.

During its long existence the society has been involved in many of the notable events in Edinburgh's history. For instance in the Jacobite rebellion of 1745 the constables were required to arrange accommodation for the King's forces and to collect blankets for them. There was no enthusiasm to do this since there was no council in existence following the capture of the city by the Young Pretender on 17 September 1745. However, the Lord Justice Clerk and other Lords of Justiciary ordered the constables to act as required "upon their highest peril", and following defeat of the Stuart cause at Culloden on 16 April 1746, the constables were required by the Sheriff to attend the burning of the rebels' colours.

A further example was the instruction by the magistrates in 1788 for the constables to meet and patrol the streets on New Year mornings as a result of increased rioting and frequent disturbances. Accordingly, the constables dined together on Hogmanay and thereafter patrolled the streets till 6 o'clock in the morning. This was the start of the "Hogmanay Patrol" which would be continued until the latter part of the 19th century.

Enactment of the Edinburgh Police Act in 1805 resulted in very material changes to the duties required of the Edinburgh constables. This Act introduced a uniform system of police throughout the whole city, and until 1856 this force was administered by a Police Commission and not by the Town Council. As a result, concerns arose about the relative duties and powers between the constables and the new police force, and following a petition from the society the council said that although they wished to retain the valuable support of the society, "it was impossible to expect that gentlemen occupying the first stations and most respectable and laborious professional employments in the city, should discharge the duties of watching over the peace of the metropolis". The council pointed out that legally the constables would be subservient to the chief magistrate of police, but they hoped that there would be no conflict between the two forces during emergencies and that they would endeavour to ensure that the police magistrate and his officers would treat every member of the society with proper respect. In 1810, in order to distinguish the society from the new police force, the society requested and received permission to use the title "High Constables of the City of Edinburgh". Since creation of the new body of High Constables, relationships with the chief constable and the police force have always been extremely friendly, and currently all society inspections and parades are held at the headquarters of Lothian and Borders Police at Fettes Avenue.

During the l9th century therefore the maintenance of law and order in the city was carried out by the new professional police force, and the role of the Society of High

Constables gradually changed inasmuch as the emphasis on attending the council on ceremonial occasions became more pronounced. In addition to the long standing tradition of attending the magistrates and council on the King's birthday there are records of the High Constables being on parade at the laying of the foundation stones of the Regent Bridge and of the new jail in 1815, at the royal visit of King George IV in 1822 and at the laying of the foundation stone for George IV Bridge in 1827 as well as many other civic outings. The High Constables also attended executions, fires and riots, and in 1828 they were on duty all night at the trial of William Burke.

Following their designation as High Constables and in view of their increasing ceremonial function, the 19th century saw a large increase in the insignia of the society. The most significant items are the moderator's gold medal and chain which were presented by the society in January 1863, and the large silver mounted batons for the use of office-bearers. The moderator's medal is still regularly used by the moderator, and the silver batons, which have been inscribed with the names of all office-bearers since about 1820, are used on all official parades.

With the exception of the moderator's gold medal, all the equipment is housed in display cases within the City Chambers. The oldest artefact is the treasurer's brass money box which was made in 1698 and is inscribed with the names and occupations of the constables who contributed to its cost; and among other inscriptions is a reference to the part played by Edinburgh High Constables during the visit of Queen Victoria to the city on 1st September 1842.

Links between the society and the council were threatened in 1857 when the council proposed to remove from the society the power to nominate their successors, and following much legal argument it was finally ruled that "the Society of Constables, or High Constables as they were allowed to be called in 1810, was not an incorporation, but was merely the aggregate body of the constables deriving their office from the magistrates of the City, but had no independent or permanent existence as a separate society". Following this judgement a full complement of new constables was elected by the council, and the former members who had raised the action were ordered to hand over all their equipment to the new office-bearers and were found liable for the expenses of the action. This seems to have been the last major disagreement between the society and the council, and relationships between successive lord provosts and the High Constables have been very cordial. Currently the society regularly parades with the lord provost and council to St. Giles Cathedral and other venues about ten times every year and also attends other important civic occasions as they occur. In addition, the lord provost attends the annual general meeting and inspects the society on parade twice per annum.

The treasurer's brass money box was originally the repository for fines levied on constables for breach of orders, and it was traditionally emptied by each group of constables before they demitted office. The moderator then distributed the proceeds to poor and needy people, and thus started the long history of charitable work carried out by the society. Examples of this during the 19th century include raising from the citizens the sum of £1422 towards a fund to relieve the widows and orphans of those who had been killed in the Battle of Waterloo, assisting the fund for the new High School in 1826 and carrying out a house to house visitation throughout the city to ingather the sum of £2050 to help distressed people in Lancashire. These charitable works were carried out at the instigation of the lord provost and council, and among many other worthy causes supported was the reconstruction of the new Royal Infirmary and the fitting out of one particular ward in 1879. It is also recorded that during the preceding ten years the society had collected £4000 for charitable purposes and had assisted the council in a health survey of slum areas in the old town.

Apart from fund raising, the society was also very active in managing the entertainment given to some 6000 poorer citizens in the Waverley Market in 1887 and these activities were repeated several times over the next few years. Those events all took place to mark some special event in the life of the royal family but the greatest benevolent activity took place during the two wars of the 20th century. In the years of the First World War the society was responsible for raising large sums for many war relief funds, and they also gave much practical help to the Grassmarket Mission and to the Courant Fund through the provision of dinners to thousands of "poor, cripple and defective children."

Between the two wars many children and old people benefited from outings supported both financially and practically by the High Constables, and during the Second World War the society organised and ran entertainment for service men and women in Edinburgh. This enterprise was known as "The Garrison Theatre" and performances were staged every Sunday evening in the New Victoria Cinema (now the Odeon Cinema) in Clerk Street. During the period 1940 to 1944 some 500,000 troops and their friends were entertained, all the proceeds went towards the war effort, and enough money remained at the end of the war to build a cottage for a disabled ex-serviceman at Salvesen Gardens, Muirhouse.

During the latter part of the 20th century the Society has regularly distributed Christmas parcels to deserving people throughout the city, and has contributed financially to deserving causes through monies raised at dinner- dances and other functions. To supplement this charitable work, several individual wards have organised similar events in their own areas of the city. In recent years the society has agreed to supplement the money raised for charity by making provision in the annual levy for a specific contribution by each member.

For many years the social highlight of the society year has been the annual dinner which is held in early December. This is a very prestigious event which is attended by the lord provost, the chiefs of the armed services in Scotland, the chief constable, the moderators of all three kindred societies and many other guests. In recent years this has been held at the Sheraton Grand Hotel, but for most of the 20th century the venue was the North British Station Hotel (now the Balmoral Hotel). The precedent for guests at the annual dinner was set in 1796 when it is recorded that this was the first occasion at which the magistrates and other gentlemen of the town were entertained. This habit was followed regularly thereafter and musical entertainment was often provided by Neil Gow and his band in the early years. Currently the entertainment is provided by official toasts and by specially invited after-dinner speakers. For many years the annual dinner and dance was a regular feature of the life of the society, but recently its popularity has waned and it is now being replaced by alternative social events.

The society runs four sports clubs for golf, bowling , angling and curling. These clubs have been operating very successfully for many years and provide an excellent forum for members to meet and to compete for the various splendid trophies that have been presented down the years. The constitution of the society has been modified at intervals over the centuries and a radical change took place in 1997 when the members agreed by a two thirds majority to permit women to become members. This was done at the request of the City of Edinburgh Council and ensures that the close association with the council will continue as the society moves forward into the 21st century as an active organisation which still maintains the best traditions of a long and honourable history.

W. R. Ferguson
Society Historian
October 2000

APPENDIX 2

INVENTORY OF INSIGNIA AND EQUIPMENT CONTAINED IN DISPLAY CASES IN THE CITY CHAMBERS IN 2002

LARGE SILVER BATONS

[1] The Moderator

A large silver-mounted baton with chased silver centre and mounted with 36 silver rings.

These rings are inscribed with the names and dates of moderators from 1904 to 1940.

The centre band is broad and massive with two richly chased wreaths of Scottish thistles, and on this centre-piece are inscribed the names and dates of moderators from 1897 to 1902.

Both ends are covered with a broad circular band of silver and these bands are divided into two segments by richly floreated silver wreaths, each segment containing a richly chased design. On one band is the Edinburgh City Arms with supporters and motto, the ancient Order of the Thistle with the motto "Nemo me impune lacesset" and the letters "E.H.C. 1865" The other band is richly chased with the Royal Arms and the Imperial Crown with the letters "V. R. 1865 "

One flat end of the baton bears the following inscription "Presented to the High Constables of Edinburgh by Charles Lawson Jun. Esq. Moderator 1862 - 1865" The opposite flat end bears the arms, supporters, crest and motto of Moderator Lawson.

This baton is generally as described in Marwick's and Robertson's histories, but was described as being of black ebony without any silver rings]

[2] The Moderator *[normally used by the moderator on parade]*

A large silver-mounted baton with chased silver centre and mounted with 32 silver rings.

31 of these rings are inscribed with the names and dates of moderators from 1940 to 2001.

The centre band is embellished with a thistle motif and is engraved :
"High Constables of Edinburgh, The Moderator's Baton, Bruce Fenwick, Moderator 1902 -1903, 1903 -1904".

Both ends are covered with a broad circular band of silver and these bands are divided into two segments by richly floreated silver wreaths, each segment containing a richly chased design. On one band is the Edinburgh City Arms with supporters and motto, the ancient Order of the Thistle with the motto "nemo me impune lacesset" and the letters "EHC 1611". The other band is richly chased with the Royal Arms and the Imperial Crown surmounting the letters "ER" .

Both flat ends of the baton are inscribed with a lion rampant within a shield surmounted by the motto "Nemo me impune lacesset".

[3] The Moderator

A large silver-mounted baton with plain silver centre band and mounted with 74 silver rings. These rings are inscribed with the names and dates of moderators from 1821 to 1897

One flat end of the baton is inscribed with the Edinburgh City Arms and the other with the initials "E.H.C."

[4] The Ex-Moderator [normally used by the ex-moderator on parade]

A large silver-mounted baton with chased silver centre band and mounted with 43 silver rings. 30 of these rings are inscribed with the names and dates of ex-moderators from 1940 to 2001.

The chased silver centre band has no inscription.

Both ends are covered with a broad circular band of silver. One band is inscribed with the Royal Arms, the Royal Crown and the letters "G.IV.R.1820". The opposite band is inscribed with the date "Anno1820", an anchor, the letters "E.H.C.", the Edinburgh City Arms and the City motto.

One flat end of the baton is inscribed :
> "Presented by the Society of High Constables for the City of Edinburgh to their Moderator, 28 September 1820",

The other flat end is inscribed :
> "James Dallas, Esq. Moderator, Mr Will Burton, Treasurer, Mr John Boog, Chaplain, Mr David Henderson, Secretary 1820"

[This baton is generally as described in Marwick's and Robertson's histories but was described as being of black ebony and no reference was made to the end inscription referring to four office-bearers at the time.]

[5] The Vice -Moderator [normally used by the vice-moderator on parade]

A large silver-mounted baton with chased silver centre band and mounted with 52 silver rings. 8 of these rings are inscribed with the names and dates of vice-moderators from 1985 to 2001.

The centre band is embellished with laurels and scrolls and is inscribed:
> "Presented to the Society of High Constables of Edinburgh by Alexander Edmonston, Vice-Moderator 1859"

One flat end of the baton is inscribed with the initials "E.H.C." and the opposite end is inscribed with the Edinburgh City Arms.

[This baton is generally as described in Marwick's and Robertson's histories but no reference was made to the silver rings]

[6] The Vice-Moderator

A large silver-mounted baton with chased silver centre and mounted with 50 silver rings. These rings are inscribed with the names and dates of vice-moderators from 1915 to 1985.

The centre band is inscribed "Presented to the Society of the High Constables of Edinburgh by James D Brown, Vice-Moderator 1915 "

One flat end of the baton is inscribed with the initials "E.H.C" and the opposite end is inscribed with the Edinburgh City Arms.

[7] The Treasurer [*normally used by the treasurer on parade*]

A large silver-mounted baton with chased silver centre and mounted with 58 silver rings. 9 of these rings are inscribed with the names and dates of treasurers from 1975 to 1999.

The centre band is inscribed "Presented to the Treasurer of the Society of High Constables of Edinburgh by George Brown, Treasurer, 1828 "

Both flat ends of the baton are inscribed with the Edinburgh City Arms and the initials "E.H.C."

[*This baton is generally as described in Marwick's and Robertson's histories*]

[8] The Treasurer

A large silver-mounted baton with chased silver centre band and mounted with 53 silver rings inscribed with the names and dates of treasurers from 1909 to 1975.

There is no inscription on the centre band.

One flat end of the baton is inscribed with the City Coat of Arms and the other with the initials "E.H.C"

[9] The Secretary [*Currently used by the secretary on parade*]

A large silver-mounted baton with richly chased silver centre band and mounted with 54 silver rings. 34 of these rings are inscribed with the names and dates of secretaries from 1940 to 2001.

The centre band is inscribed "Presented to the Secretary of the Society of the High Constables of the City of Edinburgh by James Patison, Secretary, 1828"

Both ends of the baton are covered with a band of silver with no inscription.

One flat end of the baton is inscribed with the Edinburgh City Arms and the other with the initials "E.H.C"

[*This baton is generally as described in Marwick's and Robertson's histories*]

[10] The Surgeon

A large silver-mounted baton with chased silver centre band and mounted with 58 silver rings inscribed with the names and dates of surgeons from 1831 to 1895.

The centre band has the inscription "The Office of Surgeon to the Society of High Constables of the City of Edinburgh, instituted 1831" alongside the name of William Johnston, Moderator and all office-bearers at that time.

Both flat ends of the baton are inscribed with the Edinburgh City Arms and the initials "E.H.C"

[*This baton is generally as described in Marwick's and Robertson's histories*]

[11] The Surgeon [*normally used by the surgeon on parade*]

A large silver-mounted baton mounted with 47 silver rings. 35 of these rings are inscribed with the names and dates of surgeons from 1948 to 2001.

The baton has a richly chased centre band inscribed :

"Presented to the Society of High Constables by Hamilton Wylie, M.B.C.M., Surgeon 1895"

Both ends are covered with a band of silver with no inscription.

Both flat ends of the baton are inscribed with the Edinburgh City Arms and the initials "E. H. C."

[12] The Custodier

A large silver-mounted baton with chased silver centre and two telescopic tubular inserts. The main body of the baton has a chased silver centre and is mounted with 60 silver rings inscribed with the names and dates of Chaplains from 1831 to1856 and the names and dates of custodiers from 1858 to 1886. The tubular inserts have 67 inscriptions indicating the names and dates of custodiers from 1888 to1957.

The centre band is inscribed " Presented to the Chaplain of the Society of High Constables of the City of Edinburgh by Eagle Henderson, Chaplain 1828"

One flat end of the baton is inscribed with the Edinburgh City Arms and the other with the initials "E.H.C"

[This baton is generally as described in Marwick's and Robertson's histories but no reference was made to the telescopic nature of the baton]

[13] The Custodier *[normally used by the custodier on parade]*

A large silver baton mounted with 46 silver rings. 22 of these rings are inscribed with the names and dates of custodiers from 1957 to 2001.

The baton has a richly chased centre band inscribed :
>   "Presented to the Society of the High Constables of Edinburgh by George Lisle, C.A., Secretary 1895"

Both ends are covered with a band of silver with no inscription.

One flat end of the baton is inscribed "E.H.C" and the other end shows the Edinburgh City Arms.

TREASURER'S MONEY BOX FOR COLLECTION OF FINES

A brass box with handle on lid which also has a slot for the collection of money. The box is heavily engraved and the initial engraving states " List of Constables chosen by the council of Edinburgh 21 May 1698 who caused make this box and paid for the same: William Lindsay, Moderator; John Anderson, Coppersmith, Treasurer; Alexr. Hay Vintner, Clerk" and 25 other names. The many other engravings are fully described in Marwick's and Robertson's histories and this is the oldest artefact in the possession of the society.

THE DUNBAR TROPHY

A large silvered Rose Bowl encircled with floral motif and mounted with two plaques. One plaque is inscribed with the initials "E.H.C" and the other with "The Dunbar Trophy 1912"

There are no other inscriptions on the bowl itself but it is supported on a double square wooden plinth with 8 large silver plates fixed to the faces of the plinth. One of the plates bears the City Coat of Arms and motto in the centre, and other plates are inscribed with the winners of the trophy from 1929 to 2001. These inscriptions indicate the date, number and name of the ward and the name of the ward captain at the appropriate time.

RIFLE CLUB TROPHY

Large wooden shield with substantial silvered centrepiece oval in shape with leaf motif surrounding and embossed with crouching figure firing a rifle. This is surmounted by a silvered decorated heading inscribed "Ferguson Aggregate Trophy". 10 small silver shields surround the centrepiece, 5 of which are blank. One is engraved "Edinburgh High Constables' Rifle Club" surmounted by the High Constables crest and another is engraved "Presented for annual competition by Thomas Ferguson, J.P., Moderator 1914 -15 -16" The other three shields denote winners from 1915 to 1939.

RIFLE CLUB ROSE BOWL FOR COMPETITION BY WARDS

An E.P.N.S. rose bowl inscribed " Edinburgh High Constables Rifle Club, Ward Challenge Cup, Presented by the Rt. Hon. Sir Robert K. Inches, Lord Provost, for Annual Competition, 1916". The bowl is fully inscribed with the High Constables Crest, and winners from 1916 to 1939 are listed by wards and sometimes also include the names of individual ward members.

RIFLE CLUB BOWL FOR SCRATCH COMPETITION

A beaten silver bowl on integral stand inscribed "EHC Rifle Club Scratch Bowl, presented by James D Brown, Moderator 1916".

The base of the bowl is engraved with the names of individual winners from 1916 to 1930.

R.A.F. WOODEN SHIELD

A wooden shield engraved "Royal Air Force Headquarters North Maritime Air Region" and "Ne Quis Impune Praeterite". It is also embellished with the Royal Crown and a tiger's head.

PRESENTATION TEA SET TO MRS JAMES TULLO 1894

The set, presented to the wife of Moderator James Tullo, comprises a tray, tea pot, sugar bowl and milk jug, all in EPNS. All items are engraved with the Edinburgh City Arms and with the Edinburgh High Constables' crest set within diagonally crossed batons. The tray bears the inscription "Presented along with a silver afternoon tea set to Mrs. James Tullo on the occasion of her Silver Wedding by members of the Edinburgh High Constables, 13 October 1894 "

SILVER TEA SPOONS

4 spoons with handles decorated with the City Arms and the word "Edinburgh" in blue enamel. The bowls of the spoons are inscribed "E.H.C".

2 spoons with handles decorated with a crown, crossed rifles and an enamel rifle target. The bowls of the spoons are inscribed "E.H.C. 1929".

1 spoon with handle decorated with the City Arms and the word "Edinburgh". The bowl of the spoon is inscribed "E.H.C".

WOODEN GAVEL

A wooden gavel with silver rings |unmarked| and a silver plaque inscribed "Presented to The High Constables of Edinburgh by David Wilkie Esq., Custodier 1944"

METAL WHISTLE

A metal whistle engraved "Edinburgh High Constables, Moderator and The Metropolitan".

MANUSCRIPT OF E. H. C. PIPE TUNE

The original manuscript for the pipe tune "High Constables of Edinburgh" mounted in a photographic frame with an inscription stating "Presented by Chief Constable W G M Sutherland, QPM, on behalf of Lothian and Borders Police Pipe Band - 21 April 1988". It also indicates that the tune was composed by Martin G Wilson.

RIFLE CLUB MEDAL

A large silver plated medal inscribed "E.H.C. Rifle Club - instituted 1915. Presented by Mr Tom Snailum".

The medal also lists the names and dates of all winners of the Handicap Medal from 1916 to 1932.

BADGES

[1] Traditional badge used by office-bearers with a bar set a black and white ribbon. The bar is inscribed "Past Moderator" and the rear of the badge is inscribed "James G Y Buchanan, Moderator 1949 - 50 – 51".

[2] Traditional badge used by office-bearers with a bar set on a black and white ribbon. The bar is inscribed "Moderator" and the rear of the badge is inscribed "David R Grubb, Moderator 1885 - 88".

[3] Traditional badge used by office-bearers with a bar set on a black and white ribbon. The bar is inscribed "Moderator" and the rear of the badge is inscribed "A M Bruce, Moderator 1888 - 89 ".

[4] Traditional badge used by office-bearers with a bar set on a black and white ribbon. The bar is inscribed "Past Moderator" and the rear of the badge is inscribed "Past Moderator George M Bruce, 1962 - 63".

[5] Miniature gold badge in traditional style with a miniature gold bar and crown set on a black and white ribbon. The bar is inscribed "Ex -Captain VIth Ward" and the rear of the badge is inscribed "Coronation of King George V".

[6] Miniature gold badge in the form of a shield within crossed batons topped by thistles along with separate gold crown and bar set on a red ribbon. The bar is inscribed "1897", the front of the shield shaped badge is inscribed with the monogram of Edinburgh High Constables, "1611", and around this inscription ; "To commemorate Jubilee of Queen Victoria 1837 to 1887". On the rear of the badge is inscribed "A Robertson, 8th Ward".

[7] Miniature gold badge as described in [6] above but the rear of the badge is inscribed "James Gill, Captain, 10th Ward".

SMALL SILVER CUPS

[1] Small silver-plated presentation cup with stand. The cup is inscribed "E H C 1926 27".

[2] Small silver-plated presentation cup with stand. The cup is identical to [1] above but the inscription reads "E H C Rifle Club 1927 - 28".

[3] Small shallow silver-plated salver with three styled legs. The cup is inscribed "E H C 1927 - 28".

[These small cups were presented to the society in 2002 by descendants of James Cruikshank who had been a member of Ward VII, Haymarket in the 1920s.

SMALL BATONS

6 small batons are as described below :

[1] A small silver-mounted ebony baton with a central silver band inscribed

"James Tullo, Moderator, EHC 1893-94"

[2] A small ebony baton with silver bands at centre and at each end. One end band is marked "General Commissioner of Edinburgh Police , 16th Ward " and the other end is inscribed with the Royal Crown and " V.R" No reference to Edinburgh High Constables is given..

[3] A small silver-mounted ebony baton with no markings.

[4] A small silver-mounted ebony baton having the Royal Arms on one end and the Edinburgh City arms on the other. The baton is inscribed "Treasurer Calton No 2 " on the central silver ring.

[5] A small silver-mounted baton having the Royal Arms on one end and the Edinburgh City Arms on the other. The ends are also inscribed "E.H.C." and "1611" respectively and the central silver band is inscribed "Custodier ". The baton is covered with 17 engraved silver rings listing the names and dates of custodiers from 1910 to 1925.

[6] A small silver-mounted baton covered with 20 silver rings with silver chain attached. The rings are inscribed with the names and dates of moderators from 1852 to 1873 and the ends are richly chased with the Royal Arms and the Edinburgh City Arms. A central silver band is inscribed "Presented to the Society of High Constables of Edinburgh by George Beattie Esq. Moderator 1851".

[This baton is described in both Marwick's and Robertson's histories]

LARGE WOODEN BATONS

21 Large wooden batons as follows:

Black wooden baton inscribed "EHC" and bearing the Edinburgh City Arms in addition to the Royal Arms surmounting the initials "VR". The baton is also marked "144".
Black wooden baton inscribed "EHC" and bearing the Edinburgh City Arms in addition to the Royal Arms surmounting the initials "VR". The baton is also marked "16".

Black wooden baton [68 cm. long x 32mm. diameter] inscribed "EHC" and bearing the Edinburgh City Arms in addition to the Royal Arms surmounting the initials "GR". The baton is also marked " Ward 4, 43".

Black wooden baton inscribed "EHC" and bearing the Edinburgh City Arms in addition to the Royal Arms surmounting the initials "GR". The baton is also marked "Custodier".

Black wooden baton [7 cm. long] inscribed "EHC" and bearing the Edinburgh City Arms in addition to the Royal Arms surmounting the initials "GR". The baton is also marked "Ward 19, 219".

Black wooden baton inscribed "EHC" and bearing the Edinburgh City Arms in addition to the Royal Arms surmounting the initials "GR". The baton is also marked "Ward 11, 126".

Black wooden baton inscribed "EHC" and bearing the Edinburgh City Arms in addition to the Royal Arms. The baton is also marked "45".

Black wooden baton inscribed "EHC" and bearing the Edinburgh City Arms in addition to the Royal Arms. The baton is also marked "6".

Black wooden baton [58 cm. long x 25mm. diameter] bearing the Edinburgh City Arms in addition to the initials "VR". The baton is also marked "Pr. City Officer".

Black wooden truncheon bearing the Edinburgh City Arms in addition to the Royal Crown surmounting the initials "VR". The truncheon is also marked "8th District, 92".

Black wooden baton bearing the inscription "Cal Prison" in addition to the Royal Arms surmounting the initials "VR". The baton is also marked "Calton, CSC".

Black wooden truncheon bearing the Edinburgh City Arms in addition to the Royal Crown surmounting the initials "VR". The truncheon is also marked "Calton, 17".

Black wooden truncheon bearing the Edinburgh City Arms in addition to the Royal Crown surmounting the initials "VR". The truncheon is also marked "5th District, 271".

Black wooden baton bearing the Royal Crown surmounting the initials "G IV WR". The baton is also marked "40".

Black wooden baton bearing the Royal Crown surmounting the initials "E IV WR" The baton is also marked "24".

Red baton bearing the Edinburgh City Arms in addition to the Royal Arms surmounting the initials "W IV R". The baton is also marked "Circus Gardens".

Black wooden truncheon bearing the Royal Crown surmounting the initials "ER". The truncheon is also marked "City Police 37".

Black wooden truncheon bearing the Royal Arms surmounting damaged initials. The truncheon is also marked "345".

Black wooden baton bearing the Edinburgh City Arms in addition to the Royal Arms surmounting the initials "VR". The baton is also marked "Calton CSC".

Black wooden truncheon bearing the Edinburgh City Arms in addition to the Royal Arms. The truncheon is also marked "6th District 28".

Black wooden baton bearing the Royal Crown surmounting the initials "III GR". The baton is also marked "Portsburgh".

*Silver batons, Dunbar Trophy and Ferguson Shield for shooting
on display in Mandela Room in the City Chambers 2002.*
(*Photograph by George C Robb*)

APPENDIX 3

INVENTORY OF INSIGNIA AND EQUIPMENT HELD IN TRUST FOR THE SOCIETY BY OFFICE-BEARERS AND MEMBERS IN 2002

Items held by the Moderator

[A] A gold medal with a massive gold link chain, purchased by the society in 1863. The medal is oval, with two richly chased wreaths of Scotch Thistles. On the one side are the Edinburgh City Arms with supporters, crest and motto finely chased, and on the reverse side is the following inscription : "Moderator, the High Constables of Edinburgh, Instituted 1611. Presented to the Society, January 1863"

[This medal is as described in Marwick's and Robertson's histories]

[B] Moderator's small silver-mounted baton with the central silver band inscribed "Presented to the Edinburgh High Constables by Thomas Smailum, Moderator 1920-21-22." This baton is kept complete with carrying case.

[C] Traditional silver-gilt and enamel badge used by office-bearers with a bar inscribed "Moderator" set in a black and white ribbon. The rear of the badge is inscribed "Thomas Ferguson J.P-Moderator 1914-15-16". This badge is kept complete with box.

[D] Silver cufflinks embossed in the form of the society badge. These cufflinks are complete with box inscribed "Moderator's cufflinks – in memoriam [sic] TN Miller D.F.C."

[E] Whistle inscribed "Edinburgh High Constables, Moderator".

[F] Large black wooden baton inscribed "EHC Moderator" and bearing the Edinburgh City Arms in addition to the Royal Arms surmounting the initials "GR". The cipher and Arms dates this baton to the period 1816 to 1830, and the baton is complete with leather case.

[G] Copy of History of the High Constables of Edinburgh by James D Marwick, bound in leather embossed with the Edinburgh City Arms and bearing the inscription "Personal gift to Thomas F Anderson, Moderator 1953,1954."

[H] Black leather briefcase monogrammed "EHC"

Items held by the Ex-Moderator

[A] Traditional silver-gilt and enamel badge provided with ribbon to be worn round the neck.

[B] Small silver-mounted baton marked "Treasurer".

[C] Large decorated wooden baton marked "Ex-Moderator".

[D] Traditional silver-gilt and enamel badge used by office-bearers with a bar inscribed "Ex-Moderator" set in a black and white ribbon.

[E] Whistle inscribed "Edinburgh High Constables, Ex-Moderator"

Items held by the Vice-Moderator

[A] Gold medal in the form of a shield, with chased scrolls as a border. On one side are engraved the City's Arms, crest and motto, and on the reverse side the inscription "Vice-Moderator of the High Constables of the City of Edinburgh" "Instituted 1855".

Attached to the medal is a fine gold chain of a square cable link. The medal and chain were purchased by the society in 1855. [*this medal is as described in Marwick's and Robertson's histories.*]

[B] Small silver-mounted baton with a richly chased wreath of scrolls from top to bottom. The City's Arms are chased on one end, and the Royal Arms on the other. On the centre is the following inscription "Presented to the Society of High Constables of Edinburgh by Thomas Gill, Esq., Vice-Moderator 1855". [*this medal is as described in Marwick's and Robertson's histories.*]

[C] Large decorated wooden baton marked "Vice-Moderator".

[D] Traditional silver-gilt enamel badge used by office-bearers with a bar inscribed "Vice-Moderator" set in a black and white ribbon.

Items held by the Treasurer

[A] Small silver-mounted baton chased and floreated with scrolls, initials "EHC Treasurer" and engraved on each side are the Royal Arms, V.R. and the City Arms. [*this is as described in Marwick's and Robertson's histories*]

[B] Large decorated wooden baton marked "Treasurer".

[C] Traditional silver-gilt enamel badge used by office-bearers with a bar inscribed "Treasurer" set in a black and white ribbon.

[D] A silver boatswain whistle with silver chain attached. The whistle bears the following inscription "Adopted by the Society of High Constables during their arduous duties 1831" [*this is as described in Marwick's and Robertson's histories*]

Items held by the Secretary

[A] Small silver-mounted baton chased and floreated with scrolls, engraved initials "EHC Secretary" on each end the Royal Crown with "VR" and the City's Arms. [*this is as described in Marwick's and Robertson's histories*]

[B] Large decorated wooden baton marked "Secretary".

[C] Traditional silver-gilt enamel badge used by office-bearers with a bar inscribed "Secretary" set in a black and white ribbon.

[D] Whistle inscribed "Edinburgh High Constables, Secretary".

Items held by the Surgeon

[A] Small silver-mounted baton chased and with scrolls, inscribed "High Constables, Surgeon, 1832". On either end the Royal Crowns and V.R., with the British Arms, are tastefully engraved. [*this is as described in Marwick's and Robertson's histories*]

[B] Large decorated wooden baton marked "Surgeon".

[C] Traditional silver-gilt enamel badge used by office-bearers with a bar inscribed "Surgeon" set in a black and white ribbon.

Items held by the Custodier

[A] Small silver mounted baton. This is probably the oldest baton belonging to the society. The two silver ends are fine specimens of antique silver chasing. The City's Arms and supporters are very boldly executed, and the Royal Arms, although more defaced by time and use, are still in fine preservation. The quarterings of the arms give due prominence to Scotland, and the three fleur de lis in the second quarter fix the age of the baton to be before the union of this country with the crown of Hanover. The centre plate and rings are modern. The centre ring bears the following inscription "Custodier of Batons, 1855. EHC" [this is as described in Marwick's and Robertson's histories]

[B] Large decorated wooden baton marked "Custodier".

[C] Traditional silver-gilt enamel badge used by office-bearers with a bar inscribed "Custodier" set in a black and white ribbon.

Items held by members

[A] Small ebony baton with silver bands at each end. The ends are inscribed with the Royal Arms on one end and Edinburgh City Arms on the other. These bands are generally marked "EHC", "Instituted 1611" and indicate the member's roll number.

[B] Large wooden baton decorated with the Royal Arms and the City Arms. Each baton is also marked "EHC" and indicates the member's ward number and roll number.

[C] Traditional silver and enamel badge used by members with a bar inscribed with the member's ward number set in a black and white ribbon.

[D] Whistle generally engraved "Edinburgh High Constables" and indicating the member's roll number.

Items held by ward captains

[A] Small silver-mounted baton with central silver band inscribed "Captain" alongside the appropriate ward number. One silver end cap is engraved with the City's Arms and the other with the Royal Arms.

[B] Large decorated wooden baton embellished with the Royal Arms and the City Arms. The baton is similar to that held by all members bearing the initials "EHC" at one end, the appropriate ward number at the other end and the centre is marked with the word "Captain".

[C] Traditional silver and enamel badge similar to that held by members but with a bar inscribed "Captain" alongside the appropriate ward number. This bar is set in a black and white ribbon.

[D] Whistle generally engraved "Edinburgh High Constables" and "Captain".

Items held by Convener of Captains

[A] Traditional silver-gilt and enamel badge used by office-bearers with a bar inscribed "Convener of Captains" set in a black and white ribbon.

Items held by Society Chaplain

Traditional silver-gilt and enamel badge used by office-bearers with a bar inscribed "Chaplain" set in a black and white ribbon.

Items held by Society Officer

[A] Black ceremonial baton shorter in length and smaller in diameter than the large wooden batons issued to members. The baton is suitably decorated and is marked "Society Officer".

[B] Traditional silver-gilt and enamel badge used by office-bearers with a bar inscribed "Society Officer" set in a black and white ribbon.

Items held by Lord Provost

Black ceremonial baton shorter in length and smaller in diameter than the large wooden batons issued to members. The baton is suitably decorated and marked "Lord Provost"

APPENDIX 4

BYE-LAWS OF THE SOCIETY APPROVED BY MAGISTRATES AND COUNCIL, 27 JULY 1922

1.   ALL Meetings of the Society shall, under orders from the Moderator, or Lord Provost and Magistrates, be called by printed or written notices, issued by the Secretary, except in cases of urgent necessity, when a personal intimation made by a brother Constable, City Officer, or other authorised person shall be sufficient.

2.   The Moderator may, whenever he thinks fit, convene a meeting of the Society. He shall also do so at any time on receiving a written requisition signed by at least twenty Members of the Society, which meeting shall be held within fourteen days of the date of the requisition.

3.   Subject to the provisions of Article I, all Special and General Meetings of the Society shall be called on not less than four days written notice which shall be given by the Secretary to each Member. The notice shall state the place, day and hour of meeting and the business to be transacted.

4.   The Office-Bearers of the Society shall consist of a Moderator, an Ex-Moderator, a Vice-Moderator, a Treasurer, a Secretary, a Surgeon, and a Custodier. There shall also be one gentleman from each Ward, not holding any other office in the Society, who shall be Captain of the Constables in such Ward. These Office-Bearers and Captains of Wards shall form the Committee to whom shall be entrusted the immediate management of the Society's affairs.

5.   The Committee, at a Special Meeting to be held in the beginning of March annually, shall prepare a list of gentlemen whom they decide to recommend to the Society to be put in nomination as Office-Bearers at the Nomination Meeting.

As this regulation is merely to facilitate the dispatch of business, it is hereby specially enacted and declared that such recommendation shall in no way interfere with the right of any Member of the Society to nominate members other than those recommended to any office in the Society.

6.   A General Meeting shall be held in the month of March, previous to the Annual Election, for the purpose of NOMINATING Office-Bearers. Each Ward shall have the right to nominate the gentleman who is to hold the office of Captain in the Ward, leaving the Election to the Society; the nomination to be in the hands of the Chairman, if not more than two Members of the Ward attend. In case of the Office of Captain in any Ward becoming vacant, previous to the Annual Election, the Moderator shall call a Meeting of the Ward for the purpose of electing an interim Captain. At that Meeting the Moderator shall preside. He shall not have a deliberative vote but he shall have a casting vote.

7.　A General Meeting of the Society shall be held on the first Monday in April annually, at which the Members shall by a majority of votes of those present elect from their number the Office-Bearers and Captains of Wards mentioned in Article 4, except the Ex-Moderator, who is not elected. At this Meeting, the Moderator of the preceding year shall continue Chairman until the Election is concluded.

8.　On vacancies occurring among the Office-Bearers, by resignation or otherwise, at any time previous to the Annual Election in April, a Special General Meeting, to fill such vacancies, *ad interim*, shall be convened without delay.

9.　No member shall be elected to the office of Moderator, Vice-Moderator, Treasurer, Secretary, Surgeon or Custodier, for more than two successive years, unless to fill any vacancy occurring after the Annual Meeting in each year for the election of Office-Bearers.

10.　The Moderator, or in his absence, the Vice-Moderator, or in the absence of both, a Chairman to be appointed for the time, shall preside at all meetings of the Society, and in the case of an equality of votes, shall have a casting vote in addition to his deliberative vote.

11.　The Treasurer shall keep a cash book, showing all his transactions with the funds of the Society, and shall submit a state of the Funds, duly audited, to the Nomination Meeting each year. An Auditor of the accounts of the Society shall be appointed at the annual Election Meeting in each year.

12.　The Secretary shall keep a full and correct record of all the transactions of the Society, issue circulars calling meetings of the Society and Committee and shall keep a roll, showing the names of those present at or absent from such meetings. He shall also read the minutes of the meetings of the Society at the General Meeting in March, and which shall be submitted to the Society for approval or disapproval. He shall also read, if desired, the Minutes of Meetings of Committee held during the past year.

13.　The Custodier shall have charge of all the moveable property of the Society, and he shall keep a record of it in a book for the purpose. He shall not issue to any Member batons which do not belong to the Member's Ward. Members on sending in their batons must receive a receipt for the same from the Custodier personally, or through their Captains. Each Member shall retain the batons he receives on entering the Society till such time as he ceases to be a Member of the Society, and in the event of his being elected to any office, he shall, during the tenure of office, receive official batons, &c., in addition to the Membership batons. All batons or badges passing from a retiring Office-Bearer to a newly-elected Office-Bearer, or from a retiring Member to a newly-elected Member, must be through the medium of the Custodier, who is officially appointed for that purpose.

14.　The Books of the Society shall be balanced before the day of each Annual Election, a levy on the Members of the Society being made, if necessary, by the Committee, and any Member failing to make payment of his share within fourteen days after the date of the notice demanding payment of the same shall be liable to be struck off the Roll of Members but he shall, notwithstanding, remain liable for his share of said levy.

15.　Any gentleman wishing to join the Society shall make application by filling up and delivering to the Secretary a Schedule setting forth his name, designation, residence, place of business, and the Ward in which applicant is a registered elector. Every applicant must be a registered elector of the City, and must also be either (1) bona-fide householder in the Ward in which he seeks appointment or (2) in Business within the said Ward; every applicant must also be available for Service at any time when called out. No members of the Town Council can be appointed High Constables; and in the event of any Member of the Society accepting office of Councillor he shall be held to have resigned his office as Constable. All applications must be submitted to the Members of the Ward into which the applicant seeks admission, and if approved of by them, recommended to the Committee by the Captain of the Ward.

16.   The Secretary shall submit the Schedules of application to the first meeting of Committee to be held after they have been received, and the same shall lie on the table till the next succeeding meeting when a ballot shall be taken. Should the same be approved of by the votes of two thirds of the members present at the meeting, the Secretary shall forward the names of the applicants to the Town-Clerk, to be submitted to the Lord Provost, Magistrates, and Town Council, for election. Should the applicants be elected, the Secretary shall intimate the same to them, and require their attendance at the Council Chambers on a day to be named to qualify themselves by taking the necessary oaths. New Members shall pay to the General Funds of the Society the sum of Four Guineas as Entry money.

17.   Each Member shall, on entering the Society, deposit in the hands of the Treasurer, the sum of £1,1s., which shall be deposited in a separate account, to be called the "Badge Account," and thereupon he shall receive from the Custodier a large and small baton and whistle; also a badge to be worn on all public occasions. On leaving the Society he shall re-deliver the badge, batons and whistle in good order, and shall, thereupon, receive repayment of the sum deposited by him under deduction of any fines due by him to the Society. A Member on being appointed a Captain or Office-Bearer, shall receive the badge, batons and whistle appropriate to the new office, which shall be held during the tenure of said office only. On retiring from said office without leaving the Society, he shall deliver up the badge, batons, and whistle appropriate to the office held by him to the Custodier.

18.   Any Member changing his address shall within eight days thereafter give notice thereof, in writing, to the Secretary.

19.   In addition to the meetings specified in sections 5 and 6, there shall be held three General Meetings for drill during the months of April or/and May and three General Meetings for drill during the months of October or/and November annually.

20.   The Society shall act in a body, or in divisions, as may be thought advisable, under direction and control of the Lord Provost and Magistrates; and if in a body, they shall move under the immediate command of the Moderator, subject to the like control. If in divisions, the first shall act under the direction of the Moderator, the other divisions under that of the Office-Bearers present, in the order of their rank; and, in the event of it being necessary to communicate with the officer in command, heads of divisions must depute Members for the purpose, but must on no pretext whatever leave their divisions.

21.   The Members, on being called out in case of riot or other emergency, shall, without delay, proceed to the Royal Exchange, and shall, at the request of the Lord

Provost, act under the command of the Office-Bearers present in accordance with the instructions of the Chief Constable of the City.

22. The following fines shall be exacted from Members of the Society:-

(1) Absence from General Meetings of the Society, or Meetings of the Committee when the roll is called, or leaving the Meeting thereafter without permission from the Moderator - One Shilling.

(2) Absence from Meetings of the Society called by order of the Lord Provost and Magistrates to preserve the peace of the City, when the roll is called, or leaving the same without permission from the Moderator-Five Shillings.

(3) Failure to exhibit small baton when called upon by the Moderator-One Shilling.

(4) Neglecting to bring large baton when instructed to bring it - One Shilling.

(5) Losing large or small baton, or badge, except when on duty - Ten Shillings and Sixpence in addition to the expense of replacing the articles lost.

(6) Losing whistle, except when on duty-Two Shillings and Sixpence, in addition to the expense of replacing the article lost.

(7) Lending large or small baton-Twenty-one Shillings.

(8) Any Member of the Society exchanging or handing over his batons, badge, or whistle, otherwise than through the Custodier, as provided for in Bye-Law XIII, shall be fined Five Shillings, and held responsible for said batons, badge, and whistle.

23. Absence from town, indisposition, or other necessary cause may exempt Members from attending meetings, provided they intimate in writing the reason of their inability to attend, to the Secretary, previous to the meeting being held. It shall be the Secretary's duty to submit these excuses to the Moderator who shall decide whether they are to be accepted. Should the Moderator accept the excuse the same shall be marked in the roll, otherwise the Member shall be marked absent. In the event however of a Member failing to attend four out of the total number of Drills and General Meetings in any year, irrespective of excuses, his name may be struck off the Roll of Members, at any Committee Meeting held during the following year, at which the Captain of his Ward must be present.

24. At the hour of meeting the Secretary shall call the roll and mark the names of all Members present.

25. Should a Member be absent from town or be unable from indisposition to send an excuse before the meeting he may do so in writing to the Secretary immediately on his return to town, or recovery from illness, and the Secretary shall submit such excuse to the next meeting of Committee, which shall dispose of the same.

26. A note of the fines incurred by members shall, from time to time, be handed by the Secretary to the Treasurer, and, after being certified by him, shall be sent to the Members who shall be bound to pay the same to the Captains of their Wards. Members objecting to pay such fines and their share of necessary expenses, must, within three days from date of receipt, state their reasons in writing to the Treasurer, by whom such reasons shall be submitted to the first Meeting of Committee. Unless the Committee

consider the reasons offered satisfactory, those liable must pay-otherwise the Moderator, in name of the Society, may strike the name of such Member or Members off the roll. Members in arrear shall not be entitled to vote or express an opinion on any subject that may be brought before the Society.

27. If the conduct of a Member, either in or out of the Society, shall, in the opinion of the Committee, be injurious to the character or interests of the Society, or if he becomes bankrupt, grants a trust deed for behoof of or compounds with his creditors, the Committee shall have the power to summon such Member to appear before it, to explain his conduct or position, and, if after hearing any explanation such Member may have to make, the Committee may recommend such Member to resign, and if the Member recommended to resign shall refuse or delay to resign within fourteen days from the date of such recommendation, the Committee shall bring the matter before a General Meeting of the Society, and it shall be competent for a majority of the Members present at any such General Meeting to expel any such Member.

28. One-third of the Constables for each Ward, being the four at the top of the list, shall go out of office annually on the first Monday of April previous to the election of Office-Bearers. These retiring Members may, however, be re-elected, provided they signify their wish to be so to the Secretary at least half an hour before the hour of meeting, and take the necessary oaths before a Magistrate, who will be in attendance at the Council Chambers for that purpose. Failing their doing so the vacancies will be filled up in the mode prescribed in section 15.

29. Members wishing to leave the Society shall intimate their desire in writing to the Secretary, who shall bring the matter before the first meeting of Committee, who may agree to accept the resignation on condition that all sums due by the Member are previously paid, but no resignation shall be accepted until such Member shall have paid his proportion of the current expenses of the year, and all fines due by him, and every Member until then shall be subject to the Act of Council regulating the Constitution of the Society and these Bye-Laws.

30. Every motion affecting the Bye-Laws of the Society to be brought before the Society shall be intimated in writing to the Secretary at least fourteen days before the Meeting at which it is to be dealt with and notice thereof given in the circular calling the Meeting. If approved of at such Meeting by a majority of two-thirds of the Members present the same shall, subject to the approval of the Lord Provost, Magistrates and Council, pass into law.

APPENDIX 5

COUNCIL DECISIONS AND SOCIETY CONSTITUTION

Excerpts from the City of Edinburgh District Council Minutes 1975

"On 21st March 1975, the City of Edinburgh District Council resolved that in principle the District Council continue the existing association with the Society of High Constables of the City of Edinburgh."

"On 25th April 1975, the City of Edinburgh District Council approved the revised Constitution of the Society of the High Constables of the City of Edinburgh in terms of the draft submitted to them"

Preamble to Constitution with effect from 16th May 1975:

Whereas the City of Edinburgh District Council being aware of the close association of the Society of the High Constables of the City of Edinburgh with the City and its Lord Provost, Magistrates and Council since 1611, and of the Allegiance owed and shown by the members of the Society to the Sovereign and the Lord Provost, Magistrates and Councillors of the City of Edinburgh, and being desirous, following the various changes in the organisation of local government in Scotland introduced by the Local Government (Scotland) Act 1973, of ensuring the continuance of the Allegiance of the Members of the Society to the Sovereign and to the Local Council and of the ceremonial, social and charitable duties and work carried out by members of the Society, do hereby provide, declare and enact as follows:-

(First)   That the members of the Society shall attend upon the Lord Provost and Councillors of the City of Edinburgh District Council at such times and in such manner and for the purpose of carrying out such ceremonial, social or charitable duties as the Lord Provost and Councillors may direct;

(Second) That the City of Edinburgh District Council shall make such annual allowance to the Society for defraying their necessary expenses as the Council shall from time to time decide; and (In the Second Place) that from and after the sixteenth day of May 1975 the former Society of High Constables of the City of Edinburgh shall be known as the Society of High Constables of Edinburgh (hereinafter referred to as "the Society") and the Constitution of the Society shall consist of the following Articles:-

Excerpts from the City of Edinburgh Council Minutes 1997

On 17 June 1997 the City of Edinburgh Council resolved

[1] To welcome the Society's decision to widen its membership to include women.

[2] To note that a further report would be received in 12 months time on the progress being made by the Society in admitting women members.

[3] To reaffirm the long standing relationship between the Council, The Lord Provost and the Society.

[4] To advise the Society that the Council does not require any changes to be made to the present structure of 23 wards.

Constitution with effect from 16 May 1975 including amendments to 2008

1. The Society shall consist of twenty three divisions or wards each of twelve members or such other number of divisions or wards and members as the Society shall from time to time determine.

2. All new members of the Society shall declare their allegiance as High Constables of Edinburgh as soon as convenient and in any event not later than four weeks after their election to membership of the Society in accordance with the provisions of Article Eighteen hereof.

3. Members of the Society shall re-affirm their allegiance at the Annual General Meeting of the Society.

4. Those elected to be members of the Society shall be registered electors within the City of Edinburgh. No member of the said City of Edinburgh Council shall be elected as a member of the Society and in the event of any member of the Society accepting the office of Councillor of the City of Edinburgh Council, that person shall be held to have resigned from membership of the Society as from the date of such acceptance of office.

5. On the first Monday of April in each year or on such other day in April as the Committee (constituted as hereinafter provided) may decide, the members of the Society shall meet in general meeting (herein referred to as the "Annual General Meeting") and by a majority of votes of those present shall elect from among their number the following office-bearers; a Moderator, a Vice-Moderator, a Treasurer, a Secretary, a Surgeon and a Custodier of Equipment, and shall appoint an Honorary Chaplain, an Honorary Auditor, an Honorary Historian and a Society Officer. At the same time they shall also elect from among the members of each ward, one person not holding any other office in the Society and who shall have been previously nominated by their ward, who shall be captain of such ward. The most junior surviving Past-Moderator from time to time shall hold the office of Ex-Moderator. The office-bearers so elected, who shall hold office until the next Annual General Meeting, shall, with the captains of the wards and the Ex-Moderator, (but without the Honorary Chaplain, Honorary Auditor, Honorary Historian and Society Officer) form the Committee of the Society (hereinafter called "the Committee") to whom shall be entrusted the immediate management of the affairs of the Society.

The members of the Society shall also fix the amount of the levy for the year to be paid by each member of the Society by a majority of votes of those present. Any member of the Society failing to make payment of such levy by 30th June following shall be liable to be struck off the Roll of Members but the members shall, notwithstanding, remain liable for the amount of such levy. The Committee shall have power in the case of new members to reduce, or even waive the levy.

6. At all meetings of the Society and of the Committee, the Moderator, or in absentia, the Vice-Moderator, or in the absence of both, a member to be appointed by the members present, shall preside, and in the case of an equality of votes shall have a casting vote in addition to their deliberative vote.

7. All meetings of the Society shall, under orders from the Moderator, or Lord Provost, be called by notice in writing issued by the Secretary of the Society (or other office-bearer acting for the Secretary) except in cases of urgent necessity when a personal intimation made by an other High Constable, the Society Officer, or other authorised person shall be sufficient.

8. Whenever the Moderator thinks fit, a meeting of the members of the Society may be convened. The Moderator shall convene a meeting at any time on receiving a written requisition signed by a least twenty members of the Society, which meeting shall be held not later than twenty eight days from the date of receipt of such requisition, giving to the members at least the period of notice prescribed in Article Nine hereof.

9. All meetings of the Society (other than those convened in cases of urgent necessity as provided in Article Seven hereof) shall be called on not less than seven days' notice in writing which shall be given by the Secretary (or other office-bearer acting for the Secretary) to each member. The notice shall state the place, day and hour of the meeting and the business to be transacted.

10. The Committee shall cause to be circulated with the notice calling each Annual General Meeting of the Society a list of members whom they decide to recommend to the Society to be elected as office-bearers for the following year. Any member of the Society wishing to nominate as an office-bearer a member of the Society who has not previously been a member of the Committee mentioned in Article 5 hereof, shall intimate the full name and address and the number of ward of such nominee along with similar details of the proposer and of the seconder of such nominee and of the office for which the person is nominated to the Secretary of the Society in sufficient time to allow the Secretary to circulate these details along with the list of members recommended for election as office-bearers by the Committee. This regulation shall in no way interfere with the right of any member of the Society at the Annual General Meeting of the Society to nominate for any office of the Society, a member or members other than those recommended by the Committee provided that such member nominated has previously been a member of the Committee. Only candidates who have been nominated and seconded and who are willing to be elected shall be eligible for election as office-bearers of the Society or captains of wards. In the event of competition for any particular office or captaincy, the successful candidate shall be the one who receives a greater number of the votes of those present than any other candidate. In the event of an equality of votes, the Moderator or other person presiding shall determine which candidate will be successful by exercising a casting vote.

11. The quorum for Annual and Special General Meetings of the Society shall be seventy five of the members of the Society present in person; the quorum for meetings of the Committee shall be fifteen members present in person or, in the case of a ward captain, represented by a deputy authorised by such ward captain.

12. On vacancies occurring among office-bearers of the Society or among the captains of wards by resignation or otherwise at any time previous to the Annual General

Meeting, the Committee (in the case of captains after consultation with the members of the ward) may fill such vacancies ad interim by co-option without delay.

13. No member shall be elected to the office of Moderator, Vice-Moderator, Secretary, Surgeon or Custodier for more than two successive years unless to fill any vacancy occurring after the Annual General Meeting as provided in Article Twelve hereof. The Treasurer may hold office for more than two successive years if so elected by the Society.

14. The Treasurer shall keep proper records showing all transactions with the funds of the Society and shall submit a financial statement made up to the thirty-first day of January each year, duly audited by the Honorary Auditor of the Society, to the Annual General Meeting of the Society each year. In addition, the Treasurer shall carry out such further duties related to the financial affairs of the Society as the Committee may from time to time direct.

15. The Secretary shall keep a Roll of the Members of the Society and a full and correct record of all the proceedings of the Society and of the Committee. The Secretary shall issue notices calling meetings of the members of the Society and of the Committee and shall keep a record showing the names of those present at such meetings. The Secretary shall present minutes of the General Meetings of the Society for approval by the members at each Annual General Meeting of the Society. Once so approved the minutes shall be signed by the Moderator or other member presiding at the meeting. In addition, the Secretary shall carry out such further secretarial duties as the Committee may from time to time direct.

16. The Custodier shall have charge of all the moveable property of the Society and shall keep a record of it in such form as the Committee shall from time to time instruct. Members on handing in their equipment must receive a receipt for the same signed by the Custodier. Each member shall retain the equipment received on entering the Society till such time as membership ceases. All items of equipment passing from a retiring office-bearer to a newly elected office-bearer and from a retiring captain to a newly elected captain must be with the knowledge and with the authority of the Custodier, who is officially appointed for that purpose.

17. The Committee shall hold not less than six meetings in the year between Annual General Meetings and shall hold its first meeting of each year not more than six weeks after the Annual General Meeting. No later than the second meeting of the Committee after the Annual General Meeting, the Committee shall appoint a Convenor of Captains.

18. All applications for membership must in the first instance be submitted to the members of the ward into which the applicant seeks admission and if approved by them, they shall make application by filling up and delivering to the Secretary of the Society, a schedule setting forth their full name, designation, residence, place and nature of business or profession, number on the published Register of Electors within the City of Edinburgh and the name and number of the ward which the applicant wishes to join.

The Secretary shall then submit the schedules of application to the first meeting of the Committee to be held after they have been received and the same shall lie on the table until the next succeeding meeting when a ballot shall be taken. Should the same be approved of by the votes of two thirds of the members present at the meeting, the

Secretary shall intimate to the applicants that their applications have been accepted and require their attendance within four weeks on a day to be named to qualify themselves by taking the necessary oaths, before a Notary Public or other Commissioner of Oaths selected from a list approved by the Committee. New members shall pay to the general funds of the Society a sum of Ten Pounds (or such other sum as the Committee shall from time to time direct) as entry money. Members must be available for service at any time when called out.

19. Each member shall, on entering the Society, deposit in the hands of the Treasurer (in addition to the entry money specified in Article Eighteen above) the sum of Ten Pounds (or such other sum as the Committee shall from time to time direct) which shall be deposited in a separate account to be called the "Equipment Account" and thereupon the member shall receive from the Custodier a large and a small baton and a whistle and also a badge to be worn on all public occasions. On leaving the Society, the member shall re-deliver the badge, batons and whistle in good order.

20. Any member changing address, shall, within fourteen days of such change, give notice thereof in writing to the Secretary of the Society.

21. In addition to the meetings specified in Articles Five and Eight hereof, there shall be held each year no fewer than two General Meetings for combined drill and inspection; of these meetings, at least one will be held in the Spring and at least one will be held in the Autumn. The Lord Provost or a deputy appointed by the Lord Provost shall be invited to inspect the Society at such meetings.

22. The following fines shall be extracted from members of the Society:-

1. Absence without the permission of the Moderator from general meetings of the Society or meetings of the Committee when the roll is taken, or leaving the meeting thereafter, one pound.

2. Failure to exhibit small baton when called upon by the Moderator, one pound.

3. Neglecting to bring large baton when instructed to bring it, one pound.

4. Losing large baton or small baton or badge except when on duty, one pound, in addition to the expense of replacing the articles lost.

5. Losing whistle except when on duty, one pound, in addition to the expense of replacing the article lost.

6. Lending large or small baton, one pound.

7. Any member of the Society exchanging or handing over batons, badge or whistle in their possession, otherwise than as provided for in Articles Sixteen and Nineteen hereof, shall be fined one pound and held responsible for said batons, badge and whistle.

The Committee shall have power to increase or reduce the amount of the above mentioned fines from time to time and at its discretion to waive them.

23. Fines incurred by members shall be paid to the Treasurer. Members objecting to pay such fines must, within seven days from the date of notification, state their reasons in writing to the Treasurer by whom such reasons shall be submitted to the first meeting of Committee thereafter. Unless the Committee consider the reasons offered satisfactory, those liable must pay within one month otherwise the Moderator in name of the Society, may strike the name of such member or members off the roll.

24. Absence from town, indisposition, or other necessary cause may excuse a member

from attending meetings, provided the member intimates in writing to the Secretary the reason for inability to attend, previous to the meeting being held. It shall be the Secretary's duty to submit these excuses to the Moderator who shall decide whether they are to be accepted. Should the Moderator accept the excuse, the same shall be marked in the roll, otherwise the member shall be marked absent.

25. Should a member be absent from town or be unable from indisposition or other necessary cause to send an excuse in writing before the meeting, such member shall, as soon as possible thereafter, submit an excuse in writing to the Secretary. It shall be the duty of the Secretary to submit these excuses to the Moderator who shall decide whether they are to be accepted.

26. In the event, however, of a member failing to attend four out of the total number of drills and general meetings in a period of two years, irrespective of excuses, such member's name may be struck off the Roll of Members at any Committee meeting held during the year following the said period, at which the captain of the relevant ward must be present.

27. If the conduct of a member whether in or out of the Society shall, in the opinion of the Committee, be injurious to the character or interests of the Society, or if such member becomes bankrupt, grants a trust deed for behoof of or compounds with creditors, the Committee shall have the power to summon such member to appear before a sub committee appointed for the purpose to explain their conduct or position. After hearing any explanation such member may make, the Committee may recommend such member to resign. If the member recommended to resign shall refuse or fail to resign within fourteen days from the date of such recommendation, the Committee shall expel the member.

28. A member wishing to leave the Society shall submit a resignation in writing to the Secretary who shall bring the matter before the first meeting of Committee.

29. Every motion affecting the constitution of the Society to be brought before the Society shall be intimated in writing to the Secretary at least twenty one days before the meeting at which it is to be dealt with and notice thereof given in the circular calling the meeting. A majority of at least two thirds of the members present at such meeting shall be required for the passing of such motion.

APPENDIX 6

PRINCIPAL SPEAKERS AT ANNUAL DINNERS
1931–2007

1931	The Marquis of Linlithgow	1974	Robert Coulter
1932	Lord Elphinstone	1975	The Hon. George Younger, M.P.
1933	Sir Harry Lauder	1976	Sir John Inch
1934	Sir Robert Bruce,	1977	Rt Hon Enoch Powell, M.P.
1935	The Rt Hon The Earl of Home.	1978	Lionel Daiches
1936	The Earl of Haddington	1979	Major General R E Urquhart
1937	The Earl of Airlie	1980	Nigel Tranter
1938	The Earl of Lauderdale	1981	Magnus Magnussen
1939 to 1947 No Dinners held		1982	Sir W Kerr Fraser
1948	Lord Strachan	1983	Tom Fleming
1949	The Hon Lord Blades	1984	Very Rev Dr Leonard Small
1950	Sir Archibald Sinclair	1985	Robert A McN. Crampsey
1951	The Earl of Eglinton and Winton	1986	Air Chief Marshall Sir Thomas Kennedy
1952	The Rt Hon Lord Home	1987	Robin Morgan
1953	Sir John Ure Primrose	1988	Arthur Wood
1954	His Grace the Duke of Buccleuch	1989	Dr Alastair Donald
1955	The Earl of Dundee	1990	Ivor R Guild
1956	Lord Normand of Aberdour	1991	T A Kevin Drummond
1957	Colonel Walter E Elliot	1992	Charles M Winter
1958	The Rev Dr H C Whitley	1993	Jimmy Logan
1959	Sir Edward Appleton	1994	W Gordon Smith
1960	Mason Brown	1995	Robert R H Glen
1961	J A Stoddart, M.P.	1996	Sir Peter Heatley
1962	The Hon Lord Cameron	1997	Dr Michael Shea
1963	Sir Charles Connell	1998	Rt Hon Sir Malcolm Rifkind
1964	Professor D F Macdonald,	1999	Rt Hon Sir Sir David Steel, M.S.P
1965	Sheriff Principal MacDonald	2000	William Copeland
1966	Professor Michael Swann	2001	David McLetchie, MSP
1967	Brigadier J S Sanderson	2002	Most Rev K P O'Brien
1968	The Hon Lord Kilbrandon	2003	Sir Tom Farmer
1969	Sir William McEwan Younger	2004	Rt Hon Lord McLean
1970	The Hon Lord Birsay	2005	Rt Hon Liz Cameron
1971	The Rt Hon Lord Clyde	2006	Rt Rev Richard Holloway
1972	The Rt Hon Lord Emslie	2007	Sheriff Principal Edward F Bowen
1973	John Orr		

APPENDIX 7

WINNERS OF COMPETITIONS BETWEEN WARDS IN THE SOCIETY 1929-2008

Date	Dunbar Trophy	
1929-30	Ward 5	Morningside and
	Ward 23	Corstorphine Cramond
1930-31	Ward 23	Corstorphine Cramond
1931-32	Ward 23	Corstorphine Cramond
1932-33	Ward 19	West Leith
1933-34	Ward 23	Corstorphine Cramond
1934-35	Ward 19	West Leith
1935-36	Ward 19	West Leith
1936-37	Ward 19	West Leith
1937-38	Ward 23	Corstorphine Cramond
1938-39	Ward 22	Colinton
1939-40	Ward 20	Central Leith
1940-47	NO COMPETITION HELD	
1947-48	Ward 20	Central Leith
1948-49	Ward 6	Gorgie
1949-50	New Ward	
	XIV	St Bernard's
1950-51	Ward XIX	Central Leith
1951-52	Ward XIV	St Bernard's
1952-53	Ward XII	Murrayfield Cramond
1953-54	Ward XII	Murrayfield Cramond
1954-55	Ward X	Gorgie Dalry
1955-56	Ward X	Gorgie Dalry
1956-57	Ward VI	Morningside
1957-58	Ward VII	Merchiston
1958-59	Ward VII	Merchiston
1959-60	Ward VII	Merchiston
1960-61	Ward XXII	Portobello
1961-62	Ward XXII	Portobello
1962-63	Ward IV	Newington
1963-64	Ward XIX	Central Leith
1964-65	Ward XXII	Portobello
1965-66	Ward XIV	St Bernard's
1966-67	Ward XXII	Portobello
1967-68	Ward XVIII	West Leith
1968-69	Ward XVIII	West Leith
1969-70	Ward XVIII	West Leith
1970-71	Ward XVIII	West Leith
1971-72	Ward XVIII	West Leith
1972-73	Ward VII	Merchiston
1973-74	Ward XVIII	West Leith "

Date	Dunbar Trophy *Continued*		Skittles		Quiz Night	
1974-75	Ward XVIII	West Leith				
1975-76	Ward XVIII	West Leith				
1976-77	Ward VI	Morningside				
1977-78	Ward XII	Murrayfield Cramond	Office-Bearers			
!978-79	Ward XII	Murrayfield Cramond	Office-Bearers			
1979-80	Ward IV	Newington	No competition			
1980-81	Ward VI &	Morningside	Ward XVIII	West Leith		
	Ward XVIII	West Leith				
1981-82	Ward XVIII	West Leith	Ward XX	South Leith		
1982-83	Ward XX	South Leith	Ward XX	South Leith		
1983-84	Ward XVIII	West Leith	Ward VII	Merchiston		
1984-85	Ward XIX	Central Leith	Ward XX	South Leith		
	& Ward XX	South Leith				
1985-86	Ward IV	Newington	Ward XX	South Leith		
	Ward V &	Liberton				
	WardXIX	Central Leith				
1986-87	Ward IV	Newington	Ward XVI	Broughton		
1987-88	Ward XII	Murrayfield Cramond	Ward XIII	Pilton		
1988-89	Ward VI	Morningside	Ward XVIII	West Leith		
1989-90	Ward III &	George Square	Ward II	Holyrood		
	Ward XIX	Central Leith				
1990-91	Ward XVI	Broughton	Ward V	Liberton		
1991-92	Ward XIV	St Bernard's	Ward XX	South Leith		
1992-93	Ward XIII	Pilton	Ward XIV	St Bernard's		
1993-94	Ward XIV	St Bernard's	Ward XVI	Broughton		
1994-95	Ward XIV	St Bernard's	Ward XVI	Broughton		
1995-96	Ward XII	Portobello	Ward XVI	Broughton		
1996-97	Ward XII	Portobello	Ward XVI	Broughton		
1997-98	Ward XXII	Portobello	Ward X	Gorgie-Dalry		
1998-99	Ward X	Gorgie Dalry	Ward VII	Merchiston		
1999-00	Ward XIII	Pilton	Ward XIII	Pilton	Ward V	Liberton
2000-01	Ward IX	Sighthill	Ward VI	Morningside	Ward XVIII	West Leith
2001-02	Ward XXII	Portobello	Ward VI	Morningside	Ward I	St Giles
2002-03	Ward XXII	Portobello	Ward VIII	Colinton	Ward I	St Giles
2003-04	Ward V	Liberton	Ward VIII	Colinton	Ward V	Liberton
			10 Pin Bowling			
2004-05	Ward V &	Liberton	Ward XIV	St Bernard's	Ward III	George Sq.
	Ward XIII	Pilton				
2005-06	Ward V	Liberton	Ward XI	Corstorphine	Ward III	George Sq.
2006-07	Ward V	Liberton	Ward XVI	Broughton	Ward III	George Sq.
2007-08	Ward V	Liberton	Ward X	Gorgie-Dalry	Ward XXIII	Craigmillar

APPENDIX 8

OFFICE BEARERS OF THE SOCIETY OF HIGH CONSTABLES OF EDINBURGH 1925 TO 2008

(Office Bearers from the Union of the Parliaments 1707 till 1924 are detailed in the histories by Marwick and Robertson)

Date	Moderator	Ex-Moderator	Vice-Moderator	Treasurer
1925	Thomas Dunbar	James M Manclark	No record	No record
1926	James Rae King	Thomas Dunbar	"	"
1927	James Rae King	Thomas Dunbar	"	"
1928	Anthony T White	James Rae King	"	"
1930	Anthony T White	James Rae King	"	"
1931	John Davidson	Anthony T White		
1932	Andrew Reid	John Davidson	Alexander Fulton	James Jackson
	John Davidson	Anthony T White		
1933	James Jackson	John Davidson	ThomasMenzies	George W Adams
1934	Thomas Menzies	John Davidson	George W Adams	William Laing
1935	Thomas Menzies	John Davidson	George W Adams	William Laing
1936	George W Adams	Thomas Menzies	William Laing	William Gillespie
1937	George W Adams	Thomas Menzies	William Laing	William Gillespie
1938	William Laing	George W Adams	William Gillespie	James M Cleugh
1939	William Laing	George W Adams	William Gillespie	James M Cleugh
1940	William Gillespie	William Laing	James M Cleugh	David H M Jack
1941	William Gillespie	William Laing	James M Cleugh	David H M Jack
1942	James M Cleugh	William Gillespie	David H M Jack	Marcus W Ward
1943	James M Cleugh	William Gillespie	David M Jack	Marcus W Ward
1944	David H M Jack	James M Cleugh	Marcus W Ward	T R Mossman
			T R Mossman	David Wilkie
1945	David H M Jack	James M Cleugh	T R Mossman	David Wilkie
1946	T R Mossman	David H M Jack	David Wilkie	James G Y Buchanan
	David H M Jack	James M Cluegh		
1947	David Wilkie	David H M Jack	James G Y Buchanan	James A McArthur
1948	David Wilkie	David H M Jack	James G Y Buchanan	James A McArthur
1949	James G Y Buchanan	David Wilkie	James A McArthur	James Dunbar
1950	James G Y Buchanan	David Wilkie	James A McArthur	Thomas Y Anderson
1951	James A McArthur	James G Y Buchanan	Thomas Y Anderson	David Cook
1952	James A McArthur	James G Y Buchanan	Thomas Y Anderson	David Cook
1953	Thomas Y Anderson	James A McArthur	David Cook	J Norman H Steele
1954	Thomas Y Anderson	James A McArthur	David Cook	J Norman H Steele
1955	David Cook	Thomas Y Anderson	J Norman H Steele	Thomas K Currie
1956	David Cook	Thomas Y Anderson	J Norman H Steele	Thomas K Currie
1957	J Norman H Steele	David Cook	Thomas K Currie	George M Bruce
1958	J Norman H Steele	David Cook	Thomas K Currie	George M Bruce
1959	Thomas K Currie	J Norman H Steele	George M Bruce	James W W Kemp

Date	Moderator	Ex-Moderator	Vice-Moderator	Treasurer
1960	Thomas K Currie	J Norman H Steele	George M Bruce	James W W Kemp
1961	George M Bruce	Thomas K Currie	James W W Kemp	Owen H Hadley
1962	George M Bruce	Thomas K Currie	James W W Kemp	Owen H Hadley
				Thomas K Currie
1963	James W W Kemp	George M Bruce	Duncan D Melvin	D S O Wilkie
1964	James W W Kemp	George M Bruce	Duncan D Melvin	D S O Wilkie
1965	Duncan D Melvin	James W W Kemp	D S O Wilkie	Rex de la Haye
1966	Duncan D Melvin	James W W Kemp	D S O Wilkie	Rex de la Haye
1967	D S O Wilkie	Duncan D Melvin	Rex de la Haye	Thomas Baillie
1968	D S O Wilkie	Duncan D Melvin	Rex de la Haye	Thomas Baillie
1969	Rex de la Haye	D S O Wilkie	Thomas Baillie	T N Miller
1970	Rex de la Haye	D S O Wilkie	Thomas Baillie	T N Miller
1971	Thomas Baillie	Rex de la Haye	T N Miller	John Christie
1972	Thomas Baillie	Rex de la Haye	T N Miller	John Christie
1973	Thomas N Miller	Thomas Baillie	John Christie	J Ritchie Wilkie
1974	Thomas N Miller	Thomas Baillie	John Christie	J Ritchie Wilkie
1975	John Christie	T N Miller	J Ritchie Wilkie	James W Coulthard
1976	John Christie	T N Miller	J Ritchie Wilkie	James W Coulthard
1977	J Ritchie Wilkie	John Christie	James W Coulthard	Douglas J S Miller
1978	J Ritchie Wilkie	John Christie	James W Coulthard	W T Cavaye
1979	James W Coulthard	J Ritchie Wilkie	W T Cavaye	I A T Gowans
1980	James W Coulthard	John Christie	W T Cavaye	I A T Gowans
1981	W T Cavaye	J W Coulthard	I A T Gowans	G Dick
1982	W T Cavaye	J W Coulthard	I A T Gowans	G Dick
1983	I A T Gowans	W T Cavaye	G Dick	T P L McGlashan
1984	I A T Gowans	W T Cavaye	G Dick	W T Cavaye
				W H G Mathison
1985	G Dick	I A T Gowans	E Ian Adam	W H G Mathison
1986	G Dick	I A T Gowans	E Ian Adam	W H G Mathison
1987	E Ian Adam	G Dick	Ian M Crosbie	W H G Mathison
1988	E Ian Adam	G Dick	Ian M Crosbie	W H G Mathison
1989	Ian M Crosbie	E Ian Adam	Alan W Mowat	Donald Semple
1990	Ian M Crosbie	E Ian Adam	Alan W Mowat	Donald Semple
1991	Alan W Mowat	Ian M Crosbie	W R Ferguson	Donald Semple
1992	Alan W Mowat	Ian M Crosbie	W R Ferguson	Donald Semple
1993	W R Ferguson	Alan W Mowat	Brian C A Short	Donald Semple
1994	W R Ferguson	Alan W Mowat	Brian C A Short	Fredrick Small
1995	Brian C A Short	W R Ferguson	Simon Bolam	Fredrick Small
1996	Brian C A Short	W R Ferguson	Simon Bolam	Fredrick Small
1997	Simon Bolam	Brian C A Short	Kenneth W Dunbar	Fredrick Small
1998	Simon Bolam	Brian C A Short	Kenneth W Dunbar	Fredrick Small
1999	Kenneth W Dunbar	Simon Bolam	J Richard Allan	Douglas L Walker
2000	Kenneth W Dunbar	Simon Bolam	J Richard Allan	Douglas L Walker
2001	J Richard Allan	Kenneth W Dunbar	Leonard Wallace	Douglas L Walker
2002	J Richard Allan	Kenneth W Dunbar	Leonard Wallace	Douglas L Walker
2003	Leonard Wallace	J Richard Allan	David F Rutherford	Douglas L Walker
2004	Leonard Wallace	J Richar Allan	David F Rutherford	Douglas L Walker
2005	David F Rutherford	Leonard Wallace	Robert C B Forman	Alistair N W Beattie
2006	David F Rutherford	Leonard Wallace	Robert C B Forman	Alistair N W Beattie
2007	Robert C B Forman	David F Rutherford	Gerrard A D Clark	Alistair N W Beattie
2008	Robert C B Forman	David F Rutherford	Gerrard A D Clark	Alistair N W Beattie

Date	Secretary	Surgeon	Custodier
1925–1931	No record	No record	No record
1932	Thomas Menzies	Dr T R Matson	George W Adams
1933	William Laing	Dr T R Matson	William Gillespie
1934	William Gillespie	Dr A F Wilkie Millar	James M Cleugh
1935	William Gillespie	Dr A F Wilkie Millar	James M Cleugh
1936	James M Cleugh	Dr Thomas Finlay	David H M Jack
1937	James M Cleugh	Dr Thomas Finlay	David H M Jack
1938	David H M Jack	Lt Col Wm T Finlayson	Marcus W Ward
1939	David H M Jack	Lt Col Wm T Finlayson	Marcus W Ward
1940	Marcus W Ward	Angus Millar	T Robertson Mossman
1941	Marcus W Ward	Angus Millar	T Robertson Mossman
1942	T Robertson Mossman	Dr A Paterson Robb	David Wilkie
1943	T Robertson Mossman	Dr A Paterson Robb	David Wilkie
1944	David Wilkie	James Lumsden	James G Y Buchanan
	James G Y Buchanan		James A McArthur
1945	James G Y Buchanan	James Lumsden	James A McArthur
1946	James A McArthur	Dr W Stanley Shaw	James Dunbar
1947	James Dunbar	Dr W Stanley Shaw	Thomas Y Anderson
1948	James Dunbar	Dr William S Dalgety	Thomas Y Anderson
1949	Thomas Y Anderson	Dr William S Dalgety	David Cook
1950	David Cook	Alex H Brown	J Norman H Steele
1951	J Norman H Steele	Alex H Brown	Thomas K Currie
1952	J Norman H Steele	Dr A F Wilkie Millar	Thomas K Currie
1953	Thomas K Currie	Dr A F Wilkie Millar	George M Bruce
1954	Thomas K Currie	Douglas K Cameron	George M Bruce
1955	George M Bruce	Douglas K Cameron	James W W Kemp
1956	George M Bruce	Alex H Brown	James W W Kemp
1957	James W W Kemp	Dr William S Dalgety	Owen H Hadley
1958	James W W Kemp	Dr William S Dalgety	Owen H Hadley
1959	Owen H Hadley	Dr R C Bignold	Duncan D Melvin
1960	Owen H Hadley	Dr R C Bignold	Duncan D Melvin
1961	Duncan D Melvin	Dr Lindsay Wilkie	D S O Wilkie
1962	Duncan D Melvin	Dr Lindsay Wilkie	D S O Wilkie
1963	Rex de la Haye	Dr H W S Rankin	Thomas Baillie
1964	Rex de la Haye	Dr H W S Rankin	Thomas Baillie
1965	Thomas Baillie	Dr William C Wightman	Thomas N Miller
1966	Thomas Baillie	Dr William C Wightman	Thomas N Miller
1967	Thomas N Miller	Dr P G Weston	John Christie
1968	Thomas N Miller	Dr P G Weston	John Christie
1969	John Christie	A S Flockhart	Alastair D Robertson
1970	John Christie	A S Flockhart	Alastair D Robertson
1971	Alastair D Robertson	A Gordon Miller	J Ritchie Wilkie
1972	J Ritchie Wilkie	A Gordon Miller	J W Coulthard
1973	J W Coulthard	W J Govan	Douglas J S Miller
1974	J W Coulthard	W J Govan	Douglas J S Miller
1975	Douglas J S Miller	Philip Brown	William T Cavaye
1976	Douglas J S Miller	Philip Brown	William T Cavaye
1977	William T Cavaye	T P L McLashan	I A T Gowans
1978	I A T Gowans	T P L McGlashan	George Dick
1979	G Dick	Dr E Ian Adam	T P L McGlashan

Date	Secretary	Surgeon	Custodier
1980	G Dick	Dr E Ian Adam	T P L McGlashan
1981	T P L McGlashan	Dr Alan R Milne	E Ian Adam
1982	T P L McGlashan	Dr Alan R Milne	E Ian Adam
1983	E Ian Adam	Dr Evan L Lloyd	Ian M Crosbie
1984	E Ian Adam	Dr Evan L Lloyd	Ian M Crosbie
1985	Ian M Crosbie	Dr Thomas Hannah	Alan W Mowat
1986	Ian M Crosbie	Dr Thomas Hannah	Alan W Mowat
1987	Alan W Mowat	Lyndon S Watkins	W R Ferguson
1988	Alan W Mowat	Lyndon S Watkins	W R Ferguson
1989	W R Ferguson	Michael E Harrington	Brian C A Short
1990	W R Ferguson	Michael E Harrington	Brian C A Short
1991	Brian C A Short	Dr Alan R Milne	Simon Bolam
1992	Brian C A Short	Dr Alan R Milne	Simon Bolam
1993	Simon Bolam	Dr F Owen George	James G Banks
1994	Simon Bolam	Dr F Owen George	James G Banks
1995	Kenneth W Dunbar	Dr Richard S Denison	Douglas N Spratt
1996	Kenneth W Dunbar	Dr Richard S Denison	Douglas N Spratt
1997	J Richard Allan	Dr J Douglas Stuart	John Newall
1998	J Richard Allan	Dr J Douglas Stuart	John Newall
1999	Leonard Wallace	Dr D R Kerr Fraser	Alan M Brown
2000	Leonard Wallace	Dr D R Kerr Fraser	Alan M Brown
2001	David F Rutherford	Dr F Owen George	Colin Cargill
2002	David F Rutherford	Dr F Owen George	Colin Cargill
2003	Robert C B Forman	Dr Richard S Denison	James Gray
2004	Robert C B Forman	Dr Richard S Denison	James Gray
2005	Gerrard A D Clark	Dr D R Kerr Fraser	Raymond J Pia
2006	Gerrard A D Clark	Dr D R Kerr Fraser	Raymond J Pia
2007	Raymond J Pia	Dr J Douglas Stuart	Victor J Montgomery
2008	Raymond J Pia	Dr J Douglas Stuart	Victor J Montgomery

APPENDIX 9

PERSONS HOLDING OFFICE
BUT NOT ON THE SOCIETY COMMITTEE
1925 -2008

Date	Auditor	Drill Officer	Society Officer
1925	No record	No record	No record
1926	-	-	-
1927	-	-	-
1928	-	-	-
1929	-	-	-
1930	-	-	-
1931	-	-	-
1932	-	W G T Keddie	-
1933	-	David R Keir	A C McArthur
1934	-	David R Keir	A C McArthur
1935	-	David R Keir W W Finlayson	A C McArthur
1936	-	W W Finlayson A J Corrie	A C McArthur John M Finlayson
1937	Wm Hunter Smart	A J Corrie	John M Finlayson
1938	Wm Hunter Smart	A J Corrie	John M Finlayson
1939	Wm Hunter Smart	Ronald M Donaldson	John M Finlayson
1940	Wm Hunter Smart	No drills	John M Finlayson
1941	Wm Hunter Smart	No drills	John M Finlayson
1942	Wm Hunter Smart	No drills	John M Finlayson
1943	Wm Hunter Smart	No drills	W W Murray
1944	Wm Hunter Smart	No drills	W W Murray
1945	Wm Hunter Smart	No drills	W W Murray
1946	Wm Hunter Smart	No drills	W W Murray
1947	Wm Hunter Smart	Fred P McCulloch	W W Murray
1948	Wm Hunter Smart	Fred P McCulloch	WW Murray
1949	Wm Hunter Smart	Fred P McCulloch	W W Murray
1950	Wm Hunter Smart	Fred P McCulloch	W W Murray
1951	Wm Hunter Smart	Fred P McCulloch	Wm H Young
1952	Wm D Lawson	Fred P McCulloch	Wm H Young
1953	Wm D Lawson	Fred P McCulloch	Wm H Young
1954	Wm D Lawson	Fred P McCulloch	Wm H Young
1955	Wm D Lawson	Fred P McCulloch	Wm H Young
1956	Wm D Lawson	Fred P McCulloch	Wm H Young
1957	H Forbes Murphy	John Aitken	Wm H Young
1958	H Forbes Murphy	John Aitken	Wm H Young

Date	Auditor	Drill Officer	Society Officer
1959	H Forbes Murphy	Rex de la Haye	Wm H Young
1960	H Forbes Murphy	Rex de la Haye	Wm H Young
1961	H Forbes Murphy	Rex de la Haye	Wm H Young
1962	H Forbes Murphy	Rex de la Haye	Wm H Young
1963	H Forbes Murphy	W A W Sivewright	Wm H Young
1964	H Forbes Murphy	W A W Sivewright	Wm R H Thomson
1965	H Forbes Murphy	W A W Sivewright	Wm R H Thomson
1966	H Forbes Murphy	W A W Sivewright	Wm R H Thomson
1967	H Forbes Murphy	W A W Sivesright	Wm R H Thomson
1968	H Forbes Murphy	W A W Sivewright	Wm R H Thomson
1969	H Forbes Murphy	W A W Sivewright	Wm R H Thomson
1970	H Forbes Murphy	W A W Sivewright	Wm R H Thomson
1971	H Forbes Murphy	W A W Sivewright	Wm R H Thomson
1972	H Forbes Murphy	W A W Sivewright	R M Woods
1973	H Forbes Murphy	W A W Sivewright	R M Woods
1974	H Forbes Murphy	W A W Sivewright	R M Woods
1975	H Forbes Murphy	W A W Sivewright	R M Woods
			Stanley Gordon
1976	H Forbes Murphy	W A W Sivewright	Stanley Gordon
1977	H Forbes Murphy	W A W Sivewright	Stanley Gordon
1978	H Forbes Murphy	W A W Sivewright	Stanley Gordon
1979	W W B Gray	W A W Sivewright	Stanley Gordon
1980	W W B Gray	W A W Sivewright	Charles C Allan
1981	W W B Gray	W A W Sivewright	Charles C Allan
		W W Johnston	
1982	W W B Gray	W W Johnston	Charles C Allan
1983	G C Ellis	James G Banks	Charles C Allan
1984	G C Ellis	James G Banks	Charles C Allan
1985	G C Ellis	James G Banks	Charles C Allan
1986	G C Ellis	James G Banks	Charles C Allan
1987	G C Ellis	James G Banks	Charles C Allan
1988	G C Ellis	James G Banks	Charles C Allan
1989	G C Ellis	James G Banks	Charles C Allan
1990	G C Ellis	James G Banks	Charles C Allan
1991	G C Ellis	James G Banks	Charles C Allan
	Timothy D Straton		
1992	Timothy D Straton	James G Banks	D Skeldon
1993	Timothy D Straton	John Henderson	D Skeldon
			L Robertson
1994	Timothy D Straton	John Henderson	L Robertson
1995	Timothy D Straton	John Henderson	L Robertson
1996	Timothy D Straton	John Henderson	L Robertson
1997	Timothy D Straton	John Henderson	L Robertson
1998	Timothy D Straton	John Henderson	Khelil Bachkhaznadji
1999	Timothy D Straton	John Henderson	Khelil Bachkhaznadji
2000	Timothy D Straton	John Henderson	Khelil Bachkhaznadji
2001	Timothy D Straton	John Henderson	Khelil Bachkhaznadji
2002	Timothy D Straton	John Henderson	Khelil Bachkhaznadji
2003	Timothy D Straton	John Henderson	Khelil Bachkhaznadji
2004	Timothy D Straton	John Henderson	Khelil Bachkhaznadji
			George Kirkpatrick

Date	Auditor	Drill Officer	Society Officer
2005	Timothy D Straton	John Henderson	George Kirkpatrick
2006	Timothy D Straton	John Henderson	George Kirkpatrick
2007	Robert Clark	John Henderson	George Kirkpatrick
2007	Robert Clark	John Henderson	George Kirkpatrick

Date	Chaplain	Historian
1959 to 1972	The Rev Dr H C Whitley	-
1973 to 1988	The Rev G I Macmillan	-
1989 to 1998	The Very Rev G I Macmillan	-
1999	The Very Rev G I Macmillan	W R Ferguson
2000	The Very Rev G I Macmillan	W R Ferguson
2001	The Very Rev G I Macmillan	W R Ferguson
2002	The Very Rev G I Macmillan	W R Ferguson
2003	The Very Rev G I Macmillan	W R Ferguson
2004	The Very Rev G I Macmillan	W R Ferguson
2005	The Very Rev G I Macmillan	Hamish W Coghill
2006	The Very rev G I Macmillan	Hamish W Coghill
2007	The Very Rev G I Macmillan	Hamish W Coghill
2008	The Very Rev G I Macmillan	Leonard Wallace

APPENDIX 10

OFFICE BEARERS AND
ROLL OF MEMBERS – JUNE 2008

Moderator	Robert C B Forman
Ex-Moderator	David F Rutherford
Vice-Moderator	Gerrard A D Clark
Treasurer	Alistair N W Beattie
Secretary	Raymond J Pia
Surgeon	Dr J Douglas Stuart
Custodier	Victor J Montgomery

Those marked:

|M|	have been Moderator		|C|	have been Custodier
|V-M|	have been Vice-Moderator		|c|	have been Captain
|T|	have been Treasurer		|*|	25 years' Service Star
|S|	have been Secretary		|**|	35 years' Service Star
|s|	have been Surgeon		|***|	40 years' Gold Bar
|†|	Past Convenor of Captains		|****|	50 years' Service

Ward I - St Giles

1.	J Hector Hawley-Groat |c|	Retired Dispensing Chemist	9 Campbell Road.
2.	Lt Col William P McNair |c,†|	Communication Consultant	11 Windsor Street
3.	Dr D R Kerr Fraser |c,s|	Retired Medical Practitioner	18 Midmar Gardens
4.	W Martin Smith |c|	Retired Chartered Surveyor	4 Suffolk Road
5.	David G Sibbald |c|	Architect	21 Ravelston Park
6.	Eric G S Melvin **Captain**	University Tutor	6 Cluny Place
7.	Andrew Williams	Solicitor	31 Hermitage Gardens
8.	Douglas M B Green	Retired Government Officer	41 Carlton Terrace Mews
9.	Robin H Wilson |c|	Retired Secretary, Merch. Co	8A Belwood Road, Milton Bridge
10.	Raymond J Pia |c, C| **SECRETARY**	Retired Managing Director	8 Frogston Road West
11.	John H Watkins |c|	Business Analyst	17 Cammo Grove
12.	Anthony F Nixon	Retired	10b Wester Coates Gardens

Ward II – Holyrood

13.	Valentine T Tudball **Captain**	Retired	4A Essex Road
14.	Charles I Bryden |c|	Chartered Quantity Surveyor	25 Pewlandcroft, South Queensferry
15.	Robert C B Forman |c, S, V-M| **MODERATOR**	Writer to the Signet	51 Braid Road
16.	Ian D Baikie	Chartered Surveyor	5 Cammo Brae
17.	Keith R Dyer	Chartered Surveyor	72 Forrester Road
18.	A Michael Hansen-Just	Proprietor Water Supply Company	11 Pentland Grove
19.	J Douglas Stuart |c,s| **SURGEON**	General Practitioner	1 Essex Road
20.	David J Miller	Chartered Accountant	14 Blinkbonny Avenue
21.	Alan Hardie	Managing Director	1B Glenlockhart Bank
22.	R Neil Godfrey |c|	Director, Travel Company	110 Liberton Brae
23.	Charles J Spence	Manging Director	26 Garscube Terrace
24.	W Allan Duncan |c|	Retired Manager, Insurance Co.	24 Braehead Crescent

Ward III – George Square

25.	Angus M R Tod [c]	Stockbroker	3 Lansdowne Crescent
26.	James R Laidlaw [c]	Chartered Architect	34 Colinton Grove
27.	Alex Peden **Captain**	Retired Shop Proprietor	17 Chalmers Crescent
28.	John Drummond [c**]	Retired Fruit Merchant	10 Blinkbonny Terrace
29.	Alasdair J Beaton	Airline Pilot	20 West Mill Bank
30.	Morris M Duncan [c]	Chartered Accountant	2 Wester Steil
31.	R J Neil Patrick	Solicitor	31 Gillespie Road
32.	David A Walker	Hackney Carriage Operator	107 Lanark Road
33.	Douglas L Walker [c, T]	Chartered Accountant	10/2 St Margaret's Place
34.	Gerrard A D Clark [c,S]	Solicitor	15 Comiston Drive
	VICE-MODERATOR		
35.	David L Cavanagh [c,*]	Antique Dealer	30 House O'Hill Avenue
36.	Angus J M Mair [c]	Solicitor	1 Belford Park

Ward IV – Newington

37.	Bryan J Rankin [c,*]	Chartered Accountant	4 Clarendon Crescent
38.	Richard H Barron [c]	Dental Practitioner	9 Kevock Road, Lasswade
39.	John Henderson [c,*]	Butcher	1 Belgrave Place
	DRILL OFFICER		
40.	William G R Thomson	Chartered Accountant	21A Buckingham Terrace
41.	James Drysdale [c]	Retired Partner, Electrical Sales Agency	22/8 South Oswald Road
42.	Craig A L Scott **Captain**	Advocate	21 Hope Terrace
43.	John Newall [c,C,*]	Writer to the Signet	7 Belgrave Place
44.	Peter D Clark [c,†]	Stockbroker	10 Blacket Place
45.	Alan S Marshall [c]	Chartered Architect	20 Hope Terrace
46.	Andrew C Walker [c]	Professor of Physics	20 Mortonhall Road
47.	Vacancy		
48.	Andrew Chalmers	Solicitor	89 Collinton Road

Ward V – Liberton

49.	Colin S Mcpherson	Structural Engineer	40 Drum Brae North
50.	Robert M W Clark [c]	Chartered Accountant	6 Comiston Rise
	AUDITOR		
51.	Kenneth W Dunbar [c,S,V-M,M †]	Writer to the Signet	14 Hermitage Drive
52.	Fergus Gillies	Chartered Civil and Structural Engineer	5 Silverknowes Brae
53.	David P MacLaren [c]	Golf Club Secretary	8 Winton Grove
54.	David Halliday	Managing Director	17 Clayhills Grove
55.	Davd S Brown	Chartered Accountant	1B Greenbank Gardens
56.	Stewart D M McIntosh [c,†]	Chartered Surveyor	3 Greenhill Gardens
57.	Nigel Derek Fairhead	Chartered Accountant	3 Bonaly Crescent
58.	Alistair N W Beattie [c]	Chartered Accountant	5 Bonaly Terrace
	TREASURER		
59,	Charles H B Cutting **Captain**	Architect	36 Bonaly Crescent
60.	Victor J Montgomery [c,†]	Local Government Officer	24 Braid Farm Road
	CUSTODIER		

Ward VI – Morningside

61.	Terence Holmes	Accountant	140 Craiglea Drive
62.	Thomas W Bell [c]	Retired Bank Manager	44 Greenbank Loan
63.	Ian Wotherspoon [c]	Retired	14 Margaret Rose Avenue
64.	F Owen George [c,s]	General Practitioner	41 Morningside Grove
65.	Norman M Stewart [c]	Retired Bank Manager	33/5 Easter Steil
66.	Eugene Mooney [c,*]	Retired Managing Director	4 Blackford Road
67.	Lindsay M N Lorimer [c]	Retired House Furnisher	70A Morningside Drive
68.	John M H Biggar [c]	Writer to the Signet	8 Cluny Gardens
69.	Alan R Irvine [c,†]	Retired Manager	131 Comiston Drive
70.	Ronald A Dove [c,*]	Retired Estate Agent	19 Braid Farm Road
71.	Richard S Denison [c,s]	Medical Practitioner	26 Braid Hills Road
72.	Richard A Dunbar **Captain**	Investment Director	26 Easter Steil

Ward VII – Merchiston

73.	Charles White [c,*]	Retired Property Company Director	211 Colinton Road
74.	Gordon M J G Henderson [c]	Master Butcher	22 Pentland Avenue
75.	Vacancy		
76.	Andrew Dorward [c*] **Captain**	Private Hire Operator	25 Cairns Gardens, Balerno
77.	Philip A Marshall [c]	Management Consultant	43 Craigmount Gardens
78.	John Mitchell [c]	Chartered Accountant	12 Craigleith Crescent
79.	William G Menzies [c]	Company Director, Steelfounder	33 Blinkbonny Gardens
80.	Alan C Lindsay [c]	Retired Managing Director, Motor Industry	2 Succoth Place
81.	George S Veitch [c]	Writer to the Signet	15 Merchiston Place
82.	Alistair E L Weir [c]	Retired Chartered Surveyor	Glenbrook Road
83.	Iain W St C Scott [c]	Retired Bank Official	22 Bramdean Rise
84.	John L Paterson [c]	Stockbroker	57 Murrayfield Gardens

Ward VIII - Colinton

85.	Wilson M Marshall [c]	Farmer	Carlowrie, Kirkliston
86.	Ian M Gotts [c]	Chartered Surveyor and Town Planner	10 Pentland Avenue
87.	Alasdair F Campbell [c]	Chartered Accountant	33 Barnshot Road
88.	Rev Dr George J Whyte	Minister of Religion	The Manse of Colinton
89.	T Ewart Shields [c]	Chartered Accountant	44 Craiglockhart Road
90.	Douglas N Spratt [c, C,**]	Company Director, Confectionery Co.	6 Fernielaw Avenue
91.	William R J MacEachen	Dental Surgeon	12 Laverockdale Crescent
92.	David R C Brechin [c]	Chartered Quantity Surveyor	17 Grant Avenue
93.	Fred A Ainslie [c,***]	Chartered Accountant	16 Campbell Park Crescent
94.	Alastair C Dempster [c]	Company Director	8 Harelaw Road
95.	David L Bell **Captain**	Financial Consultant	212 Colinton Road
96.	Lewis M McGill [c]	Company Director	7 Bonaly Road

Ward IX – Sighthill

97.	John M Hume |c, †|	Chief Executive	31 Hillpark Brae
98.	Brian J W Powell	Architect	11 Braehead Grove
99.	James H T Gray |c,C|	Director	36 Barnton Grove
100.	Myer Wexelstein |c|	Retired Chartered Accountant	22 Garscube Terrace
101.	George D Holmes **Captain**	Forestry Consultant	7 Cammo Road
102.	George McLeod |c*|	Retired Master Grocer	50 Drumbrae Road North
103.	Paul M Aslett |c|	Approved Driving Instructor	2 Quarry Road, Fauldhouse
104.	Lindsay D Wilson |c,†|	Retired Chartered Accountant	21 Cammo Grove
105.	Robert R Brough |c|	Solicitor	108 Whitehouse Road
106.	William Wotherspoon |c|	Building Services Manager	9 Craigmount Bank West
107.	Martin McMenigall |c, †|	Refrigeration Engineer	193 Colinton Road
108.	Gordon W Banks |c,*|	Retired Insurance Broker	18 Bonaly Road

Ward X – Gorgie Dalry

109.	Jacqueline B Easson	Recruitment Consultant	33 Drumsheugh Gardens
110.	Christopher H Barclay **Captain**	Residential Care Officer	39 Alnwickhill Road
111.	Alexander Hutchon	Salon Owner	40 Belgrave Road
112.	Vernon Williamson	Managing Director	11 Church Road, Lasswade
113.	John R T Carson	Chartered Civil Engineer	11 Kirkliston Road, S. Queensferry
114.	Leonard Wallace|c,†,S,V-M,M| **HISTORIAN**	Advocate	18 Cammo Crescent
115.	Gary L Muirhead	Business Development Manager	40 Moredun Park Drive
116.	Raymond James Abbot |c|	Senior Investment Manager	5 Barnton Park
117.	Richard J Santandreu	Computer Consultant	31 Lower London Road
118.	Steven P Donald |c|	Photographer	Green Lane, Lasswade
119.	James C Hendy |c,**|	Retired	31 North Gyle Terrace
120.	Frederick J Daynes |c|	Company Director Road Transport	Edinburgh Road, Winchburgh

Ward XI – Corstorphine

121.	Gary F White	Financial Advisor	29 Inveralmond Drive
122.	Ian Pollock |c*|	Managing Director, Road Transport Contractor	8 Craigs Bank
123.	Archie Leitch	Sales Director	5 Craigs Bank
124.	Sandy Murdoch |c,*|	Retired Master Builder	1 Craigmount Gardens
125.	D Graham Balfour |c|	Managing Director, Agricultural Consultants	3 Maybank Villas
126.	James Beveridge |c|	Retired Architect	13 Craigmount View
127.	James T Carmichael |c,***|	Retired Managing Director, Auctioneer	8 Featherhall Crescent North
128.	Fred C H McLeod |c, †,*|	Retired Chartered Accountant	53 Hillview Road
129.	Jeremy Scott	Architect	17 Frogston Gardens
130.	Stephen Osborne **Captain**	Consulting Engineer	7 Craigmount Hill
131.	Martin C Mitchell	Hotelier	Johnsburn House, Balerno
132.	Colin Cargill |c,C|	Bank Manager	268/3 Lanark Road

Ward XII – Murrayfield Cramond

133.	Colin Forsyth [c]	Building Contracts Manager	10 Queen's Gardens
134.	Mark Speirs	Storage Contractor	5 Standingstane Road, Dalmeny
135.	Ian A T Gowans [c,C,S,T,V-M, M,***]	Civil Engineer	9 Queen's Gardens
136.	David R Hall [c,**]	Retired Company Director, Meat Trade	2 Brighouse Parkgate
137.	Adam G Dzierzek	Director Property Development	1/8 Marchfield Grove
138.	Ted Dzierzek [c]	Chartered Builder	8 Queensferry Road, Kirkliston
139.	Clive Castell	Safety Consultant	10 Hillpark Brae
140.	Norman Watt **Captain**	Company Director	5 Queen's Gardens
141.	Duncan A H Hall [c]	Marine Photographer	26 Brighouse Parkcross
142.	John Lindisfarne Rushbrook [c]	Sales Manager	6 Blinkbonny Grove West
143.	Ronald R O Souness [c]	Retired Departmental Manager Suture Manufacturer	22 Barnton Park Crescent
144.	Alan Scott	Finance Director, Construction	23 Strathalmond Road

Ward XIII – Pilton

145.	Ian C Adam [c]	Non Executive Director, Financial Services	2 Cammo Road
146.	Wm Tulloch Thomson [c,*]	Retired Licensed Grocer	19 Cammo Road
147.	J Robert Thomson	Garage Proprietor	22 Dean Park Mews
148.	Andrew S Hepburn [c,†,**] **Captain**	Company Director (Engineering)	65 Ravelston Dykes
149.	Simon Bolam [c,†,C,S,V-M,M,*]	Chartered Insurance Broker	14 Ramsay Garden
150.	Ross A K Smith [c]	Insurance Broker	Gellybank Farmhouse, Cleish
151.	Alan Cameron	Pharmacist	98 Oxgangs Road
152.	Allan K Smith [c]	Farmer	Clifton Wood, Newbridge,
153.	Alan B Ness [c]	Jeweller	26 Carfrae Gardens
154.	Alistair N Huett [c]	Partner, Law and Commercial Copying	5 Murrayfield Drive
155.	Heywood Tully [c,†]	Retired Company Director, Plant Hire	43 Braid Farm Road
156.	Donald Ross [c,*]	Retired Marine Consultant	200 Whitehouse Road

Ward XIV – St Bernards

157.	Robert F Gregor [c,*]	Rural Youth Consultant	11 Queensferry Road
158.	L Campbell Milne [c]	Retired Architect	109 Craigleith Road
159.	Vacancy		
160.	John Laurie [c]	Retired Treasurer	50 Craigleith Crescent
161.	Alistair J Bowen [c,*]	Company Director	The Murrel, Aberdour
162.	Max J Mendelssohn [c,†]	Retired Chartered Surveyor	8 Craigleith Gardens
163.	David J D Miller [c]	Director	Hollytree Lodge Pool of Muckhart
164.	Christopher J C Milne **Captain**	Structural Engineer	101/8 East Claremont Street
165.	W R Ferguson [c,C,S,V-M,M,**]	Retired Civil Engineer	128 Craigleith Road
166.	Euan M Donaldson [c]	Retired Bank Manager	134 Craigleith Road
167.	Andrew R Diamond [c]	Solicitor	59 Hillview Crescent
168.	Malcolm Rust	Solicitor	30 Lomond Road

Ward XV – St Andrews

169.	Jamie Thain **Captain**	6/7 Fox Street
170.	John A Loudon [c,*]	6C Essex Road
171.	Vacancy	
172.	Ian R Mathieson [c]	11 Eildon Terrace
173.	Norman A Smith [c]	19 Lynedoch Place
174.	Norman A Fiddes	20 Coltbridge Terrace
175.	Graham Mather [c]	26 Glencairn Crescent
176.	Ross Mickel	Project/Site Manager	18/5 Abercromby Place
177.	Anthony J Thain [c]		19 Kings Grove, Longniddry
178.	John Dixon	Antique Dealer	31 Morningside Road
179.	Brian Rafferty [c,*]	30/1 Alva Street
180.	Robert W Handley	7 Boswell Road

Ward XVI – Broughton

181.	Richard Leask [c]	Chartered Accountant	207 Colinton Road
182.	Peter N S Hall [c,*]	Retired Paper Merchant	7 Ross Road
183.	E Ian Adam [c,s,C,S,V-M,M,†,**]	Retired Medical Adviser, Lothian Region	60 Hillview Terrace
184.	Bruce R Herrald [c]	Antique Dealer	Dunnichen House, Forfar
185.	Austin Flynn	Solicitor	4 Alfred Place
186.	Gordon I A Adam [c]	Commercial Director	39A Great King Street
187.	Robert H Miller [c,*]	Agricultural Merchant	Linsandel House, Eskbank
188.	Andrew G Hannay [c]	Independent Financial Advisor	10 Murrayfield Gardens
189.	Peter N M Drennan	Chartered Surveyor	9 Wardie Crescent
190.	Fraser H Kerr	Chartered Accountant	94 West Ferryfield
191.	A Walker Forsyth [c,*]	Retired Stockbroker	10 Craighall Gardens
192.	William F Malcolm [c] **Captain**	Retired Solicitor	40 Northumberland Street

Ward XVII – Calton

193.	James A Stewart [c]	Property Factor	5 Mains of Craigmillar
194.	James W Tait **Captain**	Retired Managing Director	21 Woodfield Avenue
195.	Robert G Kelly [c,*]	Retired Company Director Roofing Contractor	13 Meadowfield Terrace
196.	George M Wallace [c,*]	Retired Chartered Accountant	28 East Werberside
197.	David A G McMurray	Publisher	20 Coates Gardens
198.	James B Raeburn [c]	Director, Scottish Daily Newspaper Society	44 Duddingston Road West
199	David Campbell Bell	National Director	3 Derby Street
200.	Gary C Winney [c]	Retired Group Employee Relations Manager	7 Forthview Road
201.	Vacancy		
202.	David J T Henderson [c]	Solicitor	34 Blinkbonny Avenue
203.	John F Dundas [c]	Company Director, Masonry Contractor	71 Pentland View
204.	Vacancy		

Ward XVIII – West Leith

205.	Ewen Dyce	Company Director	31 Braid Road
206.	Roy S Milne |c|	Architect	22 Russell Place
207.	Kenneth Grant	Retired Company Director |Retail|	21A Russell Place
208.	Kenneth Smart |c,*|	Retired Media Manager	74 Barnton Park View
209.	Harvey MacMillan |c|	Retired Company Director	1 York Road
210.	Michael H Sims **Captain**	Management Consultant	46 Barnton Park View
211.	Stuart Thom	Restaurateur	31 Inverleith Row
212.	Scott Hastings |c|	Marketing Consultant	49 Warriston Drive
213.	Alan S McConnell |c|	Retired Banker	78/6 Orchard Brae Avenue
214.	William L Grant |c|	Retired	186 Newhaven Road
215.	Hamish W Coghill |c,†,*|	Journalist	5 Allan Park Crescent
216.	Norman J McRobb |c,†|	Retired Screen Printer	72 Barnton Park View

Ward XIX – Central Leith

217.	James G Allan |c|	Pharmacist	7D Devon Gardens
218.	George W Tait |c,*|	Solicitor	7 Grant Avenue
219.	Robin W Finlayson |c|	Chartered Accountant	24 Murrayfield Gardens
220.	Richard Alexander |c|	Shipbroker	31 Silverknowes Grove
221.	Ian McArthur |c,†*|	Cartographic Consultant	13A/3 Milton Road East
222.	Alan A McCreath |c|	Company Director	17/3 Kinnear Road
223.	Matthew P Henderson |c|	Chartered Accountant	1 Murrayfield Drive
224.	Charles C Graham |c|	Insurance Broker	19 Lynedoch Place
225.	George H Shaw |c,†|	Company Director, Engineering	1/4 North Werber Road
226.	John A Crerar |c,*| **Captain**	Consultant	11 Otterburn Park
227.	Vacancy|		
228.	Timothy D Straton |c,†*|	Chartered Accountant	32 Wardie Road

Ward XX – South Leith

229.	Iain McCombie |c|	Solicitor	70 Spylaw Bank Road
230.	Peter G Duncanson |c|	Retired Bank Manager	14 Appin Place
231.	Alan W Mowat |c,†C,S,V-M,M, *|	Retired Solicitor	12 Ravelston House Park
232.	W H G Mathison |c,T *|	Chartered Accountant	11 Corrennie Gardens
233.	David S Paterson |c|	Retired Bank Manager	11 Newbattle Gardens, Eskbank
234.	Alistair W Lothian **Captain**	Managing Director	12 Kinnear Road
235.	David Rutherford |c†,S,V-M,M|	Chartered Accountant	176B Whitehouse Road
	EX-MODERATOR		
236.	Gavin McLean	Solicitor	2 Hampton Terrace
237.	Mark R Miller	Company Director	14 Dundas Home Farm South Queensferry
238.	Graham Russell	Medical Pratitioner	1 Laverockbank Terrace
239.	Ross S Hepburn |c|	Managing Director	101 Whitehouse Road
240.	Vacancy		

Ward XXI – Craigentinny

241.	Robin K Valentine	Solicitor	2A Corrennie Gardens
242.	Robert E Goodwin **Captain**	Retired Electrical Contractor	1 East Court, Ravelston House Park
243.	Alan M Brown [c,C]	Retired Director Housing Association	23 Burnbrae
244.	Hugh A Rutherford [c]	Chartered Surveyor	27 Wester Coates Avenue
245.	Deirdre A Kinloch Anderson [c]	Company Director	36A Kings Road, Longniddry
246.	Fiona Brown	Fitness Consultant	71 Durham Terrace
247.	Michael Gray [c]	Chartered Architect	Damhead Farm, Lothianburn
248.	Mark T Hopton [c]	Chartered Architect	167 Colinton Road
249.	Ian K Brash [c]	Chartered Architect	Fa'side Castle, Tranent
250.	Norman M Foulner [c]	Chartered Engineer	9 Alnwickhill Road
251.	Patrick C Brown	Chartered Engineer	40 Biggar Road
252.	R Shaun Vigers	Auctioneer	27 Comely Bank

Ward XXII – Portobello

253.	Kenneth L Orr [c]	Retired Sub-Postmaster	"Lankford", Wadeslea, Elie
254.	Joseph H Gilliatt [c,*]	Retired Manager, Manufacturing Opticians	58 Wakefield Avenue
255.	Peter J Livingstone [c]	Financial Adviser	2 Lady Nairn Loan
256.	Nigel L Bruce [c,**]	Retired Director Computer Services Co	5 The Paddock, Dirleton
257.	Ian D F Thomson[c,**]	Retired Publicity Manager	4 Meadowfield Drive
258.	James H Gray [c]	Chartered Accountant	78 Thomson Crescent, Currie
259.	Stewart Anderson	Quantity Surveyor	124 Morningside Drive
260.	Brian C A Short [c,C,S,V-M,M*]	Retired Retail Acquisitions Controller	28 Newhouses Road , East Burnside, by Broxburn
261.	Andrew R Gillon **Captain**	Finance Manager	1 Great Stuart Street
262.	Vacancy		
263.	Charles A Kemp [c,***]	Retired Master Grocer	9 Southfield Road West
264.	Colin L Wood [c]	Retired Civil Servant	78 Duddingston Road West

Ward XXIII – Craigmillar

265.	Vacancy		
266.	J Richard Allan [c,S,V-M,M]	Finance Director	12 Wardie Avenue
267.	Fraser Morrison	Dental Surgeon	14 Netherby Road
268.	John E D Gordon	Finance Director	11 Belford Gardens
269.	James A McLean [c]	Solicitor	9 Blinkbonny Terrace
270.	Roderick M Maclennan **Captain**	Solicitor	13 Belford Gardens
271.	William F Raynal	Financial Services Executive	1 Wester Coates Terrace
272.	John Stewart	Banker	48 Gordon Road
273.	Ian H Murning [c]	Chartered Surveyor	86 Craiglockhart Drive South
274.	John W Kennedy	Chartered Accountant	43 Corstorphine Hill Crescent
275.	D H Tweedie [c]	Retired Informations Systems Manager	34 Bonaly Crescent
276.	James M Finlay [c*]	Retired Life Assurance Official	97 Craigleith Hill Crescent

174

APPENDIX 11

EDINBURGH LORD PROVOSTS
1919-2008

1919-1921	John William Chesser
1921-1923	Sir Thomas Hutchison
1923-1926	Sir William Lowrie Sleigh
1926-1929	Sir Alexander Stevenson
1929-1932	Sir Thomas Barnby Whitson
1932-1935	Sir William Johnston Thomson
1935-1938	Sir Louis Stewart Gumley
1938-1941	Sir Henry Steele
1941-1944	Sir William Young Darling
1944-1947	Sir John Ireland Falconer
1947-1951	Sir Henry Hunter Arbuthnot Murray
1951-1954	Sir James Miller
1954-1957	Sir John Garnett Banks
1957-1960	Sir Ian Johnston Gilbert
1960-1963	Sir John Greig Dunbar
1963-1966	Sir Duncan Mackay Weatherstone
1966-1969	Sir Herbert Archbold Brechin
1969-1972	Sir James Wilson Mackay
1972-1975	Jack Kane
1975-1977	John Millar
1977-1980	Kenneth W. Borthwick
1980-1984	Thomas Morgan
1984-1988	Dr John Mackay
1988-1992	Eleanor T.McLaughlin
1992-1996	Norman M Irons
1996-2000	Eric Milligan
2000-2003	Eric Milligan
2003-2007	Lesley Hinds
2007-	George Grubb

INDEX

179